UNIVERSITY C
'INC'

Evaluation of Events:
Scandinavian Experiences

Edited by:
Lena L. Mossberg
School of Economics
Göteborg University
Sweden

Cognizant Communication Corporation
New York • Sydney • Tokyo

Evaluation of Events:
Scandinavian Experiences

Cognizant Communication Offices:

U.S.A.	**3 Hartsdale Road, Elmsford, NY 10523-3701**
Australia	**P. O. Box 352 Cammeray, NWS 2062**
Japan	**O.B.K Inc. Primavera 205 3-3-11 Hochioji, Tokyo 192-0355**

Library of Congress Cataloging-in-Publication Data

Evaluation of events: Scandinavian experiences/edited by Lena Larsson Mossberg
p. cm. – (Tourism Dynamics)
Includes bibliographical references (p.).
ISBNB 1-882345-40-1 (HC) – ISBN 1-882345-41-X (softcover)
    1. Tourism-Scandinavia-Management. 2. Special events—Scandinavia—Management
    3. Tourism-Economic aspects—Scandinavia. 4.Special events—Economic aspects-Scandinavia.
I. Mossberg, Lean Larsson. II Series
G155.S268 E82 2000
394.26'068—dc21   99-058762

Printed in the United States of America

Printing: 12345678910 Year: 0123456789

Cover Photo: C. Lundin

Contents

List of Tables

Contributors

Tommy D. Andersson is Professor in Managerial Economics at Bodoe Graduate School of Business in Norway. Presently he works as Programme Director at ETOUR – European Tourism Research Institute – a research project in Sweden. He has been carrying out several economic impact analyses of events since 1984. Email: Tommy.Andersson@etour.mh.se

Magnus Bohlin is Senior Lecturer at Dalarna University, and received his Masters degree from University of Alberta in Edmonton, Canada, and later a doctorate degree in human geography from the University of Uppsala, Sweden. Currently he serves as president for the European Chapter of the Travel and Tourism Research Association (TTRA). Bohlin has a long list of publications, including research reports, articles and chapters in edited books. Email: mbo@du.se

Monica Hanefors is a social anthropologist with a particular research interest in tourist behavior, tourism encounters and impacts, and imagery. She holds a position as Senior Lecturer at Dalarna University in Borlänge, Sweden. Hanefors has international experience from research, teaching, and practical work in the tourism industry. She has published extensively, including two co-authored books, chapters in edited volumes, and a vast number of articles concerning the same topic. Email: hfs@du.se

Lars Hultkrantz is Professor of Economics, esp. Transport and Tourism at Dalarna University and Uppsala University, Sweden. In the tourism field he has published various econometric studies on tourist demand, and economic analysis of property-rights issues related to different topics in tourism and recreation. He has a vast publication in other fields, such as forest economics and policy, green accounting, value of travel-time savings, and telecommunications policy. Email: Lars.Hultkrantz@du.se

Lena L. Mossberg is Senior Lecturer with the School of Economics, Göteborg University in Sweden. She holds a Ph.D. in Business Administration and has interests in tourist behavior, destination image, service quality and customer satisfaction. L. Mossberg has published several books and a number of articles. In addition, she has been involved in international tourism and marketing programs, for example as a tourism management expert for the United Nations. Email: Lena.Larsson@handels.gu.se

Bente R. Løwendahl is Associate Professor of Strategy at Norwegian School of Management - BI, and holds a Ph.D. degree from the Wharton School, University of Pennsylvania. Her main research interest is the strategic management of professional service firms. Her study of the Lillehammer Olympic Winter Games, with Professor Odd Nordhaug, was sparked by her interest in the mobilization of individual experts in complex service organizations, and she has published several articles (including SJM and SMJ) and books on that and related topics. Email: bente.lowendahl@bi.no

Lars A. Samuelson is the Öhrlings Coopers & Lybrand Professor of Business Administration at the Stockholm School of Economics (SSE). He is head of the program "The Economics of Events" at the SSE which is financed by the City of Stockholm and within which this anthology has been written. He has also running programs dealing with control of and in industries as well as public organizations. Email: Lars.Samuelson@hhs.se

Olav R. Spilling is Professor and head of Center for Industrial Development and Entrepreneurship at the Norwegian School of Management - BI. His main research interest is in the field of entrepreneurship and small and medium-sized enterprises, but he has also, for some years, been following the regional development related to the Winter Olympics organized in Lillehammer, and evaluated the short and long term industrial impacts of the events. He has published a number of books and articles in the field of industrial development, entrepreneurship and SMEs. Email: olav.r.spilling@bi.no

Foreword

The aim of this anthology is to give an overview of the state of current research regarding evaluation of events, as supported by empirical research mainly within Scandinavian countries. Event management and event tourism are topics that are increasing in importance in practice as well as for academia. In practice we experience tourism as an expanding industry due to e.g. increasing standards of living in more countries giving more people the possibility to travel. And with the expanding industry follows interest in academic studies in order to establish a knowledge basis of the field.

The city of Stockholm has for several years now systematically made efforts to increase the number of tourists. Different segments of the market have been identified such as leisure tourists, scientific conferences and events. Those in charge of these efforts have, however, realized difficulties in deciding what measures should be taken in order to achieve established goals. The knowledge base was found to be meager.

So, in 1995 an agreement was made with the Stockholm School of Economics to establish a four year research program into the economics of events. As a major part of this program, it was decided that a number of Scandinavian academicians should be invited to collaborate in writing this anthology. We were happy to engage Lena L. Mossberg, a Ph. D. at the Gothenburg School of Economics, as the editor. She has enthusiastically carried this project to its completion. I would like to thank her and her fellow authors for their endeavors to share with us their knowledge of the field. Many thanks to Professor Bill Faulkner, who was kind to make valuable suggestions to chapter one and adding a part about events tourism evaluation. I would also like to thank Michael Murnaghan for improving the standard of English in this book. I would also like to express my gratitude to Gunilla Green for qualifield help with editing. Finally our thanks go to the city of Stockholm for financing this project and to Göran Långsved, the president of Stockholm Information Service, for his personal support.

Stockholm in November 1999

Lars A. Samuelson

Preface

Objectives of this book and target group

It may be regarded as an established fact that events are objects of study that have, to an ever increasing extent, drawn the attention of researchers from different disciplines in the last few years. This field of research is relatively new, but it is expanding rapidly. At the beginning of the 1980´s, a number of articles and reports were published, but it was not until the mid-eighties that a greater interest was shown by researchers in this subject. A few books have been published about events and their effects. In these books events are discussed in relation to tourism. Academic journals in the field also concentrate largely on empirical research on events and tourism. The journal most often referred to is Festival Management & Event Tourism. Specific articles on events and their effects have also been published in fairly large numbers, in tourism-related journals. Specific international academic conferences related to events have been held. Many of the international conferences in the field of tourism also have sessions focusing on the area. Also, several universities now have courses in the field of events and some are offering postgraduate programs in event management.

The reader might ask if another book on the subject is really necessary. Yes, indeed it is. Some of the books are not updated and others have a management perspective. Some books are published in U.S., with most of the examples from that part of the world. Others include many examples and illustrations of events from Australia and New Zealand. There is a need for a book which looks at events from a European perspective and includes European case studies.

Many aspects could be studied in connection with events and it might be too comprehensive to cover everything in one book. We therefore concentrate on a subset of event impacts that have received research attention in Scandinavian research projects. We will also discuss methodological approaches from a wide range of disciplines and reflect on specific issues highlighted by the research findings of this projects.

Books encompassing an overview of existing literature on events and its effects are not yet available, at least not at a level that can be used by advanced undergraduate and graduate students. They are the *primary target audience* of this book. The book can also be of great value to politicians, individuals who arrange events, and researchers. The readers should be familiar with the basic knowledge of economics, finance, marketing, and management. The book is research oriented and each author presents both the theoretical and methodological background of the study concerned. To make the parts more interesting and accessible, a great number of examples are given. Also, some relevant cases are discussed.

It is the main aim of this book to provide the readers with knowledge of and a good understanding of a number of event impacts. The benefits of this are threefold. The reader will

- get an understanding of the importance of various types of impacts in connection to events in different contexts,
- be able to discuss several methodological approaches for evaluation of events and their impacts, and
- increase the awareness of short- and long-term impacts for various types of events.

Structure of the book

The book consists of nine chapters. The first chapter gives an introduction, discusses definitions of the concept, event, and presents a framework for an analysis of effects of events. The introductory chapter will be followed by seven chapters focussing on the different effects of events.

In chapter 2 *Travel Patterns* will be discussed. A number of events, which have been studied in the terms of their geographical context will be presented. How the market is viewed in geographical terms and what differences appear between one-time and recurring events are some of the issues which will be discussed. Furthermore, various factors will be pointed out which can influence the character of demand in time and space.

Events and the impact on *Destination Image* are the subject matter of chapter 3. Events are often claimed to be image-makers. In this chapter various methodological approaches are discussed. Empirical data from one study concerning whether the perceptions for the destination have changed due to a mega event, is presented.

Chapter 4 is about *Local Identity*. The focus is on identity – a concept closely related to knowledge and participation and the possibilities for participation as part of the audience or through volunteer work. There will be discussion of whether the event keeps a local population together, and how created and developed identity might be maintained, reinforced and articulated, or even lost.

Organizational Knowledge is the subject of chapter five. The organizer of an event including developing the organization and the sites, and preparation through planning and training will be dealt with. Special focus is put on learning effects at the individual and collective level. The empirical data is from the Lillehammer Winter Olympic Games.

Financial Effects of Events on the Public Sector is the title of chapter six. The purpose of this chapter is to describe a model of the effects of events on the economy of the public sector, the municipality as well as the state. A bottom up approach will be described and exemplified. How and to what extent will tax revenues and other charges be affected? What costs will the municipality and/or the state have to bear? These effects are of interest as many events are conceived to be of value to the public sector; they will contribute to the development and economic well-being of the region.

Chapter 7 will continue the previous chapter's discussion of the bottom up approaches and will deal with their advantages and disadvantages. Then, *Top Down Approaches* will be introduced and the choice set of an event, cost-benefit analysis, and intervention analysis are discussed. Two examples are presented using a mega event to demonstrate that important insight into the impact of an event can be extracted in a fairly simple manner. An example of a natural experiment (treated and untreated group design) is given as well as an example of the use of an econometric model based on time-series data for evaluation of the net impact of an event.

The area dealt with in chapter 8 is *Industrial Structure*. The chapter will focus on the long-term industrial impacts of mega-events. The analysis is based on the case of the Lillehammer Winter Olympic Games. The intention is to contribute to the understanding of what may be the importance of mega-events to local development in the host region.

To make it easier for the reader to follow, the seven chapters on effects are structured as follows:

- Background
- Theoretical Framework (theory and methods)
- Empirical Study

In the background section, in each chapter, the importance of this type of impact study, in relation to events, is argued and discussed. The theoretical framework covers both earlier studies in the field and a discussion about relevant methods for evaluating this type of impact. In the empirical study various examples from events in Scandinavia are given. The author introduces the empirical study with a description of the type of event investigated, the conditions, and the method used. After the result is presented a discussion and a conclusion follow, which ascertain whether time, type of event or other conditions have affected the results.

Chapter 9, is the final chapter and is titled *Strategies in Practice*. The authors decided to invite someone representing a large city to present the city's event strategies. Stockholm was elected due to the fact of the city's hosting many events and as all the authors were familiar with the context. The group invited Göran Långsved, the President of Stockholm Information Services to present their tourism strategies in general and their event strategies in particular as well as how they are designed and communicated to other actors. The chapter starts with a summary of the speech. In the following part each author discusses four themes, focused on in the speech. The four themes are:

1. Events as part of the destination marketing

2. Destination marketing as part of the communities competition

3. Attitudes of the locals toward events

4. The decision process of events related to public financing

With this approach, practice and theory are combined in one chapter and discussed from a wide range of disciplines. The chapter also includes conclusions as well as some implications for event organizers.

Chapter 1
Event Evaluations

Lena L. Mossberg

School of Economics and Commercial Law, Göteborg University, Sweden

1.1 Introduction

Events have come to be bigger and bigger local, regional and national affairs, important from a social, cultural and tourism perspective. Besides the possibility of attracting tourists and increasing the awareness/knowledge of the destination, other purposes for arranging an event have been to reposition the host city/country within the international market, to celebrate an anniversary or to enhance investment and to improve the infrastructure. Arranging events also opens up other possibilities, such as strengthening the local identity and the chance to display the culture of the destination.

One reason for creating or hosting an event can often be of an economic nature and one of the main avenues for this impact is through the generation of tourist expenditure. The demand that is created is not for the actual event alone, but also for a range of related services that constitute with what is usually called the ingredients of the tourism experience: accommodation (for instance, hotel, youth hostel and boarding-house), food (restaurant, hamburger and hot-dog stand and café), travel (bus, boat, train, bike, canoe and car rental), and activities (museums, amusement parks, sports and bathing facilities). The emphasis on the tourism connection in books and articles written on events is therefore understandable. Since demand is spread among many services, it is also important to consider the context: where the event takes place and the size of the choice of these different services. An event might have considerable effects in one context and marginal in another, especially depending on the size and structure of the local economy and infrastructure.

There are many interesting questions of a social and economic nature that need to be answered about events for public sector policy purposes. An event, especially if it is a large one, can alter the life of a location for anything from a few days to several weeks. Are there also long-term effects? How do attitudes towards the location and the country change? Was the event successful? Why was the destination chosen to host the event? What tax and employment effects arise? When do they arise and for whom?

The economic roles of events are, besides acting as a temporary attraction and a catalyst, to also serve as an image maker. A positive image is assumed to have effects on tourism and industrial investment and can ultimately have bearing on the well-being of the local population in various ways. What the effects are and their scope, is, however, unclear. The 1994 Olympic Games in Lillehammer increased the number of tourists to that area (Spilling 1997) and Calgary improved its reputation as a host city after the Olympics (Ritchie and Smith,

1991). A large number of people can list several Olympic Games cities and some can name the exact year of each event. However, it is uncertain whether this knowledge is available for other events like Ice Hockey Championships and the World Cup in Soccer.

Most of the studies that have been conducted regarding effects of events have evaluated the economic aspects. They have also pointed out the methodology problems connected with evaluations of tourism promotion and more general economical impacts. There is a risk, according to Getz (1989), that tourism organizations, above all, think of mega-events and that the small events are regarded as having only local or regional significance. Also, it is not satisfactory if only the economic effects are in the limelight. The connections between events and social, cultural and ecological effects must also be illustrated as well as other effects that promote the development of society. This book highlights the importance of systematically evaluating the various impacts of events, as an adjunct to the planning and policy development activities of public and private sector organizations. It will focus on the difficulties in the evaluation process and discuss the advantages and disadvantages of various methodological approaches. Empirical findings mainly from research in Scandinavian countries will be used for illustrative purposes and to reinforce the arguments that are presented. Methodology will be discussed in all chapters and act as the connecting theme.

This introductory chapter is divided into four parts. The first part has identified the focus and purpose of the book, while the next section will elaborate on this by clarifying key definitions relating to events (and their evaluation). In the third part, events tourism evaluation will be discussed, and than finally a framework for an analysis of effects of events is presented, and the organizational structure of the subject-matter of this book is outlined.

1.2 Definitions

Most of us attend an event of one kind or another from time to time. An event is a special activity which is not a part of daily life, it is out of the ordinary and we often attend, as audience or participants together with others, perhaps with the family or with friends. There are big and small events with a weak or strong image that are either held regularly or only once. Many events are of short duration and are either one-off or recurrent. On the other hand, a tourist attraction is, such as the amusement park, stationary and is intended to attract and receive visitors for a long period of time. In contrast to a tourist attraction, therefore, an event is transient, both in time and often geographically. Unlike a tourist attraction, the event is not a seasonal phenomenon, and is, indeed, often used as a strategy to level out seasonal variations in the demand (Ritchie and Beliveau, 1974). One factor that also distinguishes the event from the tourist attraction is financing. One reason for organizing a big event could be to encourage economic contributions from external sources towards the improvement of infrastructure and business. According to Hall (1992:3), the majority of large events have substantial official intervention whether it is on a national, regional or local level. The official intervention increases with the size of the event and the marketing activities.

Defining events

Since one of the purposes of the present book is to summarize the literature on events and their effects, it seems as if a broader definition would be preferable in this matter. In that way, relevant studies that illustrate, for instance, trade fairs, recurring contests or festivals would not be excluded. However, there is a risk that too broad definitions lose their value and it could be difficult to tell the events apart. Therefore, criteria such as frequency, formal organizational arrangements, public access, and tourism significance have been included in the definition below. However, criteria relating to size have not been included at this stage. Specially the first and the third elements capture the definition of Ritchie (1984).

The event...

- is a one-time or recurring event of limited duration, which is held no more frequently than once a year,
- has a program, an organizing body, a number of participants and it is open to the public, and
- apart from the intrinsic objectives (e.g. sport, culture, religion) is developed primarily to enhance the awareness, appeal and profitability of the host city/region/country as a tourist destination.

According to this definition, the Olympic Games are an event; a festival and many trade fairs are, too. On the other hand, gatherings like board meetings and regular and routine conferences are not included, nor are theatrical performances and concerts in the ordinary program or recurring contests like football or ice-hockey matches in the national leagues. Another classification can be made, depending on whether there is an audience or not. Music and film festivals are public events, open to the public in contrast to board meetings and conferences, for which you need an invitation to be allowed to attend. Attractions are similarly not included. Attractions can be regarded as permanent, while events are limited in time (Carey 1994).

There are still difficulties when defining the concept event. In the literature, these events are called hallmark events, special events, mega-events, festivals, minor events or major events. Sometimes the concepts are separated in literature as different types of events. For example, Hall uses the term 'hallmark events' and Getz prefers the terms 'special events' and 'festivals'. Sometimes, however, the concepts are regarded as synonyms. Jago and Shaw (1998) address this problem by proposing a conceptual and definitional framework based upon an extensive literature review. Firstly, they suggest that 'event' covers two categories. One is routine and common events and the other is special events. Secondly, special event (used in a tourism sense) includes three categories: Minor special events, festivals, and major special events (or major events). Thirdly, major event contains two categories. Hallmark events and mega-events. Still, there will be events that do not fit exactly the structure. The relationships between the categories are illustrated in Figure 1.1.

They define a special event as "A one-time or infrequently occurring event of limited duration that provides the consumer with a leisure and social opportunity beyond everyday experience. Such events, which attract, or have the potential to attract, tourists, are often held to raise the profile, image, or awareness of a region" (Jago and Shaw 1998: 29). The same authors define a major event as "A large-scale special event that is high in status or prestige and attracts a large crowd and wide media attention. Such events often have a tradition and incorporate festivals and other types of events. They are expensive to stage, attract funds to the region, lead to demand for associated services, and leave behind legacies" (1998:29).

Mega events, such as World Fairs and Expositions, or the Olympic Games, are one-time major events, generally on an international scale (Jago and Shaw 1998:29). They "...are

Figure 1.1. Diagrammatic event framework

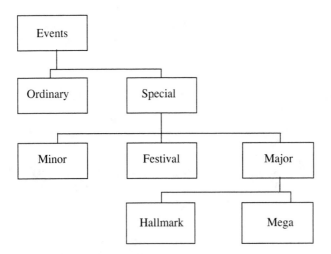

Source: Jago and Shaw. Special Events: A Conceptual and Differential Framework. *Festival Management & Event Tourism,* 5(1/2 1998): 28.

events which are expressly targeted at the international tourism market and may be suitably described as 'mega' by virtue of their size in terms of attendance, target market, level of public financial involvement, political effects, extent of television coverage, construction of facilities, and impact on economic and social fabric of the host community" (Hall 1992:2).

Hallmark event, according to Hall (1992:5) "applies to a wide range of events, including festivals and fairs, which exhibit a broad range of economic, physical and social impacts at various scales... ". Ritchie (1984) distinguishes seven categories of hallmark events: world fairs/expositions, unique festivals and carnivals, large sports events, cultural and religious events, historic milestones, classic, commercial and agricultural events and large political events. Hall (1992) has a similar classification. He categorizes according to the religious, cultural, commercial, athletic and political aim and direction of the event (Hall 1992). An example of a religious event is The Haj in Mecca, a cultural event is the Octoberfest in Munich, a commercial event is the World exhibition in Sevilla, athletic events are the Summer and Winter Olympic Games and, finally, an example of a political event is a UN conference, such as the Women's conference in Beijing. Hallmark events, therefore, have many aims and directions. Getz says (1991:51) that the concepts of hallmark events and special events are sometimes used synonymously, while others feel that a hallmark event is a special type of event that has a unique image. Getz, however, thinks that hallmark event is most appropriate in discussions about places or destinations which are known predominantly as a result of a specific event. This corresponds with Jago and Shaw's definition. An hallmark event, according to them, is "An infrequently occurring major event that is tied to a specific place whereby the destination and the event become synonymous" (1998:29). This could be true about events that are so important that the destination takes its tourism theme from the event. An event held on one single occasion will not often be a so called hallmark for the destination. On the other hand, the bull race in Pamplona, Spain, could be an example of a hallmark event.

The concept 'special event' is often used synonymously with 'festival'. The Canadian Government's Office of Tourism (1982:3) states that the main difference between the two is that festivals are usually arranged annually, while special events are often arranged on only one single occasion. Tourism South Australia (1990:2) thought it too vague to make a distinction between recurring events and non-recurrent ones. Instead they distinguish between types of audience. Another way would be to look at the theme. Festivals are related to the celebrating of social values. Falassi points out (1987:2) that both the social function and the symbolic meaning of the festival are significant for the historic development, local identity and physical survival of society. Getz (1991:54) also states social values in his distinction between special events and festivals. Sometimes the differences are invisible, according to Getz, and one reason is that all types of events tend to become more like festivals. Festivals, he says, must be open to the public and have a social cultural meaning for the host destination. Also, they always have a theme and some kind of celebration. Getz's definition reads as follows (1991:54): "A festival is a thematic celebration for the public." A festival can be "a special event that is a public-themed celebration" (Jago and Shaw 1998:29). However, not all special events are festivals. Examples are sports events of different kinds.

From an economic point of view, it is important to study to what extent an event can use already existing facilities, which can reduce the cost of the event to a large degree. Generally, one-time events use already existing capacity, while recurring events establish fixed resources, giving quite a different financial picture. On the other hand in case of very large essentially one-time event, such as the Summer Olympics, a substantial amount of new infrastructure may be necessary. Various parameters of events have been alluded to so far. These include foremost the size, image, and frequency (one-off/recurring) of the event. There are other aspects of events, such as duration and spectator/participant ratio, that provide the bases for distinguishing different types of events. The financial outcome is affected by the duration of the event, i.e. whether it is a one-day event or a multiple-day event, where visitors spend considerably more money during their stay (Anderssson and Mossberg, 1995). Furthermore, the outcome might also depend on if the visitors participate in the event (e.g. in skiing, singing, sailing) or if they are only spectators since participating visitors often have different travel patterns (which will be discussed in the next chapter). Figure 1.2 exemplifies these economic categories.

Figure 1.2. An economic categorization of public events

	One-time events	Recurring events
One day	Rock concert *(high ratio of spectators)*	The Round-Tjörn sailing-race in Sweden *(high ratio of participants)*
Multiple-day	The World Cup in Soccer *(high ratio of spectators)*	The Octoberfest in Munich *(high ratio of participants)*

The World Cup in Soccer, the World Championships in Athletics, and the Olympic Games are all, according to the above categorization, one-time multi-day events and as such they have the highest economic potential. It should be kept in mind that, even though all these events are recurring events at the global level, they are essentially one-time events so far as the host city is concerned. They differ from recurring events in many ways. The event must follow rules and regulations from an international central organization. In order for a nation/city to host the event, the nation/city must comply with specific demands. For instance, visa requirements for participants and officials often have to be waived, ticketing arrangements are constrained by provisions designed to enable member countries equal access, conditions are imposed on sponsorships arrangements to protect the interest of the parent organization and profits associated with the event are shared. The scale of the major international events referred to above is such that they are often called mega-events. The rock concert, the round-Tjörn sailing-race on the west coast of Sweden and, the Stockholm Water Festival are, on account of their size, not mega-events but they can all be categorized as special events. In the text no attempt will be made to classify events in terms of their scale and only the word 'event' will be used generically.

1.3 Events Tourism Evaluation

The widespread acceptance of events-based strategies as an approach to destination development and marketing, along with the similar use of events as a stimulus for broader aspects of business development and urban renewal, has been accompanied by a greater level of public sector support for the staging of events. This support has generally occurred through the provision of funds for such activities as the bidding process, the upgrading of facilities, security services and the establishment of agencies responsible for the planning and marketing of particular events. In some countries, for example Australia, state (or provincial) governments have committed themselves to an events-based approach to such an extent that they have established government agencies with the sole responsibility of disbursing funds to support the bidding for, and staging of, events (Mules and Faulkner, 1997). Some of this investment may simply involve changes in the timing of outlays already committed as, for instance, might be the case where the already planned upgrading of certain facilities is fast-tracked so that they will be ready in time for a particular event. In such cases, there is no net cost to the community in the longer term and, indeed, the community may benefit if this results in it having the use of these facilities earlier. This assumes, however, that the accelerated investment for the event-related facilities has not been at the expense of investments in other areas which warrant higher priority in terms of addressing community needs. The reality is that, in general, public sector investment in the staging of events does involve the shifting of resources from other areas of government responsibility and, as a consequence of this, it is imperative that the impacts of events be systematically monitored so that the costs and benefits associated with this investment can be properly evaluated.

On the basis of the above considerations, evaluation might be construed as a tool for ensuring accountability in the use of public resources devoted to events. As governments generally have become more rigorous in their demands for such accountability, event organizers and tourism agencies supporting event-based strategies are being placed under increased external pressure to develop credible methods for demonstrating the benefits derived from continued funding. This trend is equally applicable to tourism marketing generally (Faulkner, 1997). However, as observed by Faulkner in this latter context, "well-structured evaluation procedures also have an important internal role to play by virtue of the contribution they make to the organization's ongoing planning and management processes. The introduction of systematic evaluation procedures as a routine component of an organization's activities provides a framework for monitoring and assessing its performance with respect to the environment within which it operates and a rational basis for the identification of priorities and the allocation of resources. Evaluation keeps an organization in touch with changes in its environment and its performance with respect to this environment and is thus an essential prerequisite for responsiveness and adaptability" (Faulkner, 1997: 23).

The role of evaluation in event strategies at the destination level should therefore be seen as both a proactive, internally relevant means for providing the information required for rational decision making, and as a reactive, externally oriented procedure for being account-able to stakeholders (Stufflebeam and Shinkfield 1985). This dual role of evaluation has been recognised as being relevant to tourism marketing more generally by Burke and Lind-blom (1989) and Davidson and Wiethaupt (1989). Meanwhile, a growing interest in evaluation research in the tourism field has been attributed to a combination of the external pressures mentioned above and an increasing appreciation of the value of a more strategic approach to destination planning and marketing (Cook and Azucenus 1994).

In looking at applications of evaluation techniques to the events setting, it is useful to begin with the first principles of what constitutes the evaluation process. At the most basic level, the evaluation of an individual event, or a program for implementing an events based strategy, is essentially a systematic process for objectively assessing the outcomes of the event or program. This assessment is guided by three key criteria:

- Appropriateness – that is, the extent to which the stated objectives and priorities of the event/program match the needs of core stakeholders (in this case, the tourism industry, other sectors of the destination region's economy and the host community),
- Effectiveness – that is, the extent to which the event/program meets its stated objectives, and
- Efficiency – that is, the extent to which the outcomes are achieved at a reasonable cost and within a reasonable time frame.

So far as events are concerned, the appropriateness question is both a threshold issue and an extremely complex issue to resolve. The complexity arises, in the first instance, from the various agendas that are being pursued by those involved in the event. Thus, if it is a sport-ing event, the sporting organizations directly involved in the planning and conduct of the event see their primary objective as providing an opportunity for athletes to engage in elite competition. On the other hand, the tourism sector might see the event as an opportunity to promote the image of the destination and develop tourism products associated with the event. Ritchie's (1984) definition of hallmark events, which sees them as being 'developed primarily to enhance the awareness, appeal and profitability of a tourism destination' is couched very much in terms of the latter perspective and probably bears little resemblance to the objectives envisaged by the sporting organization involved. These two contrasting agenda often means that the details of the event's organization may not necessarily be conducive to the maximization of tourism benefits. However, as the organizers of sporting and other events are being placed under increasing pressure to justify government funding support in economic terms, a shift in their objectives from the purely sporting focus to tourism and other broader community objectives may be inevitable.

The issues of effectiveness and efficiency are related to the measurement of outcomes in terms of social, environmental and economic impacts of the event. These impacts need to be ultimately assessed, which takes into account alternative applications of the resources allocated to the event strategy. The remainder of this book concentrates on the monitoring of this range of impacts, and thus provides a step towards a more comprehensive evaluation of event tourism in the longer term.

Thus, many effects are derived through events – both positive and negative ones. For the purpose of creating order among the effects, a framework for analyzing events together with the structure of the book will be presented in the next section.

1.4 The Framework of the Book

Despite the fact that the number of studies of events, with different fields of interest, have increased in recent years, there are few studies that attempt to give an overall understanding or a theoretical framework. However, some progress has been made towards the designing of a framework. A broad survey of event research related to tourism is given by Getz (1991), starting from five different perspectives: the event, the visitor, the organizer, the tourism industry and the social/cultural environment at the locality. The book was revised in 1997 with a focus on the roles and impacts of events; organizers; sponsors and other partners; customers and guests; the community; the environment; and the economic perspective. Different aspects of each perspective are discussed in the various chapters. It is a management text, (as well as his first book) based on management theory and practice with all management functions covered.

Hall (1992) has a somewhat different approach; he presents a framework where an event is seen from without, how it affects and develops the socio-economic environment in the region and the culture and the country where the event is held. Within this framework, an event is, at the same time, a function of the socio-economic environment and an influence there on. The socio-economic environment is the external environment, which will affect the dynamics of the internal environment, where the event organization and the management can be found. The socio-economic environment is divided into four parts: history and importance; economic dimensions; social dimensions; and political dimensions. The importance of an event can, of course, change over time due to changes in society or changes in the event itself. Thus, the history and importance of an event are connected with the economic, social and political dimensions. It is the economic effects that provide one of the main motives for staging events. Positive, social effects are, for instance, pride, increased social interaction and strengthened identity, which could result in both increased knowledge and participation, while negative effects could imply crime, lost identity in society and a feeling of not belonging. The fact that the political dimension is included in the framework depends on the importance of different authorities on a local, regional and sometimes national level in the organization of an event. It is, thus, important not only in large events like the Olympic Games, when a city or a country bids to host the event. The four categories (historic, economic, social and political), which together make the socio-economic environment, help to explain the type and character of the values that an event represents. At the organizational level of a single event, interest is more focused on organizing, planning, directing, controlling and marketing.

A somewhat different survey of different types of effects was made by Ritchie (1984:4) at the University of Calgary. The dimensions he mentions are: economic; tourism and commercial; physical, socio-cultural; psychological; and political. The dimensions were discussed in connection with the Winter Olympic Games in Calgary – the project started several years before the event.

Faulkner (1993) builds on Ritchie's division but he has reduced the categories to three dimensions. He mentions economic, tourism/commercial, and social/environmental impacts. What Ritchie calls physical impacts, like construction of new facilities and expansion of the

Figure 1.3. A framework for monitoring the impact of tourism events

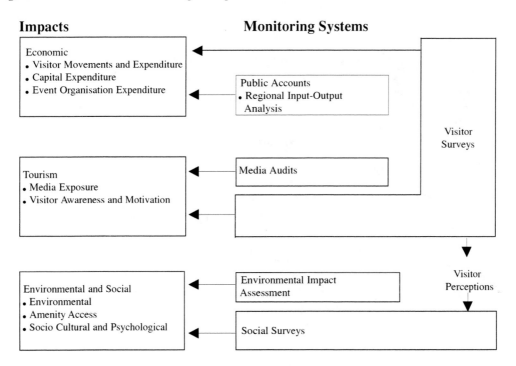

Source: Faulkner, B., *Evaluating the Tourism Impact of Hallmark Events*. Occasional Paper No 16, 1993:3, Bureau of Tourism Research, Australia.

infrastructure, are called economic effects in Faulkner's framework. He contends that they can be measured in economic terms, while negative physical effects such as environmental damage and crowding, can be included in the sociocultural and psychological impacts. The two latter effects are combined with political effects and he thinks that it is often difficult to distinguish between them. The three dimensions are identified in the left hand column of Figure 1.3. The associated systems required to monitor these impacts are shown in the right hand column.

In this book a few impact dimensions have been selected, based on importance, the experience of the book's contributors, and the availability of empirical data. The chosen effects are presented in the Figure 1.4. The intention is not to provide a comprehensive and exhaustive analysis of event effects, but rather to reflect on the status of research in this area and provide a stimulus for future research.

This book has a multidisciplinary approach. As Jafari (1977) and others more recently (e.g. Jafari and Ritchie 1981; Nash and Smith 1991; Faulkner and Ryan 1999) have suggested, tourism is a multi-disciplinary field of study and, in this setting such an approach is to be "more expedient, productive, and meaningful". In his observations on the movements of the tourist in time and space Jafari (1987) describes how the monotony of everyday life is interrupted by the journey to the destination, what happens during the journey itself and what occurs when the tourist returns to normal life. This construction is also relevant in connection with events, in order for the organizer, the community and tourism- related industries to understand the behavior of the visitor at an event, what his motives are for

Figure 1.4. The building blocks of the book

Introduction
– Chapter 1. Event Evaluations

Effects of events on...

The visitors
– Chapter 2. Traveling to Events
– Chapter 3. Effects of Events on Destination Image

The locals
– Chapter 4. The Locals – Local Knowledge, Participation, and Identity

The organization
– Chapter 5. Learning Effects – The Case of the Lillehammer Olympic Winter
  Games 1994

The economy
– Chapter 6. Financial Effects of Events on the Public Sector
– Chapter 7. Event Economics: Top-Down Approaches
– Chapter 8. Beyond Intermezzo? On the Long-Term Industrial Impacts of Mega-Events
  – The Case of Lillehammer 1994

Event strategies and authors' comments
– Chapter 9. Event Strategies in Practice

attending the event, how he makes reservations, what he does at the destination and his behavior following the visit.

A time/planning related division into "pre-bid", post-bid" and "post-event" activities was made by Roche (1994). A similar division was made when planning the World Championship in Athletics project in Göteborg (Andersson and Larsson Mossberg 1995). A number of problems were discussed from the time related division of events which was subdivided into three phases: to obtain, to implement and to evaluate an event. A similar division is also suitable as far as marketing and project theory is concerned. The purchase process for services considered in marketing has three phases; prepurchase phase, service encounter phase and postpurchase phase (Kurtz and Clow 1997). Three phases are also used as regards theories of temporary organizations and projects. Packendorff's model includes the initial phase, the implementation phase and the completion phase. In the first phase it is a matter of harmonizing a quantity of expectations, in the second phase co-ordination of different actions and finally, in the completion phase evaluating and demobilizing. Typical of events, as for many tourism enterprises, is the involvement of many organizations and projects – all with their own purposes, aims and interests – in order to plan, organize and market the specific tourism product/event. The three phases all have different implications and relevancy in the event context. There is a lot that points to the fact that a time-related division might facilitate a better understanding when studying events. In the present book, whenever possible (if relevant literature and empirical data are available), different phases will be discussed – pre event, event, and post event. Both a producer perspective and a consumer perspective will be given, according to dimension and phase.

This introductory chapter will be followed by seven chapters focussing on the different effects of events. Chapters two to eight are about effects of events on the visitors, the locals, the organization, and the economy and in this sense resembles the original framework suggested by Getz (1997). Chapter two is about travel patterns, chapter three focuses on destination image, chapter four captures the importance of local identity, and chapter five concerns learning effects at the individual and collective level. This is followed by chapters on evaluation of economical effects. In chapter six a bottom up approach is presented and the focus is on financial effects on the public sector, and in chapter seven a top down approach is discussed. Effects on the industrial structure is the subject of chapter eight. In the final chapter, titled Event Strategies in Practice, practice and theory are combined and discussed from a wide range of disciplinary perspectives.

References

Andersson, T. & L. Mossberg, L. (1995). Att få, genomföra och utvärdera VM i friidrott 1995: Ett förslag till ett övergripande forskningsprogram. In R. Puijk (Ed.), *OL-94 og forskningen V*, OL dokumentasjonstjeneste, Lillehammer Norge.

Burke, J. L. & Lindblom, L. A. (1989). Strategies for Evaluating Direct Response Tourism Marketing, *Journal of Travel Research, 28*(Fall), 33-37.

Canadian Government Office of Tourism. (1982). *Planning Festivals and Events*. Ottowa.

Carey, C. (1994). Research Needs for Developing Established Events and Attractions. In B. Ritchie & C. Goeldner, (Eds.), *Travel, Tourism, and Hospitality Research: A Handbook for Managers and Researchers*. New York: John Wiley & Sons Inc.

Cook, S. D. & Azucenus, V. (1994). Research in State and Provincial Travel Offices. In B. Ritchie & C. Goeldner, (Eds.), *Travel, Tourism, and Hospitality Research: A Handbook for Managers and Researchers*. New York: John Wiley & Sons Inc.

Davidson, T. L. & Wiethaupt, W. B. (1989). Accountability Marketing Research: An Increasingly Vital Tool for Travel Marketers, *Journal of Travel Research, 27*(Spring), 42-45.

Falassi, A.(Ed.) (1987). *Time Out of Time: Essays on the Festival*. Albuquerque: University of New Mexico Press.

Faulkner, B. (1993). *Evaluating the Tourism Impact of Hallmark Events*. Occasional Paper No. 16. Bureau of Tourism Research, Australia.

Faulkner, B. (1997). A Model for the Evaluation of National Tourism Destination Marketing Programs, *Journal of Travel Research, 35*(3), 23-32.

Faulkner, B. & Ryan, C. (1999). Innovations in Tourism Management Research and Conceptualisation. *Tourism Management, 20,* 3-6.

Getz, D. (1989). Special Events. *Tourism Management,* (June), 125-137.

Getz, D. (1991). *Festivals, Special Events, and Tourism*. New York: Van Nostrand Reinhold.

Getz, D. (1997). *Event Management & Event Tourism*. New York: Cognizant Communication Corporation.

Hall, C. M. (1992). *Hallmark Tourist Events - Impacts, Management & Planning,* London: Belhaven Press.

Jafari, J. (1977). Editor's page. *Annals of Tourism Research, 5,* 6-11.

Jafari, J. (1987). Tourism Models: The Sociocultural Aspects. *Tourism Management 8*(2), 151-159.

Jafari, J. & Ritchie, B. (1981). Towards a Framework for Tourism Education Problems and Prospects. *Annals of Tourism Research, 8*(1), 13-34.

Jago, L. & Shaw, R. (1998). Special Events: A Conceptual and Differential Framework. *Festival Management & Event Tourism, 5*(1/2), 21-32.

Kurtz, D. & Clow, K. (1998). *Services Marketing*. New York: John Wiley & Sons.

Mules, T. & Faulkner, B. (1997). An Economic Perspective on Special Events, *Tourism Economics, 2*(2), 107-117.

Nash, D. & Smith, V. L. (1991). Anthropology and Tourism. *Annals of Tourism Research, 18,* 12-25.

Ritchie, B. (1984). Assessing the Impact of Hallmark Events: Conceptual and Research Issues. *Journal of Travel Research, 23*(1), 2-11.

Ritchie, B. & Beliveau, D. (1974). Hallmark Events: An Evaluation of a Strategic Response to Seasonality in the Travel Market. *Journal of Travel Research, 14*(Fall), 14-20.

Ritchie, B. & Smith, B.H. (1991). The Impact of a Mega-Event on Host Region Awareness: A Longitudinal Study. *Journal of Travel Research, 30*(1), 3-10.

Roche, M. (1994). Mega-Events and Urban Policy. *Annals of Tourism Research, 21*(1), 1-19.

Spilling, O. R. (1997). Long Term Impacts of Mega Events - The Case of Lillehammer 1994. In *Proceeding from the Talk of the Top Conference.* 7-8 July, Östersund, Sweden.

Stufflebeam, D. L. & Shinkfield, A. J. (1985). *Systematic Evaluation,* Boston: Kluver-nijhoff.

Tourism South Australia. (1990). Planning of Festivals and Special Events. Adelaide: Planning and Development Division.

Chapter 2
Traveling to Events

Magnus Bohlin

Dalarna University, Sweden

2.1 Background

A geographers approach to the study of tourism in general and events in particular raises the question of what the spatial aspects of the phenomenon at hand are. Tourism by definition implies travel away from ones permanent place of residence to other locations which are frequented on a temporary basis. These locations are normally referred to as destinations. Clawson (1959) in an attempt to define costs associated with recreational travel described this situation in terms of a round trip. She then finished with a recreational experience consisting of five phases namely, 'anticipation', 'travel to', 'on site', 'travel back' and finally 'recollection'. (Other studies have used phases for dividing different activities in e.g. the tourism/event context, see ch. 1.4.) In spatial terms anticipation and recollection normally coincide location wise. The two travel components may or may not be identical and the on-site experience may consist of one or several geographic locations depending on the kind of trip we are dealing with. Nonetheless we have identified the three basic elements of a simple model of tourism travel, namely place of residence, routes traveled and destination.[1]

In the study of events from a geographical perspective the three components of the basic tourism model are relevant as a way of structuring our inquiry. Dealing with events the spatial outlook is normally destination based. Thus, if we concern ourselves with the viability of a particular event the questions asked refer to where do the visitors come from and how many are they. In other words where is the market located and of what size is the market at various distances from the destination and to what extent does there exist a competing supply located more or less favorable vis-à-vis the market or markets relative to the location of our event?

2.2 Theoretical Framework

Some general notes on the distance concept

Tourism presupposes travel and travel is intimately associated with the distance concept. The effect of distance has for obvious reasons received considerable attention in the field of

---

1) The spatial reduction of Clawsons phases has previously been discussed by the author (Bohlin 1975:4).

geography. Numerous studies have dealt with the impact of distance on spatial interaction as well as how it affects diffusion of information. Newton's gravity model was adopted at an early stage by those trying to model travel flows and forecast demand for tourism and recreation. The analogy from physics to human behavior is based on the assumption that e.g. two cities can be conceived as two bodies in space. The gravity between these two is related to the population size (i.e. mass) and the distance separating the two. Although these models over the years have reached increased levels of sophistication and may be more accurate in estimating future demand and thus tourist flows, they will never free themselves from the drawback of reductionism. That is to say, these models may depict reality reasonably accurately but they contribute very little, if anything at all, to the understanding of the motives and the driving forces behind the patterns recorded. What these models basically do is to portray mathematically a phenomenon the features of which are in fact already known. At any rate disregarding whether we prefer a mathematical or verbal account of the effect of distance on interaction in space, it is of ultimate significance to appreciate the friction posed by distance on travel. One of the first to introduce the concept of the friction of distance on recreational travel was Wolfe (1972). Perhaps the main merits of Wolfe's inertia model is the fact that he highlights the significance of distance on recreational travel which he portrays as a negative exponential function. If we then add the concept of intervening opportunities, which was first introduced by Stouffer (1940) we have two basic elements explaining travel behavior. The idea of an intervening opportunity is very simple. In the case of tourism it refers to the fact that when consumers are offered an opportunity to pursue their activities etc. at closer distance than before they prefer this new opportunity rather than going to the old destination. Thus by locating closer to the market one can significantly reduce the demand for more distant places. In order to assess the nature of intervening opportunities one has to realize that the concept of a tourism product is a complex one and that substitution of more distant locations in favor of those closer vis-à-vis the market may not occur automatically.

In a real situation there will be an intricate interplay between a number of factors determining whether or not this substitution effect will occur. Potential customers may accept that the nearest destination offers a somewhat inferior product as it will be made available at lower travel cost and less time being spent on traveling there. There are of course situations where travel itself is an integral part of the entire recreational experience. In such cases destinations close to the market will obviously not benefit from their proximity to the market. To what extent products are perceived as exchangeable will be tainted by psychological factors, but the perception of opportunities are also subject to having access to information. As the diffusion of information has very similar characteristics to physical interaction in space, the knowledge of more distant destinations will, ceteris paribus, always be inferior to that of those localities being relatively closer to the market. Therefore, the diffusion of information and actual travel patterns in general terms can be described as a distance decay function as it is outlined in Figure 2.1.

A major implication suggested by the distance decay function is of course that demand decreases in some exponential form outward from the origin, which is the equivalent of the tourism destination. As Figure 2.1 can be interpreted as decreasing demand or market shares with increasing distance from the destination it becomes evident that population distribution becomes a major factor to consider. Population is never evenly distributed but rather concentrated in a hierarchical system of urban centers. As a consequence it will be vital to realize that when the demand function is placed in its geographical context, as is shown in Figure 2.2, the number of potential customers is a function both of distance and number of

Figure 2.1. A general relationship between interaction and distance

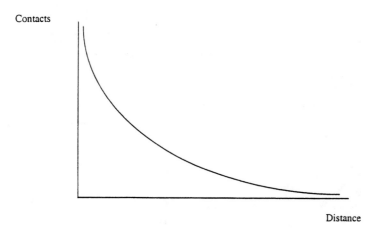

visitors. In Figure 2.2 three concentric circles are placed at equal intervals with the destination at centre indicating possible market segmentation based e.g. on travel time. As can be seen the demand function approaches zero just outside zone c. Even the presence of major urban centres in this outer zone may be of relatively limited significance as a rather small portion of the actual population is attracted to the destination. By the same token a large population within zone *b* and in particular in zone *a* will have much greater impact on the volume of demand than is the case when it is found in zone *c*.

When we are dealing with event tourism it is necessary to observe that the definition of tourism disregards the population living in the destination or its immediate vicinity. These are considered to be locals and do not qualify as tourists. The significance of making this observation is rather obvious. The local population of the destination, which could be a major city, could play a decisive role in making an event successful. Thus events located to major urban places both have an indigenous market as well as a market of tourists attending the event. This in turn leads to the observation that events which can be located anywhere will have a greater potential when located close to the market than otherwise. However, in this presentation the focus will be on events as a part of tourism travel.

Figure 2.2. Spatial significance of the demand function for event tourism

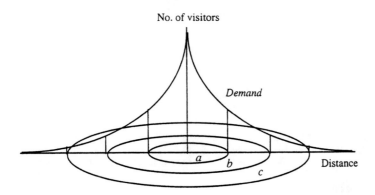

2.3 Empirical Studies

During the last decade the author, sometimes in cooperation with colleagues, has had the opportunity to study several events mainly in the province of Dalarna. These studies will be discussed in terms of results relevant to the travel aspect of events. As the case studies in question have normally had other points of departure than just the travel aspect, the available data has been reexamined to suite the theme of this chapter.

The events presented concern Falun Folk music Festival in 1989,[2] the Choir Festival in Skinnskatteberg in 1990,[3] World Championship in Nordic Skiing in 1993,[4] Vasaloppet in 1995[5] and the Swedish Rally in 1998.[6] These events all have things in common and at the same time they are very different from one another. The Folk music Festival and the Choir Festival could be grouped under the heading of music and culture events whereas the latter three events concern different sports. Similarly both Vasaloppet and the Choir Festival are related as they are, to a great extent, based on active participation by the audience itself and the other three are mainly attracting spectators.

Four of the events are recurring, although some of them have faced the threat of discontinuation as a result of large economic deficits.[7] The World Championship has been staged twice in the city of Falun, but twenty years in between the two occasions makes it necessary to consider this to be equivalent to an event which takes place just once.

The events mentioned will be discussed using both a choropleth map depicting the hinter-land of each event and an assessment made of the relation between the size of an audience and the distance traveled.[8] In order to allow for a comparison between the different events and at the same time account for the population in different parts of the country, the maps and the graphs are based on a ratio as a common denominator. It has been calculated using first the share of the visitors to the entire event coming from the province in question and then dividing this figure by the proportion which the province holds of the national popula-tion. A ratio of *one* indicates that the particular province is represented according to its population size. A value greater than *one* indicates that the province is over represented and vice-versa.

Falun Folk Music Festival

When the study of the folk music Festival in Falun was carried out the festival was relatively new. It had started in 1986 and the survey thus covered the 4th staging of the event. At the time of the study the number of visitors was estimated to be around 6.300 people. Dalarna county has a visitor ratio of 13.6 which indicates that this event at the time was still a highly local event. Even within the county of Dalarna the municipality of Falun counts for roughly 2/3 of all visitors. The equation in Figure 2.3 indicates a high degree of explanation by distance on attendance. However, the single high value for Dalarna (Falun) boosts the R^2

---

2) See Bohlin & Ternhag, 1990.
3) See Bohlin & Hanefors in 1992.
4) See Bohlin & Elbe, 1993.
5) See Bohlin, 1993 for a comparison.
6) See Bohlin & Malmberg, 1998.
7) While writing this chapter the regional newcast on Swedish TV2 broadcast that Falun Folk Music Festival has gone bankrupt.
8) A simplified way of attaining distance data was used. Thus county was used as a generalized address of the visitors and county capital was used as point for measuring the distance to the event. The distances derived are based on Vägverkets publication Vägavstånd i Sverige, 1996.

Figure 2.3. The relationship between attendance at the Falun Folk music Festival and distance to the city of Falun

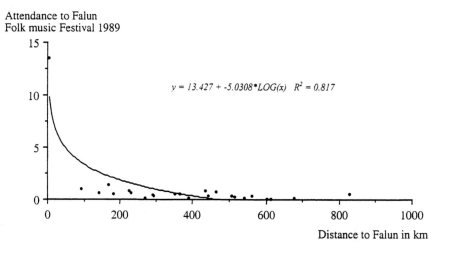

value considerably. Thus if Falun is treated as a residual the distance decay function is still possible to identify but no longer as pronounced. In order to present a more complete account of the pattern which evolves in Figure 2.3 and Figure 2.4 additional factors would have to be introduced. The original study did not have this approach and as a result the

Figure 2.4. The hinterland of the Falun Folk music Festival 1989 – attendance related to regional population

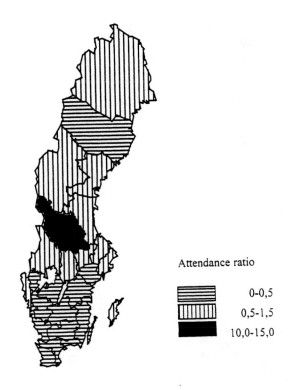

reasons behind the observed pattern remain unresolved. One would need to assess e.g. to what extent there exist regional variations in the interest for folkmusic. There are several indications that this is one relevant variable to scrutinize further.

Event visitors to Falun stay on much longer than the event itself. Almost 50% of the visitors to Falun stayed longer but in the case of Skinnskatteberg only some 10% stayed on when the festival was over. Falun and surrounding municipalities function as a rallying point. There is also a marked difference between the two festivals which is reflected in much higher visitation rates to local tourist spots in Falun in comparison to Skinnskatteberg. Still it was obvious that at the time of the Falun survey the cooperation between the local tourist office and the festival management was not functioning too well, suggesting Falun could have had even higher rates.

The Choir Festival of Skinnskatteberg

The data on the Choir Festival of Skinnskatteberg comes from a study made in 1990. At that time the festival had around 4.200 attendants of which just over half were members of different choirs. Skinnskatteberg is a small town. Most visitors stay in temporary forms of accommodation, like schools and in sleeping-cars provided by the State Railways at the train station. Two of the high points of the festival are the mass in the church and the nearby gathering of all choirs and specially invited artists performing on the stage in front of the manor house with the beautiful lake as a backdrop. The setting could not be any better on a warm and sunny summer day.

It becomes evident from Figure 2.5 and Figure 2.6 that distance only plays a part in accounting for the spatial variations in degree of attendance. Only about one third of the variation is accounted for by the distance variable. In this sense the Choir event is somewhat special. As a large part of the marketing effort is directed at choir leaders, and those participating normally attend with fellows from the same choir, an uneven distribution of choirs will most likely also show in the pattern which is later recorded. According to the festival secretariat the number of choirs is not evenly distributed. This factor has not been ascertained in any greater detail. Another factor which may also reduce the effect of sheer

Figure 2.5. The relationship between attendance to the Choir Festival and distance to the event

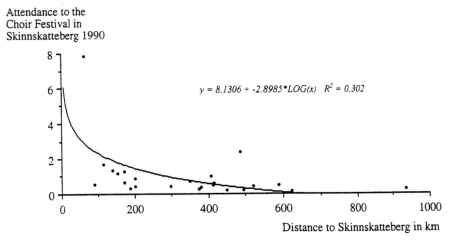

Attendance to the
Choir Festival in
Skinnskatteberg 1990

$y = 8.1306 + -2.8985*LOG(x)$ $R^2 = 0.302$

Distance to Skinnskatteberg in km

Figure 2.6. The hinterland of the Choir Festival in Skinnskatteberg 1990 – attendance related to regional population

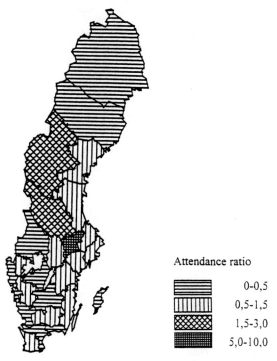

Attendance ratio

	0-0,5
	0,5-1,5
	1,5-3,0
	5,0-10,0

distance is that regularity of attendance, i.e. repeat visits more or less every year, decreases with increasing distance. This may lead to patterns of attendance which fluctuate spatially from one year to another. Time series data on attendance, which is not available, would clearify this point.

Comparing the Folk Music Festival and the Choir Festival

When comparing travel patterns generated by the choir and folk music festivals some interesting facets appear. Thus the village of Skinnskatteberg has limited supply of lodging, eating and shopping opportunities, whereas Falun as a regional capital is well furnished with this commercial infrastructure. Falun is also located in the middle of Dalarna county which in the summer time is one of the main tourist destinations in Sweden. In addition to this the Falun event attracts to a higher degree families and couples whereas the Skinnskatteberg event mainly attracts members of choirs. Thus both differences in the supply at the two destinations and the type of visitors they attract, leads to significant differences between these two events.

   It was obvious that Falun obtained a far greater economic impact than did Skinnskatteberg, but in both cases there also existed a potential for further development. The audience in Skinnskatteberg left more of a question mark as to what extent it would be worthwhile even trying to make visitors stay for another day or two. The composition of the audience may indicate that motives of these choir singers also limited their stay to the choir event, and that the only way of extending peoples stay would in fact be to add time to the event itself. The question has been raised but remains unanswered. Thus the motives of visitors has to be related to the potential of influencing the visitor's conception of time and space.

Thus if we conclude that the hinterland of the two cultural events just presented clearly demonstrates the presence of a distance decay function, still considerable irregularities occur in the patterns recorded. Different propensities to travel from various regions probably reflect the play of other variables of which regional variation in traditions may be an important factor.

World Championship in Nordic Skiing in Falun 1993

The World Championship in Nordic Skiing is a recurring event, however, it is not usually arranged in the same place. Falun has staged the event once before in the early seventies and is once again bidding for the return of the event. Considering the time which passes between events it is to be regarded as a one-time event so far as the host city is concerned.

Looking at data on place of residence of the audience to the World Championship in Nordic Skiing 1993 in Falun as shown i Figure 2.7 and Figure 2.8, a strong case for the distance decay concept can be made. Two major reasons for this situation will be put forward. Firstly, the interest in this typ of sport is probably more uniform than is folkmusic or choir membership. Secondly, this event is not recurring on a regular schedule.

The marketing of this event faced a number of difficulties which contributed to a hinterland which does not stretch very far from Falun. Not only did the weather conditions with high temperatures and insufficient snow supply in fresh memory from the pre-championship games in 1992 worry the marketing group, but mistakes were made by those in charge of marketing the event. The fact that large parts of the event were also televised probably contributed to a rather steep distance gradient as well.

Figure 2.7. The relationship between attendance at the Nordic Ski Championship and distance to the city of Falun

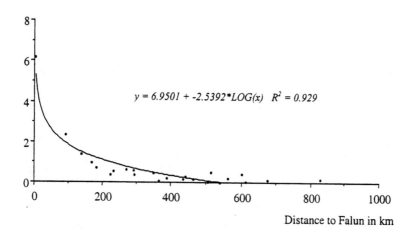

Figure 2.8. The hinterland of the Nordic Ski Championship in Falun 1993 – attendance related to regional population

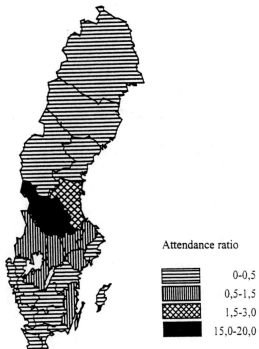

Attendance ratio

	0-0,5
	0,5-1,5
	1,5-3,0
	15,0-20,0

Despite the fact that this ski event is a World Championship, in many ways it still resembles a less renowned local event, when assessing its spatial features. Additional factors contributing to this pattern could be that this event is staged in the winter (for obvious reasons) which however, is a time of the year when trips in general are shorter both distance wise and in terms of duration. An illustration of this is given in Figure 2.9 which shows travel flows to second homes in the region of Bohuslän during the summer and winter season respectively.

Vasaloppet – a bundle of events

Vasaloppet is in many ways an outstanding event. The first competition dates back to 1922. The level of participation was low in the early phase of this event. It was not until the late fifties that this event passed 1000 participants. The 90 km race picked up momentum when it was first televised in the early sixties. TV has then normally had a rather extensive coverage of the event. It is open to elite and amateurs alike. The motives for non-elite participants are several but at the core is probably the fact that many people see Vasaloppet as a goal for their annual fitness endeavors. As such Vasaloppet is well attuned to major contemporary trends. Over the years the popularity of Vasaloppet has grown steadily. For several years the number of entries to the race was limited to 12.000. In order to relieve the pressure on Vasaloppet a parallel race was created called Öppet spår. It covers over the same distance. The participants can start within a two hour span in the morning. They attach a data chip to their boots and their passing of checkpoints as well as the final goal post in Mora is recorded

Figure 2.9.   Travel flows to second homes located in the region of Bohuslän. The share of visitors are shown by proportionate line width. Shaded regions supply visitors to Bohuslän (based on TDB-data)

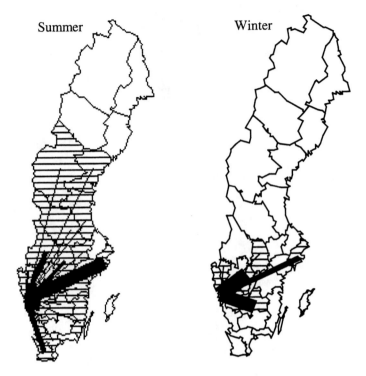

automatically. A few years ago the ceiling was raised to 15000 entries in Vasaloppet. Öppet spår is still growing, being spread out over three days. A further addition to the family of races is Tjejvasan which runs over a distance of 30 km and is restricted to females. In the summer a Vasa relay race over the 90 km takes place. The winter event now lasts a week and it draws about 30.000 participants all together and large crowds of spectators, especially to Vasaloppet itself.

When we look at the diagram depicting the relationship between distance and the participation for Vasaloppet (Figure 2.10) and at the hinterland maps of Vasaloppet, Öppet spår and Tjejvasan (see Figure 2.11), it becomes apparent that, although these three races are not identical in kind, they display characteristics which are significant. Thus Vasaloppet has a distance decay function which is much more relaxed than in the case of all the other events discussed in this chapter. Furthermore distance only explains about 40% of the variation in the participation level. And when we look at the hinterland map of Vasaloppet (Figure 2.10) it appears that distance does not play any major role in the decision process for those considering participating in Vasaloppet. As all participants in the race need to be members of a ski club in order to register they also often find an opportunity to organize their transportation through the club, chartered coaches, or through the network of members which the club provides. Thus most skiers travel in groups. This travel behavior may to some extent reduce the friction posed by distance. It is also of significance as it means that many of those managing to complete the heroic achievement of skiing the 90 km from Sälen to Mora have something to show for. This then triggers vacation travel in the summer season to places like Sälen and Mora, when the skiing hero like to show the rest of the family

Figure 2.10. The hinterland of those participating in Vasaloppet ski race in 1995 – attendance related to regional population

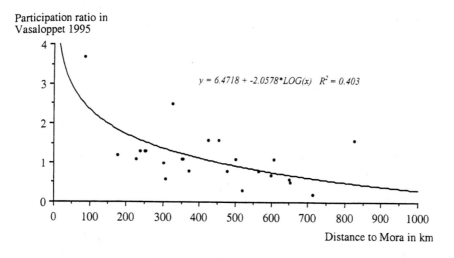

Participation ratio in
Vasaloppet 1995

$y = 6.4718 + -2.0578*LOG(x)$ $R^2 = 0.403$

Distance to Mora in km

Figure 2.11. The hinterland of the three ski races Vasaloppet, Öppet spår and Tjejvasan respectively – attendance related to regional population

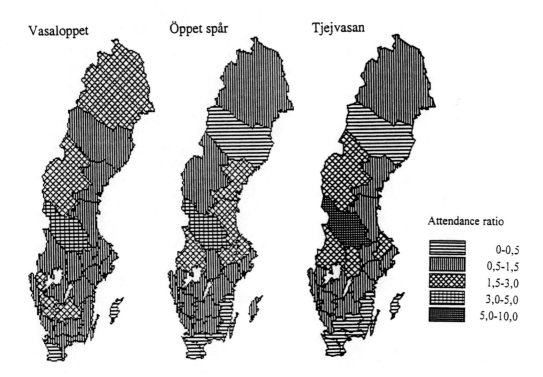

Vasaloppet   Öppet spår   Tjejvasan

Attendance ratio

0-0,5
0,5-1,5
1,5-3,0
3,0-5,0
5,0-10,0

where it all happened. This travel activity creates a considerable amount of recreational business in the area during the summer months. Another aspect which contributes to the relative insignificance of distance could be sought in the fact that Vasaloppet is an event which now (1999) celebrates its 75 anniversary.[9] It is probably the single best known sports event in Sweden. In recent times it has also gained recognition abroad not only in the ranks of elite skiers. Of the events covered in this chapter Vasaloppet has by far the highest number of foreign participants. The figure is around 20%. Looking at the choropleth map of Vasaloppet it is also obvious that those regions which have the best winter skiing conditions also show the highest rates of participation, i.e. Norrbotten, Jämtland county, Dalarna and the higland plateau in Småland. The only exception to this is perhaps the region of Västerbotten. Similarly the island of Gotland and parts of Skåne show very low levels of participation, as could be expected combining both weather, distance and transportation facilities.

We may then conclude that Vasaloppet has the least pronounced distance decay character as an event which is due to five major factors:

- Transportation to the event is relatively easy.

- The event is well known - it is an recurring event and it has been in operation for a long time.

- It has an appeal which is congruent with contemporary fitness ideals.

- It is based on participation and not just a passive spectator event.

- Repeat visitors are encouraged. Not only through traditional written information but also through e.g. medals available to those who participate several times.

Comparing Vasaloppet with its younger cousins, one might suggest that it is possible to discern a trend in participation's levels and the spatial characteristics pertaining to the market for this event. This conclusion presupposes that the three races are in fact products which are similar in kind and thus comparable. Another aspect is that these races have similar marketing strategies. Otherwise marketing in itself causes a problem when it comes to comparisons of different events as one would expect a faster diffusion process for an event which receives large marketing resources as compared to one that receives much less.

Öppet spår was established in 1984 and Tjejvasan some five years later in 1989. Thus these two products are much younger than Vasaloppet. The pattern shown in Figure 2.11 can thus be interpreted in terms of the spread of a product or an innovation. The origin, of course, is the region of Dalarna where the races take place. This region will initially have a much higher share of participants than other regions. As time passes the diffusion goes outwards and at the same time the attendance ratio tends to level off, reducing the supreme position of the initiating region making it more equal with the neighboring regions as well as the ones further away. A comparison made for Tjejvasan between 1992 and 1995 shows a very strong diffusion of the event which is also paralleled by a rapid growth in registration numbers. By 1998 the number of entrants had reached more than 7.000 which is almost three times the figure for 1992.

---

9)   Vasaloppet is slightly older but it has been cancelled three times due mainly to unfortunate weather conditions.

The Swedish Rally

This car race starts in the city of Karlstad and extends to the city of Falun. It lasts for three days. It is made up of a number of road sections which are closed off to regular traffic when the actual racing is taking place. In comparison to the Nordic Ski event the Swedish Rally, although a recurring event, has a similar clear relationship between participation and distance to the event. In this case the audience was interviewed either at the service stop in Borlänge or at the Lugnet Stadium in Falun. The distance between Borlänge and Falun is a mere 20 km. This study covers the part of the rally which takes place in the county of Dalarna, which represents about half of the entire race.

The Nordic Ski and the Swedish Rally events are similar in so far as the audience does not take any active part in the event itself. Visitors are spectators and the main driving force behind a visit is the interest in the sport itself being staged in the event. It can probably be assumed that interest in skiing and motor sport will follow the population distribution without any particular concentrations in space. Thus, one would expect as can be seen in Figure 2.7 and Figure 2.12 that there is a distance decay character to attendance scores.

Figure 2.12. The hinterland of the visitors to the Swedish Rally 1998 in the cities of Borlänge and Falun – attendance related to regional population

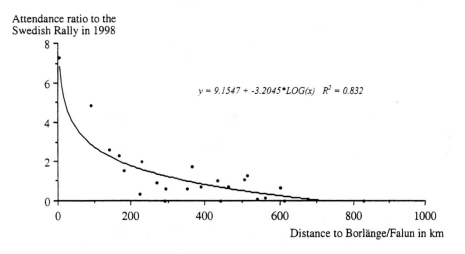

Attendance ratio to the Swedish Rally in 1998

$y = 9.1547 + -3.2045*LOG(x)$ $R^2 = 0.832$

Distance to Borlänge/Falun in km

Compared to the two music and cultural events discussed earlier, one could hypothesize that distance alone comes out stronger in the case of the Swedish Rally as it displays facets particular to a non recurring event. This is due to the fact that rally courses are replaced now and then. The layout of the rally thus changes from one year to another. In order to attend the Rally a visitor thus has to actively collect information of each individual rally as one can not rely on old information. This is probably both good and bad for the event itself. On the positive side is, of course, the fact that the product is changing, hopefully for the better, which may increase the propensity for repeat visits. On the negative side is the need to reestablish the event itself by providing the audience with up-dated information.

One aspect of the rally which makes it different from other events presented here is that each phase of the event passes extremely quickly. The rally courses are far apart and it is virtually impossible for the spectators to cover them all. Still with a sample of courses to

Figure 2.13. The hinterland of the Swedish Rally 1998 – attendance related to regional population

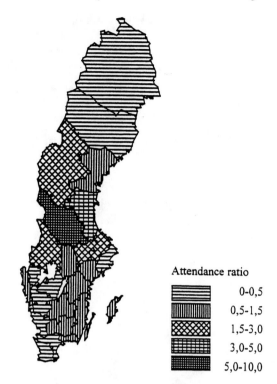

Attendance ratio

	0-0,5
	0,5-1,5
	1,5-3,0
	3,0-5,0
	5,0-10,0

cover it is very difficult to manage the time and space logistics involved. This also affects the economic impact which the rally gives rise to. Some previous desk research indicated high turnover and substantial economic impact on the communities affected by the Swedish Rally.[10] Later studies based on actual surveys of visitors, media and teams showed that these initial estimates were much too inflated. The audience do not stay on but come and go to a much greater extent than was known before. The lack of any real supply of goods and services along the race courses, which are by and large made up of road sections in the woods or in the countryside, reduces expenditures to a minimum for large parts of the rally. Spectators have to cater for their own needs. Probably another affect of this segmentation of the rally in time and space is that the media does not follow the rally in the way anticipated. The view held by several of the rally organizers that the media was an important group of high spenders proved strongly overestimated. Many of the regional and national media representatives only covered sections of the rally, often only one of three days, and several commented never staying overnight. This travel behavior reduced spending on meals and beverage, etc which would form part of the bills for over night guests. Thus primary data made it possible to kill off some of the myths regarding this particular event. The Swedish Rally in fact creates relatively little extra business activity in the places where it passes. This is to a great extent due to the very time and space structure of the event itself.

---

10) See Aronsson & Edelbring (1992).

2.4 Conclusion

To sum up a few of the things discussed in this chapter that all events have in common, it can be claimed that:

- They are subject to the distance decay function which decreases demand with increasing distance to the event. Recurring and well established events generally have a much less steep a gradient than have relatively newcomers or events which take place just once.

- Intervening opportunities may divert traffic and seriously undermine business in locations further away from the market.

- Population distribution is a significant factor to take into account when assessing the market for any event. The indigenous population within the destination is potentially more significant for an event than are tourists.

- Travel within the destination where the event takes place, we may call that micro travel, is significant when it comes to understanding e.g. the economic impact of an event.

- Events may create travel to a destination afterwards.[11] In this sense events can be of great value in selling other products which a particular destination offers.

Travel behavior and events

Tourism and recreational travel has in recent times received some attention in terms of the travel patterns that occur. A number of travel models have been put forward by Flognfeldt (1995), Opperman (1995) and Fesenmaier (1994).[12] A simplified model is given in Figure 2.14. So far very little research has been devoted to travel pattern analysis.

The significance of knowing how people in fact travel to an event lies in the possibility of placing the particular event into some sort of context. Thus if the event visitors by and large travel as *type I* in Figure 2.14 would indicate, there is little need for cooperation or concern for competition from other destinations. On the contrary, if people travel more according to *type II*, this indicates a need for consideration. What priority do visitors attach to our destination as an element in the bundle of supplies which the entire trip encompasses? Is there scope for cooperation with other destinations and in what way? If we ask people about their travel plans the itinerary may look like *type I* but we may discover that behavior does change in response to signals/information on the way. Studies done by the author indicates that event visitors may consider making detours as a result of information obtained along the road.[13]

It has been suggested that events taking place during winter months are more likely to have travel patterns like *type I,* whereas events during the warmer part of the year are more likely to include visitors whose itineraries are congruent with *type II*. The main argument

---

11) Milman and Pizam's (1995) study Central Florida suggests that increased awareness of a destination is not enough to increase visitation rates as opposed to actual familiarity, derived through previous visits. A similar observation is made by Sahlberg (1997) in his evaluation of Swedish travel data when he concludes that 90% of all Swedish travel involving an overnight stay was to destinations previously visited.

12) See e.g. also Walmsley, D.J. and Jenkins, J.M. (1992) and Woodside, A.G. and Lysonski, S. (1989).

13) The results are preliminary as yet but concern both an arts exhibition – Sculptura -97 – in the city of Falkenberg and an ongoing study including a survey of attendees at the motorcycle rally (FIM-International) in Falun in the Summer of 1998.

Figure 2.14. A simplified travel model portraying two major types of travel itineraries

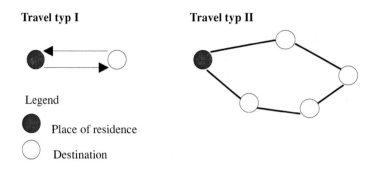

for this seems to be that, as regards recreational travel, there is less free time available to most travelers in the winter season. The main vacation period is still in the summer and this is when people are more likely to demonstrate *type II* like travel patterns.

Type II travel may also be viewed as travel on a micro scale, such as travel to various points of interest within a destination itself. The spatial concept of a destination is also a complex subject. The further away one is from a destination the greater spatial extent is one prepared to allow a particular destination to have. The closer one gets to the destination, or the more one gets to know about it, the more detail is added to the image and the more refined the boundaries which can be applied. However, in this case the spatial limit of a destination is not the key issue, but rather to what extent available supplies, which are parts of the tourism and travel production function, have a potential for being used or asked for by those attending/participating in events? A recent discussion brings to the fore the idea that, for the region of Dalarna, cooperation among the different event producers would create benefits for all and make it possible to strengthen tourism travel for cultural purposes to the destination of Dalarna.[14] Although some of this discussion concerns the adminstrative aspects of event production, other parts concern issues which lie closer to central place theory. The latter refer to the fact that by combining different goods and services one could in fact increase the attractiveness of a destination. This would in central place theory come close to the notion of orders of goods. High order events could then be achieved not only by the qualities of the event itself but through combining the event with other offers based on the supply available in the destination of the event. The latter reasoning may also include other places/destinations which are part of the product as perceived by the tourist himself. In this context of entering central place theory it is important to realize that the individual traveling always has to be the focus. It is the perception held by the tourist which set the limits. If we do not have a clear understanding of travel motives it will be very difficult, if not impossible, to ascertain whether or not a particular form of packaging is relevant or not. Two examples may illustrate the problem. When the championship in orientering (O-ringen) was held in Ronneby, local tourist officials created a bundle of programs including among other things popular orchestras with dance evenings. Participants in the O-ringen event had no interest in the products. It turned out to be a complete failure. When planning for the

---

14) These ideas were put forward in an article in a local newspaper quoting the former minister of culture Mr. B. Göransson and Dr. B. Ekman, Chairman of Musik vid Siljan (Runnberg, J.), *Kulturen är framtidens motor,* Borlänge Tidning, Saturday, 6th February, 1999, p. 20.

World Skiing Championship 1993 in Falun some people suggeted that the city of Falun should cooperate with the city of Stockholm. Some argued that this would be attractive for the international market as it would be possible to form a package tour which could include shopping and culture in Stockholm and the skiing championship in Falun. This was rejected it seems, on hearsay grounds. Some claimed, right or wrong, that winter events are not sold as packages. It is a straightforward product - the event and nothing more. As it turned out very few visitors from outside Scandinavia came to the event, although this may not have anything to do with the absence of products combining the actual event with other items and places. However, the underlying question of how people prefer to travel and how packaging may cater for such needs, still remains unanswered.

References

Aronsson, L. & Edelbring, D. (1992). *En undersökning av Svenska Rallyt 1992:* Ekonomiska effekter i Värmlands län och Karlstad kommun. Högskolan i Karlstad.

Bohlin, M. (1975). *The Spatial and Economic Impact of Recreational Expenditures and Sales in the Pigeon Lake Area of Alberta*. M.A. Thesis, University of Alberta, Edmonton.

Bohlin, M. (1993). *Vasaloppen 1992 – En studie av ekonomiska effekter,* ITR-rapport nr. 1/1993, Högskolan Borlänge.

Bohlin, M. (1995). The Development and Proliferation of a Crosscountry Ski Race in Sweden and the Involvement of the Local Community in Staging the Event. In *Proceedings of the Fourth International Outdoor Recreation and Tourism Trends Symposium and the 1995 National Recreation Resource Planning Conference* (pp. 138-144). University of Minnesota.

Bohlin, M. (1995).Turism i ett regionalekonomiskt perspektiv. In S. Berger (Ed.), *Samhällets geografi* (pp. 111-128). Nordisk Samhällsgeografisk Tidskrift, Uppsala.

Bohlin, M. & Elbe, J. (1993). *Skid-VM i Falun 1993. En utvärdering av effekter på samhälle och näringsliv.* ITR-rapport No 2/93, Högskolan i Falun/Borlänge.

Bohlin, M. & Hanefors, M. (1992). Visitor Profile, Economic, Social and Cultural Impact of Two Musical Festivals in Sweden. In F. Colbert, & C. Mitchell, (Eds.), *First International Conference on Arts Management* (pp. 79-97). Proceedings, Montreal, Canada.

Bohlin, M. & Malmberg, T. (1998). *Svenska Rallyt 1998 - Resultatsammanställning*. Tjärwood HB, Borlänge.

Bohlin, M. & Ternhag, G. (1990). *Visitor Profile and Economic Impact of Falun Folk Music Festival,* paper presented at The Sixth Annual Conference of Cultural Economics at Umeå University, June 11-13, 1990. 15 pp.

Clawson, M. (1959). *Methods of Measuring the Demand for and Value of Outdoor Recreation*. Reprint no. 10, Fourth printing 1972, Resources for the Future, Inc. Washington D.C.

Flognfeldt Jr, T. (1995). *Areal, Sted og Reiserute*. Fagbokforlaget: Bergen-Sandviken.

Fesenmaier, D.R. (1994). Traveler Use of Visitor Information Centres: Implication for Development in Illinois. *Journal of Travel Research, XXXIII* (1), 44-50.

Milman, A. & Pizam, A. (1995). The Role of Awareness and Familiarity with a Destination: The Central Florida Case. *Journal of Travel Research, XXXIII*(3), 21-27.

Oppermann, M. (1995). A Model of Travel Itineraries. *Journal of Travel Research, 33*(Spring), 57-61.

Runnberg, J. (1999). Kulturen är framtidens motor, *Borlänge Tidning,* Saturday 6, February, p. 20.

Sahlberg, B. (1997). Human Relations and Travel Patterns - A Global Network, *Revue de Tourisme, 1/97,* 25-33.

Stouffer, S. A. (1940). Intervening Opportunities: A Theory Relating Mobility and Distance, *American Sociological Review. 5*(6), 846-849.

Walmsley, D.J. & Jenkins, J.M. (1992). Cognitive Distance: A Neglected Issue in Travel Behaviour. *Journal of Travel Research, XXXI*(1), 24-29.

Woodside, A.G. & Lysonski, S. (1989). A General Model of Traveler Destination Choice. *Journal of Travel Research, XXVII* (4), 8-14.

Wolfe, R.L. (1972). The Inertia Model, *Journal of Leisure Research, 4*(Winter), 73-76.

Vägverket, 1996. *Vägavstånd i Sverige,* Heimer & Company, Reklambyrå AB, Falun.

Chapter 3
Effects of Events on Destination Image

Lena L. Mossberg

School of Economics and Commercial Law, Göteborg University, Sweden

3.1 Background

Mega-events are short-term events with long-term consequences for the host city. One consequence often referred to, is a new or renewed positive image for the city through media, particularly TV. The positive image is assumed to have effects on, for example tourism and industrial investments. Getz states "With global media attention focused on the host city, even for a relatively short duration, the publicity value is enormous..."(1997:57).

Research of the past 25 years has shown that image is an important concept in understanding tourists' destination selection processes. Tourists hold images of alternative destinations and their choice of vacation destinations is greatly influenced by their perception of destination images (Hunt 1975; Um and Crompton 1990; Ahmned 1991; Crompton 1992; Milman and Pizam 1995). Many research streams can be found but so far, most studies have examined the relationship between image and behavior (Baloglu and MacCleary 1999). A clear relationship has been found between positive perceptions of destinations, and positive purchase decisions (Pearce 1982; Telisman-Kosuta 1989). Researchers have also investigated the impact of previous visitation or familiarity on destination image (Pearce 1982; Phelps 1986; Ahmed 1991; Milman and Pizam 1995). Familiarity has been proposed as both a positive and negative factor in image evaluation, according to MacKay and Fesenmaier (1997). In most studies, familiarity has been associated with a more realistic impression of a destination (Hunt 1975; Gartner and Hunt 1987). The relationship between tourists' distance to the destination and image has been an other research area (Hunt 1975; Crompton 1979; Ahmed 1991). Additionally, a growing interest in models on destination image formation has been seen over recent years (MacKay and Fesenmaier 1997; Baloglu and MacCleary 1999).

Perceptions can change very fast, e.g. when natural catastrophes (such as oil spills) or industrial catastrophes (such as Tjernobyl) occur. Studies have been carried out focusing on negative effects. For example, the demonstration in Tiananmen square in Beijing (Gartner and Shen 1992), the consequences of war in Croatia (Vuconic 1999) and the impact of the unsettled political situation on the image of Northern Ireland (McGuckin and Demick 1999). However not many have been found that concentrate on positive effects and perceptions due to a certain event, except studies of Olympic Games. The Winter Olympic Games in Calgary, Canada, led to an enhanced reputation for the host city (Ritchie and Smith 1991) and the 1988 Seoul Olympics had a positive effect in increasing long-term visitation to the country (Kang and Perdue 1994). Another study was conducted by Jaffe and Nebenzahl (1993), who examined the effect of the promotional aspects of the 1988 Seoul Olympics on the image of certain electronic products made in South Korea. They concluded that event-related publicity can affect product-country images. Questions still remain whether large events may alter consumers' perceptions of products in general from a specific destination and/or country, and the destination as a tourist site.

3.2 Theoretical Framework

This chapter is based on research focusing on the World Championships in Athletics. This event is one of the largest events in the world. Only the Olympic Games and the World Cup in soccer are larger. In August 1995 the World Championships in Athletics were held in Göteborg. Almost half a million people gathered in Göteborg to see the games or to take part in the festivities arranged in connection with the event (Sjögren 1996). Almost 1000 journalists were accredited (Bohlin 1996). The aim of the study was to find out whether the presence of a mega-event with extensive media attention has any effects on foreign tourists' image of the destination.

The theoretical framework for the empirical study in the chapter is divided into four parts. Many research areas on destination image can be of interest for the event context, but those selected are of particular importance for the study discussed, because of its clarification of image formation and awareness levels. It is also assumed to be relevant for future studies in the same direction. First, the framework covers definitions of destination image. The next part captures the importance of the image formation stage before the trip, including the influences of information sources. Following, is the third part about awareness levels, image objects and events, and finally, the measurement of destination image is discussed.

Defining destination image

A destination image is in short the tourists' mental picture of a specific destination or as Crompton suggests an image as "...the sum of beliefs, ideas and impressions that a person has of a destination." (1979:18). Um and Crompton recognized the formation of overall image from evaluation of an object "The image of a place as a pleasure destination is a gestalt. It is an holistic construct which, to a greater extent, is derived from attitudes towards the destination's perceived tourism attributes" (1990:432-433). People develop both cognitive and affective responses and attachments to destinations (Proshonsky et al. 1983). Similarly, Oxenfeldt (1974-75) looked at image (in a general sense) as an overall or total impression which is formed as a result of the evaluation of individual attributes which may contain both cognitive and emotional content. Gartner (1993) suggests that its cognitive component (sum of beliefs and knowledge of attributes of the objects or product), and its affective component are distinct but hierarchically related. The initial image formation stage has proven to be the most important phase in the buying decision process when selecting a destination (Mercer 1971). In general, potential visitors have limited knowledge of the destination's attributes if they have not visited it before. Only the destinations the individual is aware of will be considered in the selection process. This awareness implicates an image of the destination. The same applies to selecting a product when comparing various brands. Destination image is a simplified mental representation and can be considered as a destination brand.

Destination image formation

Many have tried to capture a process of image development linked to tourism promotion and destination choice. Gunn (1988) states that the tourists' perception of destination image is revealed through two processes – organic (person-determined) and induced (destination-determined). Person-determined image reflects the individual differences in information processing and interpretations and destination-determined image reflects the actuality of the destination, according to MacKay and Fesenmaier (1997). What is communicated via mass communication (e.g. TV, radio, and newspapers) together with word-of-mouth form the organic components of destination image. Strategic promotion of the destination's tourist attractions forms the other part (induced), which is planned and intended promotion. In most cases it is difficult to change the organic part while it is, to a great extent, possible for the official tourist organizations to change the induced image through positioning. According to Phelps (1986) experience of a destination results in the formation of a primary image. Phelps distinguishes between primary and secondary image. The latter is based on organic and induced image, which influence on tourists expectations. Fakeye and Crompton (1991) propose three stages: organic, induced, and complex. The first stage represents an awareness and is present prior to destination promotion. The next stage is formed when promotions are viewed and evaluated against organic image. Complex image evolves from experience of visiting the destination. The same authors find that informative materials were assumed to be most effective at the organic stage, persuasive materials at the induced stage, and reminding materials at the complex stage. Gartner (1993) suggests that the type and amount of information sources received influence the formation of the cognitive component of image, but not the affective component. Similar results were found by Holbrook (1978) and Woodside and Lysonski (1989). Baloglu and McCleary (1999) contend that variety (amount) of information sources, type of information sources, age, and education influence perceptual/cognitive evaluations. These and the social and psychological characteristics of the perceiver together influence the affective component.

Awareness levels, image objects and events

In some cases an individual's awareness of the destination is marginal or it might even be absent. The literature developed in marketing on branding can be useful in this context of understanding awareness levels. In the literature, brand awareness is the ability of an individual to recognize or recall a brand as a member of a certain product category. It "involves a continuum ranging from an uncertain feeling that the brand is recognized, to a belief that it is the only one in the product class" (Aaker 1991:61). The same author has created the awareness pyramid concerning brands (Figure 3.1).

At the base of the pyramid, the individuals are not aware of the brand. At the next level they recognize the brand. Their ability for recognition is based upon an aided recall test. Individuals are given a set of brand names from a given product class and are asked to identify the ones they already are aware of. At the subsequent level (brand recall), the individuals are asked to name the brand in a product class. The names are not provided. It is a so called unaided recall test. 'Top of the mind' is the first named brand in an unaided recall task. It is ahead of the other brands in an individual's mind.

It is assumed here that this awareness pyramid can be applied not only to brands but also to other image objects. According to Dowling (1993), images exist on different levels (country image, company image, brand image, etc.), and manifest themselves hierarchically and

Figure 3.1. The awareness pyramid

Source: Aaker 1991:62.

automatically in the consumers' minds. In the following, awareness is discussed in connection with events and destination image at city, state and country level. The awareness levels from the pyramid are presented vertically in the matrix and the event is seen as a brand (Figure 3.2). Horizontally, the image objects on different levels are shown and different examples are presented.

Figure 3.2. Awareness levels and image objects – a synthesis

	Destination image – City level	Destination image – State level	Destination image – Country level
Top of Mind	Mentioning specific event/Vancouver first	Mentioning specific event/British Columbia first	Mentioning specific event/Canada first
Event Recall	Able to recall specific event/Vancouver	Able to recall specific event/British Columbia	Able to recall specific event/Canada
Event Recognition	Recognizing specific event/Vancouver	Recognizing specific event/British Columbia	Recognizing specific event/Canada
Unaware of Event	Unaware of specific event/Vancouver	Unaware of specific event/British Columbia	Unaware of specific event/Canada

A fundamental assumption within the research on product-country images is that individuals' images of countries influence their images of the countries' products, and conversely, consumers' images of certain products may influence their images of countries as well (Whitelock and Sequeira 1991). It can be assumed that tourists' images of a country influence their images of destinations and events in the country and vice versa. Many combinations may exist. It is not certain that the images of the country/state/destination influence the images at all levels.

As regards the left-hand column in Figure 3.2, an individual can be unaware of Vancouver as a tourist destination. He/she can also be aware of the specific event, but it does not have to be the case. Others know of Vancouver and the event but do not recognize British Columbia. An individual can, for instance, be unaware of Vancouver and British Columbia or he/she might be aware of one of them. Others name Vancouver in an unaided recall task (brand recall) but are unaware of Vancouver's location in Canada. Many, e.g. school children in Europe are aware of Canada but do not know where it is geographically and are not able to name any states or cities in the country.

It can also be assumed that different events lead to different image effects. The different kinds of image effects may depend partly on the type of event. For example, the World Championships in Athletics, the World Cup in Soccer, the Olympic Games are all one-time multi-day mega-sport-events. Through past patronage or other forms of exposure, for example television, individuals will develop some attitudes (positive or negative) regarding the event type. These attitudes will serve to frame the image of the particular event type, in this case sport events (Gwinner 1997). Also, the size, the particular theme, and the power of attraction of the event, are all features that can exert an influence, and also whether it is a matter of a one-time event at one location, recurrent at regular intervals, or recurrent at different locations at different periods of time and with different regularity. The Olympic Games can be considered in a category of its own due to its history, size and importance. For instance, the Winter Olympic Games in Lillehammer, Norway, increased the number of tourists to the place after the event (Spilling 1996). Still, no study can be found concerning the longevity of the image effect. Furthermore, it cannot be taken for granted that the publicity is necessarily favorable. In connection with the Lousiana World's Fair, the publicity was not only scarce, it was also disadvantageous (Dimanche, 1996). Local media were critical of the fair and this impression was reflected in national and international media. Many recurring events are assumed to influence individuals' images to a higher extent than one-time events, since they occur year after year and therefore may become associated with the destination. The bull race in Pamplona, Spain, is one example, the Octoberfest in Munich another, and The New York Marathon, a third.

Destination image analysis

Measuring destination image is not a new phenomenon; a large amount of research has been carried out. The conceptual framework for destination image measurement has traditionally been based on structured methodologies, specifically scales (e.g. Hunt 1975; Crompton 1977; Goodrich 1977; Crompton 1979; Pearce 1982; Haahti and Yavas 1983; Crompton and Duray 1985; Kale and Weir 1986; Gartner and Hunt 1987; Gartner 1989; Calantone et al. 1989; Ahmed 1991; Chon 1991; Javalgi et al. 1992; Chalip and Green 1997).

As shown in Table 3.1 various approaches and instruments were used. In general, for the scale development, the first step consists of a literature search where a domain of construct has to be specified. The next step is to generate a sample of items and many of the studies (see Table 3.1) have had an open approach to eliciting the constructs salient to a segment (based on e.g. literature search and focus groups). After the constructs are identified, dimensions are often developed with factor analysis (see e.g. Ahmed 1991; Javalgi et al. 1992; Echtner and Ritchie 1993; Chalip and Green 1997) and then Likert or semantic differential scales are in most cases used to rate the constructs. Following this, further data is collected and tested (a procedure for developing scales, see e.g. Churchill 1987).

Table 3.1.   The objective and methodology of previous destination image research

Reference	Objective	Methodology	Dimensions
Ahmed (1991)	To measure the image of Utah	Structured – 22 attributes – bipolar adjective (Likert type)	Four dimensions (factor analysis): 1. Parks 2. Activity 3. Culture 4. Night life
Chon (1991)	To measure pre-travel and post-travel images of South Korea	Structured – 26 attributes – 7-point Likert scale	Seven dimensions (Cronbach's alpha): 1. Shopping attributes of South Korea (4 attributes) 2. Attributes related to the people of South Korea (4 attributes) 3. Historical and cultural attractions (3 attributes) 4. Safety and security concerns (3 attributes) 5. Scenic beauty of South Korea (2 attributes) 6. General travel related resources (3 attributes) 7. General attitudes towards South Korea (6 attributes)
Javalgi et al. (1992)	To measure the image of European destinations in America	Structured – 21 attributes – 9-point Likert scale	Five dimensions (factor analysis): 1. Place with well-known landmarks and history (6 attributes) 2. Place to experience cultural variety (4 attributes) 3. Place with fine amenities (6 attributes) 4. Area for viewing wildlife and scenery (3 attributes) 5. Area for price/value (2 attributes)
Echtner and Ritchie (1993)	To develop techniques to measure destination image	Structured and unstructured – 34 attributes – 6-point Likert scale – 3 open-ended questions	Eight dimensions (factor analysis): 1. Comfort/security (10 attributes) 2. Interest/adventure (6 attributes) 3. Natural state (4 attributes) 4. Tourist facilitation (4 attributes) 5. Resort atmosphere/climate (3 attributes) 6. Cultural distance (3 attributes) 7. Inexpensive (2 attributes) 8. Lack of language barrier (2 attributes)
Chalip and Green (1997)	To develop a destination image scale	Structured – 40 attributes – 6-point Likert scale	Nine dimensions (factor analysis): 1. Developed environment (8 attributes) 2. Natural environment (6 attributes) 3. Value (4 attributes) 4. Sightseeing opportunities (5 attributes) 5. Risk (4 attributes) 6. Novelty (4 attributes) 7. Climate (3 attributes) 8. Convenience (3 attributes) 9. Family environment (3 attributes)

One problem in only using scales is that the scale items are not necessarily salient to the respondents' perceptions. Irrelevant constructs can be included and others omitted, state Selby and Morgan (1996). If respondents are only asked to assess different attributes on a scale, it is not possible to identify the unique and holistic components of the destination's image. Reilly (1990) is one of few who have used open-ended questions in destination measurement studies. He concludes that the use of free elicitation of descriptive adjectives provides a powerful method for measuring destination image. The respondents were asked to describe their mental pictures of Montana. They mentioned both the attributes and also their holistic impressions of these attributes. However, it is difficult to fully capture destination image through open-ended questions. The level of detail depends largely on the cooperation of the respondents, as unstructured techniques are time consuming. Also, open-ended questions are hard to analyze statistically and comparisons between destinations can be difficult. Some aspects do not require open-ended questions. Aspects such as safety, cleanliness, living standards etc. can be measured with a reliable and valid set of scales.

Echtner and Ritchie (1993) have developed a conceptual framework for destination image measurement. They use both structured and unstructured statements and they talk about three continua: 1/ attribute-holistic, 2/ functional-psychological, and 3/ common-unique. The first continuum (attribute-holistic) is supported by earlier research about people's information processing within psychology and consumer behavior. This means that a product is viewed both in terms of pieces of information about specific characteristics or attributes and as a whole (MacInnis & Price 1987). This emphasizes that a destination's image consists not only of perceptions of separate attributes (such as climate, hotels, service, etc.) but also of more holistic impressions (mental pictures of the destination). Functional and psychological characteristics can be perceived as either individual attributes or holistic conceptions. On the attribute side there are a number of perceptions about the destination's individual characteristics (from functional to psychological). On the holistic side, the functional impressions consist of mental pictures of physical characteristics of the destination, while the psychological can be described as the destination's atmosphere. Finally, concerning the common-unique continuum, destination image can be based on perceptions about characteristics ranging from common to the more unique ones.

Echtner and Ritchie developed the scales for the structured questions through an eight-step procedure. Eight dimensions appeared from a factor analysis (see Table 3.1).The unstructured questions were developed from earlier literature and with the help of an expert panel. The unstructured questions intended for measuring the holistic and unique components of image were the following ones (1993:5):

> 1. "What images or characteristics come to mind when you think of XXX as a vacation destination? (functional holistic component)
>
> 2. How would you describe the atmosphere or mood that you would expect to experience while visiting XXX? (psychological holistic component)
>
> 3. Please list any distinctive or unique tourist attractions that you can think of in XXX. (unique component)"

Many of the instruments are designed to be appropriate and rigorous and they have been tested to be valid and reliable. Chalip and Green (1997) assume that their scale can be used for destination image measurements at all levels: city, state, national as well as international. Echtner and Ritchie write that their "...generalized framework can be used to compare and contrast the images of most, if not all, tourist destinations" (1993:12). The framework of the latter can probably be used in all settings but the dimensions in this study and in the others are quite different from each other. In most of the studies, dimensions about culture, natural environment, activities and low costs are included but many of the others differ. Reasons for this can e.g. be the use of factor analysis with various dimensions and a free choice of name for each. The items in one dimension can be about the same but be called something different. Another reason concerns the targeted segments including the respondents' socio-cultural background. A third reason concerns the questioning of respondents regarding image. Is the aim to study perceptions of one specific destination/ specific destinations, national or international or is it the respondents' next/last tourist destinations that they are asked to rate/compare? In e.g. the Australian scale, no items related to language barriers are included. Echtner and Ritchie's scale, on the other hand, includes two items on this matter. In a Swedish context, no comprehensive scale has been developed, but it is assumed that language items are relevant in rating international destinations. Also, the Australian scale includes many outdoor activities such as tennis and golf. This is not included in the American scale.

3.3 Empirical Study

This part of the chapter presents and discusses some of the problems covered in the data collection of the study. It also shows the selected instrument, which was based on and compared with earlier studies on destination image. Thereafter follows the findings presented in a number of tables and figures.

Data collection

In order to achieve the aim of the study it is necessary to consider when and where to measure destination image and who to approach. A number of studies have employed different ways to assess this specific image. For example, they have researched:

- The image of one destination - with respondents from one or several countries/regions (Crompton 1977, 1979; Haahti and Yavas 1983; Crompton and Duray 1985; Kale and Weir 1986; Tourism Canada 1987; Reilly 1990; Ahmed 1991).

- The image of several destinations in comparison to each other - with respondents from one or several countries (Hunt 1975; Goodrich 1977; Richardson and Crompton 1988; Gartner 1989; Calantone et al. 1989; Javalgi et al. 1992; Echtner and Ritchie 1993).

- The image of one destination before and after the trip (Pearce 1982; Phelps 1986; Chon 1991).

- The change of destination image over a long period of time (Gartner and Hunt 1987).

If the aim is to evaluate the effects of one specific event (one time- or recurring) the third or the fourth approaches seem to be the best ways. The event is unique and takes place in one destination (with a few exceptions like sport tournaments). Measuring the destination image once or comparing different destinations does not seem to be useful. The image effects can only be seen in pre- and post measurement or over a long period of time.

It is difficult to develop a generalized scale to be used to compare all type of destinations, e.g. countries, regions and cities. Foreign respondents can e.g. be asked to rate and to compare the image of the Nordic countries. On the city level, however, it is difficult to compare. If foreign respondents are to be asked, one difficulty related to lack of, or vague, image has to be considered (see Figure 3.2). An important aspect to consider is if the respondents have experienced the destination before. The degree to which destination image is crystallized depends partly upon whether respondents have visited the destination recently or have plans to go there in the future (Chalip and Green 1997).

Another issue relates to the selection of respondents. The respondents can e.g. be a sample of a national and/or an international population and they can be tourists or non-tourists. The respondents can also be selected as participants or business people, national and/or international. Of major concern is whether or not the respondents have visited or participated in the event. The respondents selected in this study (Mossberg 1995;1997) were non-Swedish travelling by ferries from England, Germany, and the Netherlands with Göteborg as their destination. The data was collected by means of questionnaires during the voyage to Göteborg or directly upon arrival terminal. The pre study was conducted two to three months prior to the event and the post study three to four months after the event (two separate populations). The result is based on data from 618 respondents in the pre study and 525 respondents in the post study. The respondents did not visit Göteborg at the time the event was going on neither did they intend to nor participate in the event. This approach was selected to discover whether the tourists' perceptions had changed as a result of the event's intense communication e.g. in media and by organizations such as tourist boards. Alternatively, if the respondents were chosen because they participated in or visited the event, the result would probably have been different. In this case they could have been asked during the event and their experience of the destination could be compared with their expectations.

The respondents in the post study were not the same as in the pre study. The background variables were gender, age, nationality, and former visits to Sweden. Although the samples were not matched, there was an important between-samples homogeneity concerning the respondents' sociodemographic characteristics, which, to some degree, guarantees the similarity of the samples (see Table 3.2).

Table 3.2.   The respondents

	Pre study		**Post study**	
Age (mean)	39.35 years		39.94 years	
Gender (%)	49.7 male		49.7 male	
	42.1 female		42.7 female	
	8.3 (no answer)		7.6 (no answer)	
Nationality (%)	British	39%	British	40%
	German	20%	German	20%
	Dutch	24%	Dutch	21%
	Norwegian	3%	Norwegian	2%
	Others	6%	Others	6%
	No answer	8%	No answer	11%
Former visits to Sweden (%)	Visited Sweden	33%	Visited Sweden	30%
	Not visited Sweden	59%	Not visited Sweden	61%
	No answer	8%	No answer	9%

The instrument

The framework of Echtner and Ritchie (1993) for measuring destination image was assumed to be highly relevant. As mentioned before, they use both structured and unstructured techniques and they talk about three continua 1/ attribute-holistic, 2/ functional-psychological and 3/ common-unique. A combination of techniques is often required (Selby & Morgan 1996) and in this case it was relevant as the respondents had the chance to mention the specific event in the unstructured part. The same three open, unstructured questions were asked in order to measure the holistic and the unique components of image.

The researcher grouped the attributes used in previous studies (Hunt 1975; Crompton 1977; Goodrich 1977; Crompton 1979; Pearce 1982; Haahti and Yavas 1983; Crompton and Duray 1985; Kale and Weir 1986; Gartner and Hunt 1987; Gartner 1989; Calantone et al 1989; Ahmed 1991; Chon 1991; Javalgi et al 1992; Echtner and Ritchie 1993; Chalip and Green 1997) into a list of attributes. One problem was that the scales for most of the studies were developed for countries and states and they were assumed not wholly appropriate for use at city level. Some of the attributes in this study were modified to suit a city level. Also, the framework available for place images was considered. These studies concentrate on the industrial aspect rather than tourism (Bramwell and Rawding 1996). The list was discussed with experts from the Tourist Board and from a marketing research company. It was also presented and discussed during one methodology seminar (the participants were senior researchers and Ph.D. students, all with an interest in tourism), and in one Marketing class of Master-level students (80 participants). The final list consisted of 26 attributes and 23 of these were in congruence with the study of Echtner and Ritchie. Each item was accompanied by a 7-point scale (1 = strongly disagree, and 7 = strongly agree). The scale items used and the results from the pre and post study are presented in Table 3.4.

Findings

In Table 3.3 the most frequent answers to the three open-ended questions are shown. The table only includes answers with more than 5 % frequency. The respondents could mention more than one characteristic/description/attraction for the same statement.

Table 3.3. The most frequent descriptions regarding the open-ended questions

	Pre study	Post study
1. Images or characteristics evoked when thinking of Göteborg as a vacation destination		
– friendly	7%	8%
– clean	8%	9%
– ancient buildings/historical	9%	12%
– port/sea town	10%	9%
– cold and dark (weather)	2%	11%
2. Descriptions of the atmosphere or mood expected while visiting Göteborg		
– friendly/helpful/warm	34%	40%
– peaceful/relaxed	19%	19%
3. Distinctive or unique tourist attractions in Göteborg		
– bridges/canals/harbor	8%	6%
– Liseberg	8%	9%
– Churches and historical buildings	5%	6%

Table 3.4. Mean values for selected image scale items

Dimensions/attributes in this study	Mean value pre study	Mean value post study
Dimension 1. Comfort/Security (6 attributes)	**5.34** tot.dim.	**5.41** tot.dim.
Local standards of cleanliness and hygiene are high	5.63	5.69
High standard of living	5.63	5.55
Quality restaurants and hotels are easy to find	4.90	5.10*
Göteborg is a safe place to visit	5.44	5.47
Local people are friendly	5.36	5.42
High quality of service	5.07	5.22
Dimension 2. Interest/Adventure (6 attributes)	**4.53** tot.dim.	**4.58** tot.dim.
A holiday in Göteborg is a real adventure	4.35	4.46
Everything is different and fascinating	4.37	4.51
Many places of interest to visit	4.77	4.83
Göteborg is a city of events	4.47	4.42
Fairs, exhibits and festivals are frequent	4.37	4.40
Good sport facilities are available	4.82	4.88
Dimension 3. Natural state (2 attributes)	**5.04** tot.dim.	**5.16** tot.dim.
Göteborg is a restful and relaxing place to visit	4.97	5.09
Offers a lot in terms of natural scenic beauty	5.11	5.22
Dimension 4. Tourist facilitation (2 attributes)	**4.88** tot.dim.	**4.88** tot.dim.
Many packaged vacations to Göteborg are available	4.77	4.63
Good tourist information is readily available	4.99	5.13
Dimension 5. Resort atmosphere/Climate (3 attributes)	**4.45** tot.dim.	**4.51** tot.dim
Good shopping	4.99	5.11
Has good nightlife	4.40	4.58*
Pleasant weather	3.96	3.85
Dimension 6. Cultural distance (3 attributes)	**4.19** tot.dim.	**4.10** tot.dim.
Life style and customs are similar to ours	4.56	4.37
Food is similar to ours	4.22	4.07
Local architectural styles are similar to ours	3.78	3.86
Dimension 7. Inexpensive (2 attributes)	**3.99** tot.dim.	**3.97** tot.dim.
Prices are low	2.92	2.94
Goods and services are expensive	5.05	4.99
Dimension 8. Lack of language barrier (2 attributes)	**4.29** tot.dim.	**4.37** tot.dim.
Few people understand English	3.21	3.53*
Many people speak English	5.37	5.20

(The scale ranged from 1 to 7, where 1= strongly disagree and 7 = strongly agree.)

*= significant changes t-test 5% level

The only major difference (Table 3.3) between the two studies concerned the weather dimension (2% in the pre study, and 11% in the post study). This is not surprising since the post study was carried out in the autumn. In both studies, the tourists perceive Göteborg as a friendly, clean and relaxed seaport with old buildings.

In Table 3.4 the eight dimensions and the mean values for the image scale items are presented. Relatively small changes have occurred between the evaluations. The attributes with low scores in the pre study were also low in the post study, and the ones with high scores stayed high. Only three attributes, marked with stars in Table 3.4, show significant changes. The values for event-related attributes did not change (t-test 5% level).

The results were also summarized using graphical techniques, something demonstrated as highly relevant as it allows for easy comparison (Selby & Morgan 1996). As mentioned earlier, destination image was looked at from three continua - attribute-holistic, functional-psychological and common-unique. As it is difficult to handle three dimensions, the analysis was based on two-dimensional diagrams as Echtner and Ritchie recommend. The input data consists of the results from both the structured statements and the open-ended questions (see Table 3.3 and Table 3.4).

The mean values of several functional attributes are presented in the upper left quadrant of Figure 3.3. The values shown in parenthesis are the results from the post study. They include hotel and restaurant quality, good shopping, tourist information, costs, quality of service, scenic beauty and living standard, which all were given high values. In the lower left quadrant, different psychological attributes are shown such as friendliness, safety, knowledge of languages, restfulness and cleanliness (which were given the highest values).

Figure 3.3.   The attribute/holistic and functional/psychological components of destination image (pre and post)

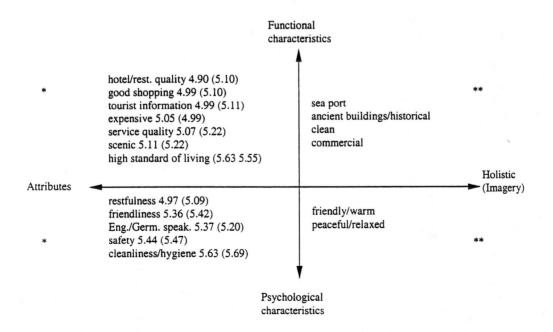

*   Information in quadrant supplied by scale items
** Information in quadrant supplied by open-ended questions

Figure 3.4. The common/unique and functional/psychological components of destination image (pre and post)

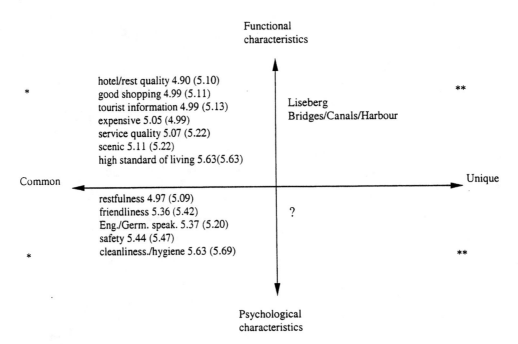

*   Information in quadrant supplied by scale items
** Information in quadrant supplied by open-ended questions

The data from the open-ended questions has been used for the right-hand side of the figure. Data from question 1 primarily formed the functional holistic image and question number 2 contributed the psychological characteristics of the holistic image. The functional-psychological and common-unique components of destination image are illustrated in Figure 3.4. The data for the left-hand side is the same as above but it is not possible to measure unique components using structured questions. Therefore, the answers from question number 3, supply the data for the right-hand side. The respondents were asked to mention specific and unique tourist attractions at the destinations.

Most of the respondents did not know of any tourist attractions. The only unique attraction was Liseberg (an amusement park). Many respondents mentioned general attractions associated with water (without names), such as bridges, canals or the harbor. Not many mentioned attractions associated with psychological characteristics. Therefore, this quadrant is empty in Figure 3.4.

Finally, in Figure 3.5, the attribute-holistic and common-unique components of image are shown. In this case, the scale items provided data for only one of the quadrants, which encompasses the common attributes of image. This figure also indicates, as do the other figures, that there is a considerable consensus between the two samples. The common and unique attributes are a scenic destination, high standard of living, and a safe and clean destination. The common and holistic components of Göteborg's image for the respondents are that the destination is a sea port, there are old buildings, and the city is clean and commercial. Looking at the holistic and unique components, it was found that the atmosphere is friendly and peaceful. Examples of both functional and psychological common attributes are provided in the upper left quadrant of the figure.

Figure 3.5. The attribute/holistic and the common/unique components of destination image (pre and post)

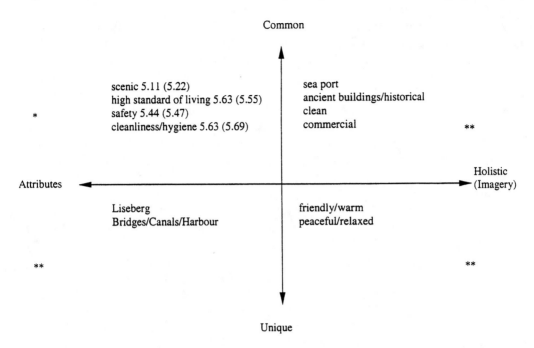

* Information in quadrant supplied by scale items
** Information in quadrant supplied by open-ended questions

It was hypothesized that the media exposure related to the event had a positive effect on foreign tourists' images of the host destination concerning attribute-holistic components, functional-psychological components, and common-unique components. Significant differences could only be found for three of the 26 structured items. These changes were small. Furthermore there were only minor differences concerning the open-ended questions between the two studies. Hence, the respondents' images of the destination did not become more positive due to the intensive media coverage related to the event.

3.4 Conclusion

Events are often claimed to be image-makers. The Olympic Games seems to be 'something else' in an image creating perspective. A lot of people know when and where the games have taken place over the years. However, it is doubtful if people in general know where other sporting events, such as the World Championships in Ice Hockey, Soccer or Athletics have been located. In this context it is interesting to study whether the perceptions about the destination image have changed due to a mega-event other than the Olympic Games. It is plausible that the intensive media coverage before and during the event increases the awareness of the destination.

A more holistic and complete measurement of destination image can be obtained by using the method developed by Echtner and Ritchie, instead of only using structured methodologies and evaluating separate attributes, which would often be the case in other studies. The method has been used before to compare different destinations. This study shows that the method is also suitable for evaluating destination image at different times to see if a change in perceptions has occurred. Diagnosing a destination's perceived image gives a valuable guide when making modifications or additions to the destination's marketing strategies. The open-ended questions provide information about tourists' perception of the destination. In this case a very fragmented picture occurred. Furthermore, the results show that the tourists' picture of the destination in question is very unclear, which can be related to the high rate of respondents visiting the destination for the first time. The awareness about tourist services in Göteborg among those are low. Most of the respondents do not know of any tourist attractions at all. When answering the question 'What images or characteristics come to mind when you think of Göteborg as a vacation destination' the majority did not mention anything, despite the fact that all had chosen Göteborg and were on their way there. This could be a result of e.g. the city's unclear positioning, the lack of unique tourist attractions or internationally well known individuals. The open-ended questions might therefore give an indication of whether promotional campaigns have achieved the desired results. Another explanation for the unawareness of any tourist attractions may be that many of the respondents participated in various package tours, because the tour itself can serve as an attraction. The package includes a long journey on a cruise ship and a short tour/a day visit at the destination.

As the evaluations only included foreign tourists not visiting the event, it is not obvious that there are no image effects on other segments. According to the local tourist organization, and from the main actors among the congress and trade fairs' organizers, the image of Göteborg as a city, with desirable qualities for arranging events, has improved due to the mega-event. The city has become more attractive for arrangements such as trade fairs, congresses, and conferences. As well it has to be pointed out that tourist numbers in the area have increased ever since. Thus, if the respondents had been chosen because they participated in or visited the event, the result would probably be different. According to what Bohlin discussed in the previous chapter, the distance seems to be of less importance for the tourists to the events if they are participating. There is a great difference in participation comparing for example Vasaloppet with the World Championship in Athletics. In the latter, most attendees are spectators, but in Vasaloppet almost everyone participates in the competition. It has to be kept in mind that for a mega-event, such as the World Championship in Athletics, the sport and the sportsmen/women are in focus. The main target group is very wide and includes individuals (mainly TV-viewers) with an interest in athletics around the world. The athletics enhance their own image and maybe the image of their own countries. The destination where the event is held can be of minor importance to this sport interested public.

There are also others factors which have to be considered why there is an increase in number of tourists visiting. A lot of other events and fairs are arranged continuously, the exchange rate is positively effected, as is the increasing number of Swedish tourists travelling domestically. Additionally, the awareness of the country of Sweden as a tourist destination may have increased.

The World Championships in Athletics gave Göteborg a great opportunity to attain global media attention for a limited period time. The post-evaluation was undertaken two to three months after the games. Despite the short time lapse, very few of the foreign tourists travelling to Göteborg connected the championships with Göteborg. Gunn's model (1972) described tourists developing organic images of a set of alternative destinations from various non-tourism information sources, such as TV, radio and newspapers. It was certainly an intensive international media coverage, but unfortunately, media simply did not expose tourist attractions in Sweden and Göteborg. Moreover, the newspaper articles merely focused on the sport activities, since most of the invited media representatives were sport journalists.

References

Aaker, D.A. (1991). *Managing Brand Equity, Capitalizing on the Value of a Brand Name.* NY: The Free Press.

Ahmed, Z. (1991). The Influence of the Components of a State's Tourist Image on Product Positioning Strategy. *Tourism Management,* (Dec), 331-340.

Baloglu, S. & McCleary, K. (1999). A Model of Destination Image Formation, *Annals of Tourism Research, 26*(4), 868-897.

Bohlin, M. (1996). Utländska tidningars bevakning av Göteborg under 1995. *Evenemang, Affärsmöjlighet och Imageskapare,* Institutet för hotell-, restaurang- och turismforskning, Handelshögskolan, Göteborgs universitet.

Bramwell, B. & Rawding, L. (1996). Tourism Marketing Images of Industrial Cities. *Annals of Tourism Research, 23*(1), 201-221.

Calantone, R., Benedetto, A., Hakam, A. & Bojanic, D. (1989). Multiple Multinational Tourism Positioning Using Correspondence Analysis. *Journal of Travel Research, 28*(Fall), 25-32.

Chalip L. & Green, C. (1997). The Destination Image Scale. Unpublished paper, Griffith University, Australia.

Chon, K.-S. (1991). Tourism Destination Image Modification Process. *Tourism Management,* (March), 68-72.

Churchill, G. (1987). *Marketing Research.* Fourth edition, The Dryden Press.

Crompton, J. (1977). *A Systems Model of the Tourist's Destination Selection Decision Process with Particular Reference to the Role of Image and Perceived Constraints.* Ph.D. diss. Texas A&M University, College Station.

Crompton, J. (1979). An Assessment of the Image of Mexico as a Vacation Destination and the Influence of Geographical Location upon that Image. *Journal of Travel Research, 17*(Spring): 18-23.

Crompton, J. (1992). Structure of Vacation Destination Choice Sets. *Annals of Tourism Research, 19,* 420-432.

Crompton, J. & Duray, N. (1985). An Investigation of the Relative Efficacy of Four Alternative Approaches to Importance -Performance Analysis, *Journal of the Academy of Marketing Science, 13*(Fall), 69-80.

Dimanche, F. (1996). Special Events Legacy. The 1984 Lousiana World's Fair in New Orleans. *Festival Management & Event Tourism, 4*(1/2), 49-54.

Dowling, G. R. (1993). Developing Your Company Image into a Corporate Asset. *Long Range Planning, 26*(2).

Echtner, C. & Ritchie, B. (1993). The Measurement of Destination Image: An Empirical Assessment, *Journal of Travel Research,* (Spring), 3-13.

Fakeye, P. & Crompton, J. (1991). Image Differences Between Prospective First-Time and Repeat Visitors to the Lower Rio Grande Valley. *Journal of Travel Research, 30*(2), 10-16.

Gartner, W. (1989). Tourism Image: Attribute Measurement of State Tourism Products Using Multidimensional Scaling Techniques. *Journal of Travel Research, 28*(Fall), 16-20.

Gartner, W. (1993). Image Formation Process. In M. Uysal & D.R. Fesenmaier (Eds.), *Communication and Channel Systems in Tourism Marketing* (pp. 191-215). New York: Haworth Press.

Gartner, W. & Hunt, J. (1987). An Analysis of State Image Change Over a Twelve-Year Period (1971-1983). *Journal of Travel Research, 28*(Fall), 16-20.

Gartner, W. & Shen, J.Q. (1992). The Impact of Tiananmen Square on China's Tourism Image. *Journal of Travel Research, XXX* (4), 47-52.

Getz, D. (1997). *Event Management & Event Tourism.* New York: Cognizant Communication Corporation.

Goodrich, J. (1977). A New Approach to Image Analysis Through Multidimensional Scaling. *Journal of Travel Research, 16*(3), 3-7.

Gunn, C. (1988). *Tourism Planning,* 2nd ed. New York: Taylor and Francis.

Gwinner, K. (1997). A Model of Image Creation and Image Transfer in Event Sponsorship. *International Marketing Review, 14*(3).

Haahti, A. & Yavas, U. (1983). Tourists' Perception of Finland and Selected European Countries as Travel Destinations. *European Journal of Marketing, 12*(2), 34-42.

Holbrook, M.B. (1978). Beyond Attitude Structure: Toward the Informational Determinants of Attitude. *Journal of Marketing Research, 15*(November), 545-556.

Hunt, J. (1975). Image as a Factor in Tourism Development. *Journal of Travel Research, 13*(Winter), 1-7.

Jaffe, E.D. & Nebenzahl, I.D. (1993). Global Promotion of Country Image: Do the Olympics Count? In: N. Papadopoulos & L.A. Heslop (Eds.), *Product-Country Images, Impact and Role in International Marketing,* International Business Press.

Javalgi, R., Thomas, E. & Rao, S. (1992). U.S. Pleasure Travellers' Perceptions of Selected European Destinations, *European Journal of Marketing, 26*(7), 45-64.

Kang, Y. & Perdue, R. (1994). Long Term Impact of a Mega-Event on International Tourism to the Host Country: A Conceptual Model and the Case of the 1988 Seoul Olympics. In M, Uysal (Ed.). *Global Tourist Behavior* (pp. 205-225). International Business Press.

Kale, S. & Weir, K. (1986). Marketing Third World Countries to the Western Traveler: The Case of India. *Journal of Travel Research*, *25*(Fall), 2-7.

McGuckin, M. & Demick, D. (1999). *Northern Ireland's Image – Platform of Pitfall for Gaining the Competitive Edge?* Paper presented at the European TTRA Conference 29th and 30th Sept, 1st and 2nd Oct. in Dublin. Ireland.

MacInnis, D. & Price, L. (1987). The Role of Imagery in Information Processing: Review and Extensions. *Journal of Consumer Research*, *13*(March), 473-91.

MacKay, K. & Fesenmaier, D. (1997). Pictorial Element of Destination in Image Formation. *Annals of Tourism Research, 24*(3), 537-565.

Mercer, D. (1971). The Role of Perception in the Recreation Experience: A Review and Discussion. *Journal of Leisure Research, 3,* 261-276.

Milman, A. & Pizam, A. (1995). The Role of Awareness and Familiarity with a Destination: The Central Florida Case. *Journal of Travel Research, 33*(3), 21-27.

Mossberg, L. L. (1995). *The Importance of Events in Tourist Destination Positioning.* Paper presented at the CHRIE and IAHMS joint conference 26-28 October, 1995 in Göteborg, Sweden.

Mossberg, L. L. (1997). The Event Market. *Annals of Tourism Research, 24*(3), 748-751.

Oxenfeldt, A.R. (1974-75). Developing a Favorable Price-Quality Image. *Journal of Retailing, 50*(4), 8-14.

Pearce, P. (1982). Perceived Changes in Holiday Destinations. *Annals of Tourism Research, 9,* 145-64.

Phelps, A. (1986). Holiday Destination Image - The Problem of Assessment: An Example Developed in Menorca. *Tourism Management*, September, 168-80.

Proshonsky, H.M., Fabian, A.K. & Kaminoff, R. (1983). Place-Identity: Physical World Socialization of the Self, *Journal of Environmental Psychology, 3,* 57-83.

Reilly, M. (1990). Free Elicitation of Descriptive Adjectives for Tourism Image Assessment, *Journal of Travel Research, 28*(Spring), 21-26.

Richardson, S. & Crompton, J. (1988). Cultural Variations in Perceptions of Vacation Attributes, *Tourism Management*, June, 128-36.

Ritchie, B. & Smith, B.H. (1991). The Impact of a Mega-Event on Host Region Awareness: A Longitudinal Study, *Journal of Travel Research, 30*(1), 3-10.

Selby, M. & Morgan, N. (1996). Reconstructing Place Image. *Tourism Management, 17*(4), 287-294.

Sjögren, S. (1996). Besökarnas utgifter under VM-dagarna - en sammanställning och analys av statistik. *Evenemang, Affärsmöjlighet och Imageskapare*, Institutet för hotell-, restaurang- och turismforskning, Handelshögskolan, Göteborgs universitet.

Spilling, O. (1996). Mega-Event as Strategy for Regional Development: The Case of the 1994 Lillehammer Winter Olympics. *Entrepreneurship & Regional Development*, (8), 321-343.

Telisman-Kosuta, N. (1989). Tourist Destination Image. In S. Witt & M. Moutinho (Eds.). *Tourism Marketing and Management Handbook,* Prentice Hall.

Tourism Canada. (1987). *Pleasure Travel Markets to North America: Japan, United Kingdom, West Germany, France, Highlights Reports.* Ottowa.

Um, S. & Crompton, J. (1990). Attitude Determinants in Tourism Destination Choice. *Annals of Tourism Research*, 17: 432-448.

Whitelock, J. & Sequeira, C.A. (1991). Methodological and Theoretical Issues in the Research into Country of Origin Effects on Product Evaluation. *EMAC Annual Conference,* Dublin.

Woodside, A.G. & Lysonski, S. (1989). A General Model of Traveler Destination Choice. *Journal of Travel Research, 27*(4): 8-14.

Vukonic, B. (1999). *Aggressive Marketing is Not Always Successful Marketing.* Paper presented at TTRA Conference 29th and 30th Sept, 1st and 2nd Oct. in Dublin, Ireland.

Chapter 4

The Locals - Local Knowledge, Participation, and Identity

Monica Hanefors

Dalarna University &
School of Economics and Commercial Law, Göteborg University, Sweden

4.1 Background

In the last couple of decades, special music events have become a prominent part of the cultural calendar in Sweden during the summer months (Aldskogius 1993:55). One such music event is the Choir Festival of small town Skinnskatteberg, located right near a lake in a rather picturesque part of the region of Västmanland in Sweden. In 1981 Skinnskatteberg was a community in crisis, following the break up of the traditional iron industry and trade, and the recently closed local board factory. Working opportunities had been declining and many locals were forced to leave Skinnskatteberg since the late 1970s.

Because of the acute crisis the local government, together with the Swedish Farmers Federation's newspaper 'Land', made efforts to start the Choir Festival. The work with the Choir Festival is said to have strengthened the solidarity among people in Skinnskatteberg. Likewise, it is claimed that managing the Festival has become a concrete, common goal for the local population.

The development of music festivals and similar events in Sweden goes back about 20 years in time. As part of a government policy to spread the supply of concert music, a series of festivals was created under the auspices of national 'Rikskonserter' (The Swedish Concert Institute) during the seventies in Sweden (see e.g. Bohlin and Ternhag 1990). The idea behind this has several components. Not only has there been a political ambition to distribute musical experiences to a wider audience outside the major metropolitan areas of Sweden, but also an attempt to find settings that offered the beauty of the Nordic summer (cf. Bohlin and Hanefors 1992b). Since then the development of musical festivals has been rapid. If early festivals had a mixed repertoire, their successors have developed into genre specific events, focusing solely on, for example, rock, folk, or choral music.

In 1990 approximately 130 different music events were reported, and according to Aldskogius (1993:57) they numbered 410 in the summer 1993, including also ballet and music theater. All of these events are not necessarily to be considered festivals, according to the definitions discussed and presented by, for example, Wilson and Udall (1982:3), Falassi (1987:1), and Jago and Shaw (1998). The two latter authors suggest that there are certain core attributes to be found in a special event such as the music festival: "attracting tourists or tourism development", "raising awareness, image, or profile of a region", "offering a social experience", and "being of limited duration and out of the ordinary" (1998:28). Their suggestion fits well with the features of the annual Choir Festival, that takes place in Skinnskatteberg.

This chapter of the book will concentrate mainly on research focusing that Choir Festival, and it was undertaken during a couple of months during the latter part of 1990.[1] The research sought to discover:

- if local identity, gained through a festival like the Choir Festival, keeps a local population together, and
- how created and developed identity is handled, i.e. maintained, reinforced and articulated, or even lost, through the Choir Festival.

4.2 Theoretical Framework

The subject of festivals has attracted continued interest from researchers within various disciplines (Saleh and Ryan 1993:289). However, the literature on the impacts of such, and other, events is dominated by studies, that have primarily focused on the economic situation (Burns and Mules 1986; Rey 1987; McDonald 1990; cf. Fredline and Faulkner n.d.). "A number of studies have examined social impacts using secondary data (. . .) but this approach is limited", say Fredline and Faulkner (op. cit.) and argue that relatively few studies have involved direct measurement of residents' perceptions as an indicator of the impacts of events. One example is pointed at (Jeong and Faulkner 1996), where the "approach places the impacts within the population's frame of reference" (op. cit. p. 8). This was also the aim of the Festival research in Skinnskatteberg.

After ten years of festival activity the local government claims that the Choir Festival has put Skinnskatteberg on the Swedish map, and also given the town and county a good name and reputation, complementing the pride it has lent to the local inhabitants. Hall notices that: "Governments and private industry generally hold that hallmark events, as with tourism, are 'a good thing', otherwise why would they be held?" (1992:5).

However, the local government argument is supported by, for example, Getz in 1989 (p.127) and 1991 (p. xi) (see also, concerning various events, e.g. Ritchie 1984; Burns et al. 1986; Decore 1986; Getz and Frisby 1987, 1988; Travis and Croize 1987; Kaspar 1987; Ashworth and Goodall 1988; Witt 1988; Getz 1989; Hall 1989 a, b, 1992, 1996; Ritchie and Smith 1991; Roche 1994; Backman et al. 1995; Wicks 1995; Light 1996).

During the initial planning phase of the Choir Festival research it became quite obvious that the local government's concern about the realization of the research was partly induced by the appearance of an intra-community conflict. This automatically led me to question whether an event touristic in character like the Choir Festival, really can have the positive effects stated by local governments and, sometimes, researchers, "whether festivals are good medicine for the souls, a glue that galvanizes communities together" (Cousineau 1991:1) – that is, other effects than strictly economic[2] ones? This question seems especially relevant, when it is known that "Without a broad-based support, it is unlikely that any community event will be successful" (Wicks 1995:177).

---

1) This research was conducted parallel to Magnus Bohlin's research focusing more directly on 'visitor profile and economic impact' of the Choir Festival (see Bohlin & Hanefors 1992 a, b).

2) The only visible effect on employment in Skinnskatteberg as a result of the Festival is the two persons employed by the Choir Festival office. They are full-time year round jobs. Due to the fact that local authorities in Sweden levy their own income tax, employment is important as it generates revenue locally. The municipal tax is around 30 %, and is therefore the major portion of the income tax in Sweden. About two-thirds of this

In research into the impacts of tourism (i.e. not particularly events) the encounter between the visiting guests and the local host population is among the major anthropological concerns. Often the hosts receive most of our research attention and just as often they are described as the losers in the encounter (see Nuñez 1978 for an early, and interesting, example). Looking also at more recent research focusing on the same theme, occurrences of words like 'dignity', 'self respect', 'adjustment' and 'identity' are frequent when the hosts are the focus. Likewise, when the hosts are allowed to describe their situation themselves (Hanefors 1990) they tell a similar story. It has been shown that tourism might contribute to the tourist receiving hosts' identity; either through creating a completely new identity (e.g. D'Sousa 1985; Fees 1989) or strengthening one, that is already present (e.g. Smith 1982; Browne and Nolan 1989), thereby adding to the local hosts' pride (e.g. den Otter 1985). Similarly, a certain identity might be maintained through a recurrent event in a host society, even if the original significance of the event has been transformed, due to tourists/tourism (Dewailly 1984).

Identity is a concept that, in order to express it simply, implies someone's identification or feeling of identification - who and what someone is to the self and to others. It is also the meaning an individual connects with him or herself, as part of a social situation or a social role. The identity gives structure and content to the sense of self, and to someone's self-esteem, and ties an individual to a social system.

There is a continuous interaction between individual identities within a group. There is also interaction between an identity and human environment's possibility, willingness, and way for perceiving the identity of a certain individual or group. Therefore, identity can be said to be both dependent on relations and reflexive in nature. By this it is possible to understand that an identity might keep a local population together and likewise that it might be a deliberate way to present oneself to the surroundings; individually or collectively. Hypothetically, a common identity could be lost, maintained, or reinforced respectively through communication in such a manner that, for example, a Choir Festival entails. The alternative is that an identity is created and developed (e.g. Babou-Arnaud 1989), to be maintained, reinforced and articulated through that Festival.

4.3 Empirical Study

Methodology

In the social sciences it is common to find that social, cultural, and ethnic identities are treated as totally separated concepts referring to, for example, one individual's identification with a specific social position, to cultural tradition or to an ethnic group. The research in Skinnskatteberg does not follow this premise, because the same distinction is not made here. Due to the aim of the study and the focus of the research, stated above, I discuss in terms of social and individual identity only, based on the feasibility for an individual to

---

accrue to the municipality directly and the rest goes to the county. The latter then filters back to the municipality through the medical services provided by the county. The tax revenue received by Skinnskatteberg is roughly estimated to be 120,000 SEK. In case of Skinnskatteberg the situation is slightly different. The last two Festivals have shown considerable deficits, which have been covered by grants from the municipality. For 1990 it is in the range of 600,000 SEK (Bohlin & Hanefors 1992 b).

obtain identity together with other individuals as well as in relation to these individuals. This decision draws on the fact that it is quite possible to view the approximately 5,400 local inhabitants of Skinnskatteberg[3] as a group of individuals sharing certain common denominators: they live in close proximity to one another, are able communicate with one another and reciprocally admit each others' existence. In other words, some important basic prerequisites for a shared identity are prevalent.

The most usual and urgent claim on any method used in social science, if general awareness of methods is excepted, deals with the need for the method to relate directly and intimately with the aim and objective of the specific research task. As soon as the researcher has decided to find the answer to one or more questions or problems – as soon as a study's aim is developed and precise - the choice of a suitable method becomes acute. The aim should, at best, be fruitful and simple, while still stimulating, and the method should serve that aim and, hence, the researcher should never be a slave to procedure and technique (Taylor and Bogdan 1984:8).

In anthropology it is normal to undertake studies with participant observation – traditionally the most usual method with anthropologists. This method means that the anthropologist spends considerable time together with the group being studied, to reach a holistic, inner perspective. However, this method is not always preferable, partly since it is relatively time consuming, and therefore it was not the sole alternative in the Skinnskatteberg Choir Festival research. Instead, it was divided methodologically into both quantitative and qualitative phases. This is not the usual way to do things, and when in a recent article Formica (1998) presents state-of-the-art research focusing on festivals and other special events, nothing of the sort is included. Instead, Formica says that normally the articles are descriptive in nature, and there are approximately seven times more quantitative than qualitative studies focused on in those articles (p. 134). Besides, Formica, reports on no anthropological contribution at all, but says "Researchers and academians seemed most interested in investigating monetary issues (. . .) whereas the investigation of socio-psychological issues related to festivals and special events was left almost unexplored" (p. 135).

In a perfect world, all researchers, whether they use qualitative or quantitative methods, are equally concerned about the accuracy of their data. In spite of that certain researchers refuse to highly value both types of methodologies, and claim that seeing things, from a different perspective, is totally worthless. To me it seems that both qualitative and quantitative methodologies are more than sets of data gathering techniques. Rather, they represent ways of approaching reality, and have to do with researchers themselves - with the researcher's worldview. I not only have a high regard for the technique linking methods, but I also advocate using both qualitative and quantitative methods if this is considered to give a better result in a specific study. The linking of methods is also argued for by, for example, Pearce and Caltabiano (1983), Theuns (1989), Crandall (1987), and Dann et al. (1988).

Because of the reasons mentioned above, and because of the aim of the study, the Skinnskatteberg Festival research is methodologically divided into three intertwined phases:

- the first was a phase of participation and observation during the three days, when the 1990 Choir Festival took place, expected to give both experience and knowledge of the festival structure, as well as a being a basis for the next phase,
- the second was a quantitative phase of design, distribution, and analysis of a questionnaire distributed by mail to certain local inhabitants in Skinnskatteberg, and

3) This is the number of inhabitants in Skinnskatteberg municipality (one of the smallest municipalities in Sweden regarding inhabitants, but still 662 km²) out of which 55 % (approximately 3,000) live in central Skinnskatteberg.

- finally, the third phase constituted personal interviews with a small number of locals, which predominantly intended to give further insight into social strategies.

There were, however, further reasons for linking methods. First, this research' divided focus - that is, on the one hand the individual and social identity among the local population, that was discussed above, and on the other hand, the social strategies caused by the Festival. The latter seemed important to include because they emanate from the various effects of the Festival. It is easy to imagine that if the locals articulate the opinion that the Choir Festival creates/strengthens/destroys individual identity in any way, that they also make certain efforts to handle the social situation implied by the Festival. Second, the Choir Festival is part of a process of change in the community - a change that involves, and is partly directed by, the community members together. And the dynamics of such a negotiation, implied by change, are very difficult to pin down solely through a survey.

Questionnaire

Knowledge and participation are two inter-related and interacting ingredients of the concept of identity - with knowledge you are able to participate and while participating you acquire knowledge. . . Another explanation for why these two areas were obvious foci goes back to a conversation I once had with my then nine year old daughter, who explained to me why a certain girl in her class was more popular than all the others - a girl who everyone uncritically admired and wanted to be friends with. *You see, Mum,* my daughter said, *it seems like we know everything about her, that's why, and we feel sort of close to her!*

Accordingly, the questionnaire was designed around arguments of knowledge and participation. In all 498 male and female adult locals, between 18 and 75 years old, chosen from the Skinnskatteberg population, were asked in the questionnaire to answer 20 questions about themselves, the community, and the Festival. Moreover, respondents were requested to declare their positions on 22 different arguments, of a positive and negative nature. The respondents were also invited to express individual opinions in their own words, an offer that activated 20 % of them. These also added their names and telephone numbers in the questionnaire, because I had explained that I might want to follow up the questionnaire with an interview. Since the research concerned identity, the selection of respondents excluded any locals, who were not Swedish citizens at the time of the research, while including locals, who for some reasons, e.g. studies, were not living in Skinnskatteberg at the moment.

Two of the questionnaires did not reach their addressees - bringing the number to 496.

To improve response rates two reminders were sent, after three and five weeks. In all 289 usable questionnaires were returned, providing a net response rate of 58 %, i.e. 51,5 % men and 48,5 % women. This rate of return was considered to be sufficient to meet the aim of the research, especially when also looking at the structure of the non replies. The distribution among the respondents concerning age and occupation corresponds completely to the structure of the total Skinnskatteberg population.

Even though research like this will give certain generalized data about the opinions of the local population, as for example if they are generally for or against the Festival, we must never be tempted to treat the locals as a homogenous group of people as a result of this, which often is the case in other research. The answers and opinions shown in the questionnaires include wide variations that are, of course, related to the individuals behind them. For example, the locals, who live nearby one of the Festival sites, and/or are disturbed by it, are more likely be more negative towards the event than those who live elsewhere (see e.g. Pizam 1978; Brougham and Butler 1981; Teo 1994). Or, the business community is not to be expected to show equal support, that is "certain businesses may be very supportive of an event whereas another might rather strongly oppose it based upon the effect the event has on their firm" (Wicks 1995:178; see also Hall 1989c concerning big events). Similarly, the politicians in the local government, however small his/her involvement in the Festival might be, would probably express an opinion similar to that of one questionnaire respondent: *As an active community politician I am naturally, and always, a strong protector of the Choir Festival.* A similar, positive opinion was also to be expected among any locals economically gaining from the Festival, as for example the 68 year old woman, who exclaimed: *I have never had the time to visit the Festival; there is a constant queue outside my kiosk – everyone is happy and you can hear singing everywhere.*

The awareness of such variations caused a number of personal, structured interviews were made with a few strategically chosen respondents. These were chosen on the basis of variation of social background, and the comments they had made in their questionnaires. Their comments told me that here I had certain individual locals with strong opinions about the Choir Festival, who can articulate interesting opinions. Eventually, I made telephone contact with several of them, however many did not want to be interviewed at this point. The reason could be that some time had passed since they answered the questionnaire, but it could also be interpreted as their not being concerned about the Festival anymore. Nine respondents, out of who five men and four women, declared that they wished to participate in an interview. My intention, of course, was not to make any generalizations from these interviews, but rather to find possible explanations for the previously collected qualitative and quantitative data.

Experience of the Festival

The annual Skinnskatteberg Choir Festival 1990 was held during three days of the Midsummer week at the end of June, when the weather in Skinnskatteberg is most agreeable. Choirs from all over Sweden participate and the program that year included 213 choirs. A festival is a themed, public celebration (Getz 1993) and, as mentioned in the first chapter of this book, it may be defined as a special and/or cultural event "consisting of a series of performances of works in the fine arts, often devoted to a single artist or genre" (Hall 1992:5). The Skinnskatteberg Festival is also a typical "community event" (Wicks 1995:178) in that it includes a small food court, craft sales area, children's' activities, and a variety of other local/regional attractions. The main part of the Festival, however, consists of workshops and concerts, out of which the former is a mixture of lectures/seminars and a more direct transmission of new knowledge where the participants themselves are active. The theme of the workshops is of course, choral singing – which might be anything from general knowledge about voices to various types of actual choral singing.

In 1990 the overall theme of the Festival was folk music, but the theme differs from one year to another, as do the artists invited. Usually the artists are both well known and popular, both to the choir members and to the more or less passive listeners of the audience, but they may have another music specialty than choral singing. One year, for example, a popular female singer was invited, even though her repertoire is Swedish pop-music, and at the 1990 Festival the invitation went to a male guitar-player and singer, with still a different repertoire of romantic ballads and more traditional Swedish melodies.

The concerts are held indoors and outdoors; the church, the school, the manor, the old railway station, as well as the Skinnskatteberg Manor Meadow, sloping beautifully down to the lake 'Övre Vättern', serve as concert locations. During 1990 a Nicaraguan peasant mass was held in the Skinnskatteberg church. Swedish priests joined the South Americans and choirs from all over Sweden joined the rhythms of the visiting choral singers. In all my life I never saw a church so filled with people - it was indeed a remarkable, spiritual experience. However, the concert usually attracting most choirs and audience is the final outdoor one, Sunday afternoon. Normally thousands of people gather on the Meadow - one year even 10,000 - bringing their blankets, or small camping chairs, and baskets with coffee, cakes, or wine, bread, cheese and fruit. The number of people in the Festival audience in 1990 was estimated to be approximately 4,200 (Bohlin and Hanefors 1992a:11).

Participation

The interest in cultural phenomena, both in general and in music, is high among the local inhabitants of Skinnskatteberg. Most of the respondents state that they are very interested in music, however not particularly choir music. During the interviews it becomes clear that there is a feeling of both development and change in the Festival - from being a Festival that meant singing *in every single copse of Skinnskatteberg,* it has increasingly become more *professional and more elevated as regards its music score.* Several ask: *Is the musical level really appropriate?* One man says: *The Festival should have more general music – more music everywhere in Skinnskatteberg. If you are a family of five, like we are, you cannot go to the concerts, if you are ordinary people, that is. Why isn't it a Festival without expensive artists?"*

As many as 60 % of all respondents agree with an argument such as 'I think culture is important'. This does not necessarily mean that they take any active part in the Festival's workshops, as is apparent from the first of the figures (Figure 4.1), although they are open to everybody. The opinions of 92 % of the locals are best illustrated by this quotation: *the workshops are not for us from Skinnskatteberg and, besides not many know where the workshops are.* Instead, many of the locals act as audience.

Figure 4.1. Local participation in 'workshops' (n=289)

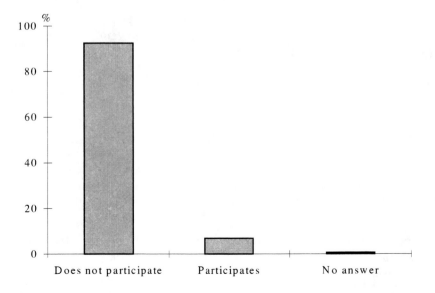

Figure 4.2. Local participation in audience (n=289)

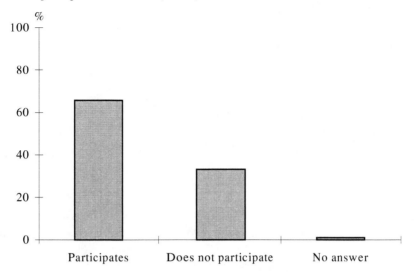

The second figure (Figure 4.2) shows that 66 % of the respondents participate as audience during the Choir Festival, even though some of them complain over the difficulty to do so. The same complaint is heard from several others who are not able, perhaps because they are too old, to visit any part of the Festival or even the spectacular open-air concert, that is the concluding event of the Festival. *Some years ago there were a number of park benches placed on the Meadow. We thought that was really good, but the benches disappeared for some reason. Not so good!* Worth noting here is that the price of a ticket to that concert is the same for the locals, as for the visitors.

Even though most locals are not engaged in any way in the Festival arrangements, as many as 15 % of the respondents work voluntarily with the Festival (Figure 4.3). For example, they take part in the planning process or they sell soft drinks, parking tickets and the like. There is no particular professional group more interested in voluntary work than other. Older respondents seem to be more engaged than the rest, which is not surprising, since these might have more time to spend than their younger counterparts. From the questionnaires it is also evident that another 15 % would like to become engaged, which means there is a great potential for involving the local people and thereby to gain support and understanding for the event, that itself is perceived as being costly. This thought is supported by Wicks (1995), who argues not only that volunteers are "an integral part of event production, but in small towns or rural areas where there are a limited number of volunteers to draw from, each contributor becomes important" (p. 181).

However, the respondents who say they would like to be engaged in voluntary work, do not seem to know how, or feel that the Festival committee does not approve of their interest. One of the respondents adds: *It seems as if the school children in Skinnskatteberg have a natural task and position within the arrangements – maybe performing themselves, or selling things, hot dogs, soft drinks, or the like, in order to earn money for the school study tours. It really is a shame that they have to pay a fee to be able to sell something in their own school yard!*

The respondents that are either engaged in the Festival work or know someone else that is, are generally more favorable towards the Festival than others, although the general opinion in Skinnskatteberg seems to be positive regarding the Choir Festival.

Figure 4.3. Voluntary work/engagement during the Festival (n=289)

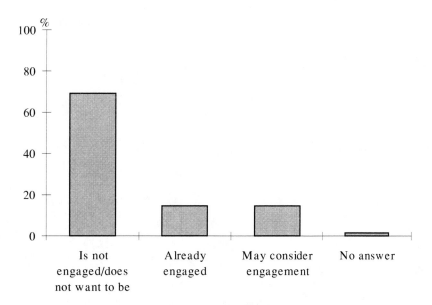

A majority of the respondents do not agree with the statement 'The Choir Festival is good for me personally'. One of the most infuriated respondents instead writes: *Stop this shit and reduce our taxes with the money instead.* A more nuanced comment was: *Naturally, I think it's wrong that the tax-payers have to cover the Choir Festival's losses, especially since we are told to save one thing after another in this community, which affects, for example, children and old people. This makes me a bit doubtful towards the whole arrangement, despite my great interest in choral music.* In one of the interviews one man said: *Right from the start I think the idea was for the Festival not to be commercial, like it is now. Then it was just a Festival for us and others to like the place.*

Despite such opinions, as above, and other similar ones, the same picture is seen when the locals are asked if/how their views correspond with the following argument 'The Festival visitors from elsewhere like Skinnskatteberg'. Instead, the respondents are generally positive, as is shown in (Figure 4.4) – approximately 130 respondents support this argument, and only approximately 9 % think it does not correspond with their opinion. These figures are supported by the locals' reactions to another argument 'I would prefer that Skinnskatteberg did not hold this Festival', that only 14 % of the locals think reflects their thoughts.

Consequently, the local opinion, concerning participation, is possible to interpret as 'us versus them' – 'us' being the locals and 'them' the visitors. Because the locals feel they are not involved, to any large extent, that is neither able nor allowed to participate – they feel rather alienated from most of the arrangements before, during, and after the Festival, except in an economic sense.

There is a notable conflict concerning the Festival within the municipality, as mentioned earlier in this chapter. This conflict is also visible in the findings from the questionnaires, where the respondents do not identify with the Festival, but think that Skinnskatteberg, as a town and county, acquires an identity through it. It appears that the local inhabitants of Skinnskatteberg think that the Choir Festival means little to them. 131 respondents express that the argument 'The Choir Festival is good for me personally' corresponds very badly or rather badly with their own opinions.

Figure 4.4. 'The Festival visitors from elsewhere like Skinnskatteberg' – an argument corresponding with local opinions (n=289)

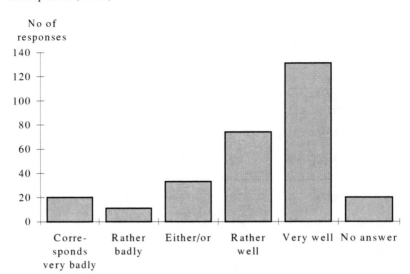

However, when the respondents are asked a direct question about what the Festival means to the municipality as such – 199 respondents agree to the argument 'The Choir Festival is good for Skinnskatteberg'. Similarly a large majority (84%) think that the Festival paints a portrait (read identity) of Skinnskatteberg and that the Festival is good on a town or county level (Figure 4.5).

The Festival gives publicity to Skinnskatteberg, is the comment in one of the questionnaires, *no one would know anything about Skinnskatteberg, if the Festival wasn't there – it has given a certain image to the place, even though I don't think anyone moved here because of that*. This is the common opinion in spite of the fact that the same respondents sometimes also consider the Festival to be a too expensive venture for the municipality.

Figure 4.5. Does the Choir Festival paint a 'portrait' of Skinnskatteberg? (n=289)

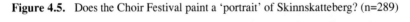
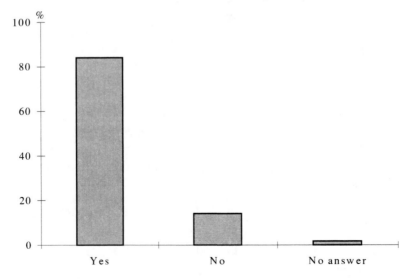

Knowledge

The argument 'I am not (enough) informed about the Festival' applies to almost 4/5 of the respondents. Several of the rest express no opinion at all, when it comes to that particular argument, which is also interpreted as poor knowledge. This is confirmed by the surprisingly varied answers given, when the respondents were asked to estimate the number of visitors and the number of locals engaged in the Festival. For example, the estimation of visitors began with numbers under 1,000 and then there were a couple of hundred diverse suggestions up till 30,000.

The Festival and its many visitors from outside the town do not seem to be a disturbance to everyday life in Skinnskatteberg. Two of the proposed arguments were very negative in character: 'There are far too many people coming to Skinnskatteberg during the Festival' and 'The Festival visitors disturb life in Skinnskatteberg'. However, the locals do not agree – 150 respondents answer that the first argument does not correspond with their opinions at all (e.g. corresponds very or rather badly), and 201 gave the same answer to the second – these are definitely not the opinions of the locals (Figure 4.6). There is no noticeable variation between those respondents living close to any concert site (17 % of the respondents), that could be expected, and those living further away.

Figure 4.6.   The Festival as irritant – two arguments not corresponding with local opinions (n=289)

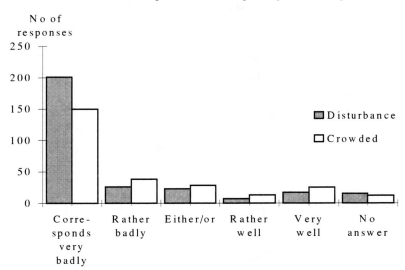

However, the interviews revealed other attitudes, such as: *It's great fun when something happens there, when there are a lot of people in this small place and when there is something to do once a year. But, despite the intention that one should go there to listen to the music, the Festival has become an excuse to drink in public, I think. Everyone, including the choir members themselves, seem to be half drunk all the time. This means, that they might as well take away all the choirs and call it a 'drinking festival' instead. Cheaper for Skinnskatteberg, and surely more fun for the visitors, who seem to come here primarily to get drunk!*

Only a few (6 %) of the respondents agree with the argument that they gain economically from the Festival (see Figure 4.7) and 1/4 of the total think that the Festival is costing them money personally. Some of them say: *If the Festival is not paying its costs, it should not be*

Figure 4.7. 'I gain economically from the Choir Festival' – an argument not corresponding with local opinions (n=289)

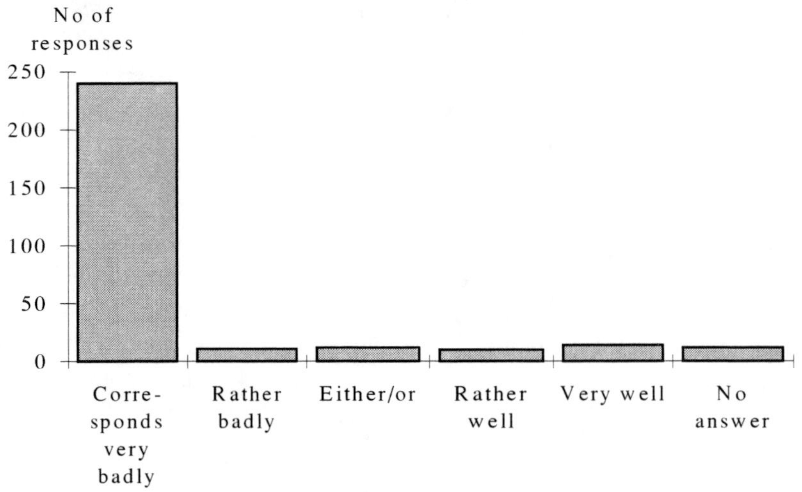

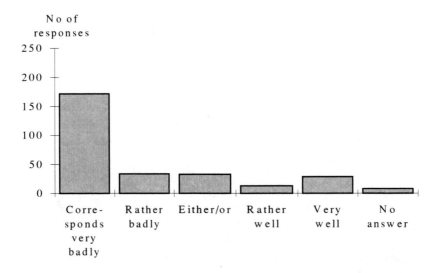

allowed to continue, while others are not that hard in their opinions: *One Festival every third year would be more than enough.*

There is a strong feeling (62 %) among the respondents that the community loses money as a result of the Festival. Even so, the majority of the respondents want the Choir Festival to remain in Skinnskatteberg. The argument 'I would prefer Skinnskatteberg not to hold the Choir Festival' does not reflect the opinion of the locals, as is shown in Figure 4.8. Instead, only 14 % of the respondents answer that this is their position, while 172 respondents say this corresponds very badly with what they think.

Figure 4.8. 'I would prefer Skinnskatteberg not to hold the Choir Festival' – an argument not corresponding with local opinions (n=289)

4.4 Conclusion

This research focused on the local Skinnskatteberg identity, possibly gained through the Choir Festival. The answer is that whatever identity the locals have, it is not due to the Festival. Instead, strong, and loudly articulated, feelings about the Festival, became apparent from this research. But the local feelings and opinions are rather strung along a continuum than representing the separate views of two opposite groups. The Festival pros on the one side of the continuum expressed themselves as this older woman did *The Choir Festival is a totally fantastic event. I am there every year and enjoy it intensely. The air and all the community is filled with singing* or this man, who had been engaged in the Festival since its beginning, *The thing I have experienced as the most important is that the Festival has demonstrated 'the impossible' to be possible!*

The opposing side, who were in a slight majority among the participating respondents, sometimes expressed their dislike of the Festival in resentful words. *I have neither been a part of the Festival and nor did I ever visit it. Therefore I am not the least interested in your questions. I must be free to do as I want!* was the comment from an older man in one of the questionnaires. A young woman argued in the same manner: *If a Festival like this should be allowed to exist, the people responsible must be economically minded – not any cultural day-dreamers!* She blamed the local government, as did most of the respondents in interviews and in their questionnaires.

Nevertheless, this research was initiated by the local government and the Festival committee themselves, even though they clearly recognized the many negative voices among the locals towards the Choir Festival. Not to be overlooked, however, is that there is a widespread cultural interest among the local population in Skinnskatteberg, even though not all of them are particularly interested in choir music. Maybe it is a good idea for the local government and the Festival committee to satisfy more than one cultural need? One respondent stressed that Skinnskatteberg has neither a cinema, nor a local assembly hall. *People here want to dance, go to the theater and the pictures.* She considered *the human climate in Skinnskatteberg to be difficult*, which is easily understandable, when as many as 60 % of the locals claim they are interested in culture.

The respondents' potential interest to join the Festival's voluntary workforce and the positive attitudes towards visitors and towards keeping the Festival in Skinnskatteberg imply that there is a good opportunity for the local government and the Festival committee to act upon this, in order to reach a greater understanding of the Festival, as well as for future community costs. Also, as pointed out earlier in this chapter, identity is acquired through interaction between individuals. Therefore, there must be a common arena to interact upon. Why not the cultural arena?

Development of the Choir Festival over the past decade

The seemingly rhetorical question above was also posed to the local government during the presentation of this research in Skinnskatteberg. However, it received no answer, and the somewhat negative research result was not received in the same happy manner as was the parallel study's result, that promised an increasingly good Festival economy.

Nevertheless, during the past decade the Choir Festival has changed in several important ways, affecting both locals and visitors. First of all, after this research was conducted the Festival committee introduced and carried out a plan to save money. Primarily it included a strategy to decrease administration costs, but also costs related to marketing, light and sound, and invited artists. Another change is the wider spectrum of music during the Festival, possibly to satisfy more locals. Moreover, the locals, who want to hear the Festival concerts, pay less for their concert tickets than do 'outsiders'. For example, two locals pay the price of only one ticket to enter the popular Manor Meadow concert. The committee's aim is to give the Skinnskatteberg locals as much as the visitors – *this is our Festival*. Therefore, the local markets have been developed, and more activities are directed especially towards the locals. *All ages, all groups must feel they are welcome during the Festival.* Other examples are, that local youths now have their own concert on the Manor Meadow and that during the Festival days all flag-poles in Skinnskatteberg are flag-adorned. It seems as if both local knowledge and participation have been improved, and local identity may be developed through and supported by the Festival.

The Choir Festival in Skinnskatteberg has survived despite economic hardships and local hesitation. In the program for 1996, the Festival committee greet presumptive choral singers and audience like this: *We don't give up. The Choir Festival is far too important. Important for Choir Sweden, for the region, and for you, as an individual and dedicated singer. But it's not the same, old Choir Festival - we have listened to opinions and changed many things. The ideas that directed our planning are: the Festival is foremost a singing festivity, it mustn't cost you too much, and it should provide experiences to bring home with you.*

References

Aldskogius, H. (1993). Festivals and Meets: The Place of Music in 'Summer Sweden'. *Geografiska Annaler, 75 B 2*, 55-72.

Ashworth, G. & Goodall, B. (1988). Tourist Images: Marketing Considerations. In B. Goodall, & G. Ashworth (Eds.), *Marketing in the Tourism Industry: The Promotion of Destination Regions* (pp. 213-238). London: Croom Helm.

Babou-Arnaud, I. (1989). Publicity and Theme Tourism. *Espace*, 98, 39-41.

Backman, K., Backman, S., Uysal, M. & Mohr Sunshine, K. (1995). Event Tourism: An examination of Motivations and Activities. *Festival Management & Event Tourism, 3*(1), 15-24.

Bohlin, M. & Ternhag, G. (1990). *Visitor Profile and Economic Impact of Falun Folk Music Festival.* Paper presented at the 6th Annual Conference of Cultural Economics at Umeå University, Sweden.

Bohlin, M. & Hanefors, M. (1992a). *Körstämman i Skinnskatteberg - en studie av samhällsekonomi och lokal identitet.* ITR-rapport No 2/92. ITR, Högskolan i Falun/Borlänge, Sweden.

Bohlin, M. & Hanefors, M. (1992b). Visitor Profile, Economic, Social and Cultural Impact of Two Musical Festivals in Sweden. In F. Colbert, & C. Mitchell, (Eds.), *First International Conference on Arts Management* (pp. 79-97). Proceedings, Montreal, Canada.

Brougham, J. E. & Butler, R. W. (1981). A Segmentation Analysis of the Resident Attitudes to the Social Impact of Tourism. *Annals of Tourism Research, 8*(4), 569-590.

Browne, R. J. & Nolan, M. L. (1989). Western Indian Reservation Tourism Development. *Annals of Tourism Research, 16*(3), 360-376.

Burns, J., Hatch, J. & Mules, T (Eds.) (1986). *The Adelaide Grand Prix: The Impact of a Special Event.* Adelaide, Australia: The Centre for South Australian Economic Studies.

Cousineau, C. (1991). Festivals and Events. A Fertile Ground for Leisure Research. *Journal of Applied Recreation Research, 16*(1), 1-2.

Crandall, L. (1987). The Social Impact of Tourism on Developing Countries and Its Measurement. In Brent Ritchie, J. R. & Goeldner, C. R. (Eds.), *Travel, Tourism, and Hospitality Research, A Handbook for Managers and Researchers* (pp. 413-423). New York. . . Singapore: John Wiley & Sons.

Dann, G. M. S., Nash, D. & Pearce, P. (1988). Methodology in Tourism Research. *Annals of Tourism Research, 15*(1), 1-28.

Decore, L. (1986). *Introduction.* International Events: The Real Tourism Impact. *Proceeding of the 1985 Canada Chapter Confererence* (pp. 2-3).Travel and Tourism Research Association, Canada.

Dewailly, J. M. (1984). Le temps libre et les loisir. *Actes du Congres Mondial de Marly-le-Roi*, 24-28 Sept, Paris.

D'Sousa, J. (1985). Does Tourism mean Development? *Contours*, 2(4), 22-23.

Fees, C. (1989). *Christmas Mumming in a North Cotswold Town: With Special Reference to Tourism, Urbanisation and Immigration-Related Social Change*. Ph. D. diss., University of Leeds.

Formica, S. (1998). The Development of Festivals and Special Events Studies. *Festival Management & Event Tourism*, 5(3), 131-137.

Fredline, E. & Faulkner, B. (n.d.) *Resident Reactions to a Major Tourist Event: The Gold Coast Indy Car Race*. Griffith University, Australia: Centre for Tourism and Hotel Management Research, Faculty of Commerce and Management.

Getz, D. (1989). Special Events. Defining the Product. *Tourism Management,10*(2), 125-137.

Getz, D. (1991). *Festivals, Special Events, and Tourism*. New York: Van Nostrand Reinhold.

Getz, D. (1993). Festivals and Special Events. In M.A. Khan, M.D. Olsen, & T. Var, (Eds.), *VNRs Encyclopedia of Hospitality and Tourism* (pp. 945-955). New York: Van Nostrand Reinhold.

Getz, D. & Frisby, W. (1987). *Report on a Survey of Community-Run Festivals in Ontario*. University of Waterloo, Canada: Department of Recreation and Leisure Studies.

Getz, D. & Frisby, W. (1988). Evaluating Managament Effectiveness in Community-Run Festivals. *Journal of Travel Research*, 27(1), 22-27.

Hanefors, M. (1990). *Turismens sociala och kulturella effekter*. ITR-rapport No 2, Högskolan i Falun/Borlänge, Sweden.

Hall, C. M. (1989a). Hallmark Tourist Events: Analysis, Defintion, Methodology and Review. In G.J. Syme, B.J. Shaw, D.M. Fenton, & W.S. Mueller (Eds.), *The Planning and Evaluation of Hallmark Events* (pp. 3-19). Avebury: Aldershot.

Hall, C. M. (1989b). Hallmark Events and the Planning Process. In G.J. Syme, B.J. Shaw, D.M. Fenton, & W.S. Mueller (Eds.), *The Planning and Evaluation of Hallmark Events* (pp. 20-39). Avebury: Aldershot.

Hall, C. M. (1989c). The Impacts of the 1987 America's Cup of Freemantle, Western Australia: Implications for the Hosting of Hallmark Events. In Welch, R. (Ed.), *Geography in Action*. Dunedin, Australia: University of Otago, Department of Geography.

Hall, C. M. (1992). *Hallmark Tourist Events: Impacts, Management & Planning*. London: Belhaven Press.

Hall, C. M. (1996). Hallmark Event and Urban Reimaging Strategies. In L. Harrison, & W. Husbands (Eds.), *Practising Responsible Tourism: International Case Studies in Tourism Planning, Policy and Development*. (pp. 366-379). New York: John Wiley & Sons.

Jeong, G. & Faulkner, B. (1996). *Resident Perceptions of Mega-Events Impacts: The Tajeon International Exposition Case*. Ms. submitted for publication.

Kaspar, C. (1987). The Role and Impact of Mega-Events and Attractions on National and Regional Tourism Development. Introduction. *Proceedings of the 37ʰ AIEST Congress* (Vol 28, pp.11-12). Calgary.

Light, D. (1996). Characteristics of the Audience for 'Events' at a Heritage Site. *Tourism Managament*, 17(3), 183-190.

McDonald, S. (1990).*The 1990 Adelaide Festival: The Economic Impact, Vol II - Methodology and Results: Details*. Adelaide: The Centre for South Australian Economic Studies.

Nuñez, T. (1978). Touristic Studies in Anthropological Perspective. In V.L. Smith (Ed.), *Hosts and Guests: The Anthropology of Tourism* (pp. 207-216). Oxford: Blackwell.

den Otter, E. (1985). *The Influence of Tourism on the Music of Peru*. Leiden University, Netherlands: Institute of Cultural and Social Studies.

Pearce, P. L. & Caltabiano, M. L. (1983). Inferring Travel Motivations from Travelers' Experiences. *Journal of Travel Research*, 22(2), 16-20.

Pizam, A. (1978). Tourism's Impacts. The Social Cost to the Destination Community as Perceived by Its Residents. *Journal of Travel Research*, 16(4), 8-12.

Rey, P. (1987). Economic Impact of Special Events using Examples of World Cup Athletics, Canberra. In *Australian Standing Committee on Tourism. The Impact and Marketing of Special Events. Papers of the Australian Travel Research Workshop, 12-14 Nov, Mt. Buffalo Chalet, Victoria*. Australian Standing Committee on Tourism, Canberra.

Ritchie, J. (1984). Assessing the Impact of Hallmark Events: Conceptual and Research Issues. *Journal of Travel Research*, 23(1), 2-11.

Ritchie, J. & Smith, B. (1991). The Impact of Mega-Event on Host Region Awareness: A Longitudinal Study. *Journal of Travel Research, 30*(1), 3-10.

Roche, M. (1994). Mega-Events and Urban Policy. *Annals of Tourism Research, 21*(1),1-19.

Smith, V. L. (1982). Tourism to Greenland: Renewed Ethnicity? *Cultural Survival Quarterly, 6*(3), 26-27.

Taylor, S. J. & Bogdan, R. (1984) *Introduction to Qualitative Research Methods. The Search for Meanings.* 2 ed., New York. Singapore: John Wiley & Sons.

Teo, P. (1994). Assessing Socio-Cultural Impacts: The Case of Singapore. *Tourism Management, 15*(2), 126-136.

Theuns, H. L. (1989). Multidisciplinary Focus on Leisure and Tourism. *Annals of Tourism Research, 16*(2), 189-204.

Travis, A. & Croize, J. (1987). The Role and Impacts of Mega-Events and Attractions on Tourism Development in Europe: A Micro Perspective. *Proceedings of the 37th AIEST Congress* (Vol. 28, pp. 59-78). Calgary.

Wicks, B. E. (1995). The Business Sector's Reaction to a Community Special Event in a Small Town: A Case Study of the 'Autumn on Parade' Festival. *Festival Management & Event Tourism, 2*(3-4), 177-183.

Witt, S. (1988). Mega-Events and Mega-Attractions. *Tourism Management, 9*(1), 76-77.

Chapter 5

Learning Effects – The Case of the Lillehammer Olympic Winter Games 1994

Bente R. Løwendahl

Norwegian School of Management BI, Norway

5.1 Background

This chapter focuses on the organization that staged a 'mega-event', namely the 17th Olympic Winter Games in Lillehammer, February 12-28th 1994, and the learning effects resulting from this event. The chapter is based on a study carried out in 1992-1994, primarily by myself and my colleague professor Odd Nordhaug at Norwegian School of Economics and Business Administration. In addition, during and after the Games we had with us two excellent Ph.D. students, Knut Haanæs and Harald Hvidsten, financed by the Norwegian School of Management. Data collection and analysis was financed by our respective institutions (Norwegian School of Management and Norwegian School of Economics and Business Administration) as well as by the LOOC, which covered our direct expenses.

We were invited in as researchers, first contacted in the summer of 1991 and formally starting our research in the early fall of 1992, to support the work of the personnel department of LOOC (The Lillehammer Olympic Organizing Committee) in their efforts to analyze and document the learning effects. Their primary focus was on the employability of their employees after the Games, and they believed they could help the employees document how their individual competence had been enhanced through their employment by LOOC. From our perspective, one of our main reasons for focussing on this particular organization was its temporary nature, as well as its rapid evolution from start-up through numerous growth and change phases, to closure in 1994. We saw this event organization as a laboratory for future knowledge intensive organizations, and were particularly interested in studying how the organization mobilized the appropriate competence when and where it was needed, as well as how they handled the transitions. In traditional organizations, major change processes typically result from market shifts or crises, i.e. situations which arise unexpectedly. Such situations are very difficult for researchers to gain access to and to mobilize sufficient resources for, and hence, participation during the critical change phases is unusual. We therefore see event organizations as especially amenable to studies of change processes, since the timing of the transition points to a large extent is planned and known in advance.

The emphasis in our study was on competence development and learning effects. We refer to Spilling's chapter in this volume, as well as other studies published by Spilling (1996, 1997) and Hervik et al. (1990) for more information about economic effects of the 1994 Olympic Winter Games in Lillehammer.

5.2 Theoretical Framework

Theoretical background

Our study was designed for the discovery of grounded theory, in order to develop new conceptual dimensions, and hence we did not outline a theoretical framework ex ante (Glaser and Strauss 1967). However, we do not believe it is possible to go into a study with a 'tabula rasa'-approach, as we had both worked for a number of years in the area of competence development before we started this study. Nordhaug has published substantially in the areas of organization theory, organization development, and human resource development (see e.g. Nordhaug 1993), whereas Løwendahl has published widely in the area of resource based strategic management applied to professional service organizations (see e.g. Løwendahl 1997). Some of the dimensions of individual competence developed by Nordhaug (1993 or earlier works in Scandinavia) have also been included in Løwendahl's work on competence as a strategic resource in professional service firms, and hence served as a starting point for our conceptual development. The dimensions developed, however, were truly grounded and inductively developed, and included both new dimensions and extended and improved dimensions compared to the previously existing frameworks. Hence, the underlying theoretical foundations are not referred to in further detail here. As for the doctoral students, insights from the present study also served as a foundation for Haanes' further development of theory on the mobilization of resources (1997). Hvidsten currently works as a consultant, and has not completed his doctorate.

Research design

The original study was designed as a longitudinal case study aimed at identifying key dimensions in the mobilization of competences (including management and organization) in a complex project organization. The case represented an 'extreme situation', which made the factors and processes of interest 'transparently observable' (Eisenhardt 1989, citing Pettigrew 1988), thus representing theoretical rather than random sampling. The case was chosen for its size and complexity, its visibility and its dependence on highly competent people from an extremely wide variety of professional backgrounds. The original study had four main foci: to define key dimensions of individual competence, to identify aspects of managerial competence critical to the mobilization of individual competences, to describe aspects of organization design and redesign critical to ensuring the right competence in the right place at the right time, and to observe and learn from the handling of exceptional situations in which the necessary competence was not immediately available. Our overall aim was to learn from successful as well as less satisfactory solutions, rather than to evaluate the quality of LOOC's planning and implementation.

The present chapter was written about five years after the completion of the 1994 Olympic Winter Games, and is based on an ex-post reanalysis of both primary data and previously documented results (mainly in Norwegian, in Løwendahl & Nordhaug 1994). Here, the emphasis is on the importance of learning effects when evaluating mega-events, and looks into the learning effects both for individual participants, for other organizations involved, and for society at large (through theory building and new concepts). Even though their impact is difficult to assess and quantify, learning effects may be among the most important lasting effects of mega-events, especially for ad hoc events such as the Olympic Games.

Data collection and analysis

The primary data were collected for three consecutive phases. Data for phases I and II were gathered primarily in a series of semi-structured interviews with selected employees from a broad range of 'units', men and women from different age groups, with varying tenure and experience within the organization, from different backgrounds, and from all levels in the managerial hierarchy. Phase I of the study (autumn 1992) concentrated on the present tasks and the competence required of the individual employees, as well as on the expected tasks and the expected competences required for the implementation of the Winter Games. Phase II of the study (autumn 1993) included three types of interview: (1) Additional interviews with employees in operational units not involved in phase I of the project, thus broadening the scope, (2) follow-up interviews with some of the employees from phase I, focussing on changes in present and expected tasks and competence one year after the first interview, and (3) interviews with managers and other employees, emphasizing aspects of managerial competence.

Phase III of the study was concerned with the actual implementation of the Olympic Winter Games, with expected and unexpected tasks, competence in use, competence required but not readily available, and the solutions of managers and other employees to such challenges. Data for phase III were collected through participant observation during the 16 days of the Olympics plus two days prior to the Opening Ceremony. This involved interviews at all managerial levels at three arenas (Håkons Hall, the Ice Hockey rink; Lysgårdsbakkene, the Ski Jumping and Ceremony arena; and Birkebeineren, the Nordic and Biathlon skiing arena), observations at management meetings in all three arenas plus staff meetings at the central personnel support function, day-long observation of four personnel managers in four different arenas, interviews with managers in central staff functions regarding specific challenges in the arenas, interviews with central members of top management, and an analysis of both public and intraorganizational documentation.

Approximately 20 interviews were conducted in each of the two first phases. Phase III included more than 60 interviews with both full-time employees and volunteers, as well as numerous informal discussions with people working in different parts of the focal arenas and with the personnel staff. The two senior researchers and the two assistants made up the research team in phase III, usually working in pairs on the interviews and observations. We lived in 'barracks' together with the LOOC employees, ate the same lunch and dinner as the employees, suffered the same cold wait for the buses as they did, and had full access to all administrative sections in the three arenas and to the central personnel staff. Although in many respects we were participants in the organization, we very rarely performed any operational tasks in the way of helping out. We were not wearing the same uniform as the employees, which meant that our role as 'outsiders allowed to ask questions' was enhanced and respected. Nonetheless we felt very close to being members of the organization, sharing in many of their emotional moods such as tension and anxiety before the Opening Ceremony, relief when the first days went well, sadness when the final day drew closer, and pride when it was all over and the success was proven.

Access to the organization was surprisingly open, and people working at all levels of operations were positive about being observed and interviewed. Prior to the Games we had made an agreement with the Arena Managers of each of the three focal arenas, whereby they accepted our presence provided we did not disturb anyone or in any way prevent them from doing their jobs properly. We also had an agreement with the director of personnel, and were given an office within the personnel staff area at headquarters, as well as free access to their building and to all meetings in the department. The central personnel staff and the personnel managers in each arena also constituted our support function, providing us with information and advice as to who to contact and at what time. Final interviews with top management were conducted a week after the Games were over, including all three members of the top management 'troika', as well as the Sports Director, because they did not want to give any personal opinions until all parts of the Games were completely over.

All interviews and observations were transcribed from our field notes. All four researchers shared all information, and the data were scrutinized for major themes. Detailed documentation of key interviews as well as insights written up by managers of different units (and consultants involved) is provided in Løwendahl and Nordhaug (1994).

5.3 Empirical Study

Introduction

The organizing process of the Olympic Winter Games was described to us as *rather similar to fireworks; you build firing ramps, you plan every single detail, you wait forever in anticipation, and then the actual event is over so quickly it feels almost unreal!* When the Lillehammer Olympic Organizing Committee (LOOC)[1] was awarded the right to organize the 17th Olympic Winter Games, in Seoul on September 15th 1988, enthusiasts had already been working seven years, hoping for this decision. And in 1988, another five and a half years of preparations lay ahead. Clearly such mega-events are severely skewed towards the period *ahead* of the actual event. Hence, this chapter will focus more on the different phases of the pre-event stage which lasted for more than a decade before the actual event in February 1994, than on the event and post event stages. However, the latter will also be discussed, with a main focus on learning effects for individuals, companies, and society at large.

Winning the event

In retrospect it is difficult to pin-point one specific starting point for the process of winning The XVII Olympic Winter Games for Lillehammer, but one person who was frequently credited for early enthusiasm was a German immigrant and hotelier, Wolfgang Müller. He had previously seen unique tourism potential in the combination of the snow and the picturesque surroundings of Lillehammer. Even as early as in the late 1970s, he dreamed about a 'compact' Olympic Winter Games in Lillehammer. When in 1980 the event sites of Falun and Åre in Sweden lost the struggle for the 1988 Winter Games to Calgary, due to the distance between the two sites (Falun and Åre), his ideas were turned into action. During the following months, a group of people worked hard to put together a proposal. Gudbrandsdal's savings bank was enlisted, with its managing director Ole Sjetne and his colleague Petter Rønningen, to secure the financial support. By the beginning of 1982, the local government was familiar with the plans, and had agreed to support a further investigation into the project, provided it would be paid for by banks and the business community. They

---

1) The Organizer of the 1994 Olympic Winter Games in Lillehammer changed names and organization structure several times during the pre-event phase, but in order not to confuse the reader, the term LOOC will be used for the organizer throughout.

saw the Olympic Games as an instrument for growth, new jobs, tourism, and better living conditions in the local community, and agreed to 'register as organizers'. Goals and strategies were developed, as well as printed materials. In the winter of 1985, a government guarantee for the expansion of roads, telecommunications and TV/radio was obtained, thus further strengthening the image of commitment to the mega-event. And in fall 1986, the application was sent.

In the ballot in Lausanne in 1986 Lillehammer did not win. Albertville won a crushing victory. But Lillehammer was only eliminated in the 5th round, and only two other contestants received more votes: Sofia and Falun/Åre. In addition, the IOC, voted that the next Olympic Winter Games were to be organized in 1994, only two years later than the Games in Albertville. As a result, the enthusiasts were by no means ready to give in, and the campaign to get the 1994 Games to Lillehammer was immediately initiated. By this time, the enthusiastic Lillehammer committee had learned a lot more about what would be needed to win the Games. They decided to focus on the Olympic Games as a national, rather than just a local, issue and pulled in the government and national politicians for support. Even Prime Minister Gro Harlem Brundtland became a central promoter of the Lillehammer Olympic Games. In order to strengthen the candidacy further, construction of Kristin's Hall (skating rink etc.) and the Hafjell ski resort began, and alpine competitions were organized in Kvitfjell in order to let competitors discover the challenges they would meet here in a potential Olympic competition.

In the end, four candidates submitted their applications for the 1994 Olympic Winter Games: Lausanne, Östersund/Åre, Sofia and Lillehammer. Sofia was regarded to be Lillehammer's toughest competitor, but in the end Östersund/Åre received 39 votes compared to Lillehammer's 45. When Juan Antonio Samaranch, president of the IOC, made the announcement: *and the decision is ... LILLYHAMMER!,* the committee at Lillehammer could hardly believe what they heard. But they knew that it was now that the real work started!

Preparing for the event

Financial resources; planning and budgeting

No sooner was the 'bid' for the 1994 Olympic Winter Games won, before the budgets had to be recalculated. The application included a government guarantee for NOK 1.8 billion, but when Petter Rønningen and his newly hired manager of finance Bjørn Brenna completed the calculations of 'every detail' of what it would take to deliver 'The best games ever', this amount more than quadrupled (NOK 8.5 billion). Major investments in sports arenas, accommodation, press and TV-centers, and infrastructure were required, and after negotiations with government, the final budget approved settled at NOK 7 billion. President Gerhard Heiberg was severely pressured to accept the much lower budget figure of NOK 5.5 billion, but insisted that he would not be willing to take the responsibility for such a low quality event. Now that Norway and Lillehammer had won the Games, we had to prove that we could deliver 'the best Winter Games ever'.

Physical infrastructure; construction of arenas

The physical construction part of planning was a great success, and most people were proud, locally as well as nationally. In late fall of 1991, midway between the decision and the

Games, the newspapers reported that construction of the ten arenas had an impressively steady course. All the facilities seemed to be on schedule. The total construction budget was set at NOK 1.45 billion, and at this stage approximately 80% of the contracts were signed, i.e. for approximately 1.1 billion. Not only were the time frames maintained, but the construction projects were also 'on budget'. In addition, several of the arenas won both architectural awards and public acclaim for their aesthetic as well as functional qualities – most notably the 'Viking Ship' skating rink in Hamar.

The organization

The agreement with the IOC stated that a committee would be created for the planning and implementation of the Games. The Lillehammer Olympic Organizing Committee (LOOC) was hence established in Lillehammer as an incorporated company, with 51% government ownership, 24.5% ownership by the Norwegian Olympic Committee (NOK), and 24.5% ownership by the Lillehammer Municipality. This structure was highlighted by LOOC management as very positive, for two reasons: First of all, the relationship with the government was very constructive, as LOOC was allowed to make their own decisions without government or parliamentary interference, 'except in exceptional cases'. *We knew that if we interfered, we could not hold the management of LOOC entirely responsible for budget problems, so we had to keep our distance. But we had substantial influence through our control routines as well as through our majority of votes on the board of directors,* said Henning Gorholt, project director for the Ministry of Culture (Løwendahl & Nordhaug, 1994:88). Secondly, the fact that both the Lillehammer Municipality and the Norwegian Olympic Committee (NOK) were equity owners and board members was seen as extremely positive, as they could then be held jointly responsible for the decisions made by LOOC. This was important, in order to secure the best interests for the event as a whole. Without the ownership, Lillehammer and NOK would not have had to worry about costs, and would have had more freedom in terms of securing their own special interests as opposed to the best overall.

Whereas the formal organization was critical to the external legitimacy of LOOC, the internal organization of the planning and implementation activities was probably even more critical towards a successful completion of the event. The issue of most concern to us was how they made sure the right person was available at the right place at the right time, when the actual service delivery was to take place. This included both the appropriate competence and the decision making authority to handle unexpected details.

The internal organization changed frequently, but for simplicity, its structure can be discussed in terms of two fundamentally different phases: the pre-event planning organization and the arena organization designed for implementation.

The functional planning organization

Most of the early organization structure was inherited from Calgary, which meant the adoption of a functional organization form. In the beginning, the structure was flat, and all functions controlled by managing director Petter Rønningen. However, as the number of tasks and employees rapidly grew, the flat structure became unmanageable, and several functional divisions were established, each led by a director. Some of the people who had been recruited early found themselves 'degraded', not because they had done a bad job, but because more and more layers of management were added on top of their operational positions. Every manager recruited into the organization at the early stages put his (they were all males, in the beginning) own stamp on the organization, and what were considered appropriate reporting structures evolved through a combination of what worked and did not work relative to the tasks at hand, and the images of good organizations brought in by the managers. The organization which evolved turned into an interesting combination of the functional organization inherited from Calgary, a blend of North Sea Construction Projects, a small touch of government departmental organization, and a 'pinch' of army roles and commands.

The early organization models were severely criticized by a number of participants, and clearly represented a compromise of the interests of the most powerful managers at any given point in time. Four aspects of the organization were subject to particularly severe criticism during the planning phase:

- The extreme emphasis on business-related aspects of the project. As one of the middle-managers stated it, *maybe there is a bit too much concrete and banking represented in top management here?* The debate as to which areas of competence should be represented in top management was going on all through the planning phase, in particular in terms of the role of the sports managers and the impact of cultural events on project management.

- The 'downplaying' of the sports aspects of the event. Even as late as three months before the opening of the games, a major newspaper debate was initiated where among others the highly respected senior Børre Rognlien, responsible for ice skating, was quoted in Aftenposten (22.10.93) saying that:

  LOOC is designed to be a planning and administrative organization. ... But LOOC must come one step further and become an execution style organization. The position of the sports manager, Martin Burkhalter, is too far down. His line of work must be reevaluated and upgraded. All other areas should be subordinate to sports.

- The insufficient respect for the cultural aspects. Some stated that the 'fight' for power between sports and culture was extremely difficult. When the Manager in charge of Cultural events, Bente Erichsen, resigned after major disagreements over budgets and plans, in particular with respect to the opening and closing ceremonies (see e.g. Erichsen 1994), the debates reached a peak. Erichsen had started her work for LOOC in January 1991, and resigned amid tremendous press interest in February 1993.

- The extreme 'masculinity' of management. A single female director, Torill Broch See-berg, was hired after severe public criticism of the lack of feminine participation, in 1991. (See e.g. Erichsen, Hugdahl, Lundsgaard, Seeberg, Sønsteby and Verde 1994). She was 'head-hunted' from the public sector, thus 'satisfying' two deficiencies in one hiring, and given a prominent position as responsible for external information and public affairs.

In retrospect it is easy to criticize an organization which was clearly far from ideal, but after the manifested success of the transformation and implementation, our interest has been more focussed on what we can learn from this successful transition. Despite the criticism, the planning organization managed to get their budgets and plans in place on time, the physical structures were in place, the budgets were not exceeded, government reports were delivered as agreed, and qualified personnel was recruited and retained for all key positions of the organization. Our impression was that the organization seemed to be a kind of 'reversed pyramid', where the degrees of freedom were much more prominent at the bottom of the pyramid than on top. When interviewed after the Games, president Heiberg confirmed this observation, and said he felt that one of his most important tasks had been to be the 'linking pin' vis-à-vis the external stakeholders, while protecting the operational employees as much as possible from the extreme pressures excerted from all sorts of interest groups. We will revert to the topic of stakeholder management below.

From planning hierarchy to arena management

The reorganization from the pre-event planning organization to the arena organization for implementation involved a major transition. During the summer of 1992 the arenas were established and the arena managers selected, and while the functional organization lived on in its traditional hierarchical form, the arena organizations slowly emerged during the fall of 1992 and the spring of 1993. As people were recruited for key positions, test events were implemented and the completed arenas came to life. The first step in this transition was made in the summer of 1992, when the arena managers were appointed. Petter Rønningen, who was to take charge of the operations during the Games, spent a lot of his time in late 1991 and early 1992 trying to find the right managers. He decided to entirely disregard both the directors of the existing planning hierarchy and the senior sports managers. Rønningen was criticized by many who felt that their candidates 'deserved' the jobs as arena managers, either because they had done such a good job for LOOC for so long, or because now, finally, it was critical to put sports into the 'driver's seat'. Yet bargaining and negotiations had no effect.

> *I disagreed with those who claimed that the arena managers should come from sports,* *Rønningen said in an interview after the Games (Løwendahl & Nordhaug, 1994: p.128).* *Take the Birkebeiner ski- and biathlon arena as an example. 1052 'workers'* [2] *from a* *large number of different functional specialties needed leadership, coordination, and* *support, in order to do a good job. This was more than just producing a good cross-* *country competition. We needed a good leader, someone with proven results from previous* *leadership roles. This should be an experienced leader, ideally someone with competence* *from previous project management. But it should also be a leader who would be respected* *and accepted by the sports managers. Odd Martinsen (the arena sports manager) should* *be allowed to be purely concerned with operational issues, whereas the arena manager* *should ideally also be well connected to the post-event utilization of arenas and* *competence locally.*

Many of the arena managers he chose had been involved in the construction of their own arenas. According to Rønningen, construction engineers had a highly relevant competence, as they were used to hiring and pulling together people with diverse backgrounds for temporary assignments, quickly and with a clear focus on results. The management principles applied to the arena organizations were the same as throughout LOOC: the manager in charge of a unit was given complete freedom in terms of hiring and firing the people he wanted. Hence, Rønningen's decisions in terms of arena managers were not interfered with

---

2) In Norwegian, there was a clear distinction between the employees of LOOC, the contracted consultants etc., and the volunteers during the planning phase. However, during implementation all 'workers' on all levels were called 'funksjonærer' and treated equally. For lack of a better word, 'workers' is used here as a substitute for 'funksjonær', hence the term 'worker' is used for all levels of the organization.

by Heiberg or any other member of top management, and similarly Rønningen did not interfere with the employee choices of his arena managers. In retrospect we concluded that the choice of arena managers must have been one of the keys to the success of the Lillehammer Games.

The layout of the arena organizations was extremely flat, with a large number of functional units represented. According to Rønningen, it was important to give each arena all the resources required to make as many decisions as possible locally; at least 85-90% of the decisions should be made without referring to the main operations center (HOS). Positions were staffed by a combination of LOOC employees and volunteers, further supported by additional external units such as the army, the police, and the catering company (Partena). Other external partners, such as Norwegian Telecom (Telenor) and the Norwegian Broadcasting Corporation (NRK) had managers formally included in the organization of each arena. The arena organization existed in parallel with the hierarchical planning organization throughout 1993, in what was described as a matrix structure. Budget responsibility was retained by the functional directors, whereas most of their personnel was 'occupied' in the arena organizations. Hence, whenever an arena needed to exceed budgets for any specific function, the resource utilization had to be authorized by the functional director who had made and accepted the budget for that function.

The transformation from planning to implementation occurred subtly, and for a long transition period most of the employees said they were 'living in the matrix' in the sense that they reported to both the arena managers and to their functional managers. Few of the functional tasks disappeared before the actual implementation, and hence most employees worked in dual positions. In addition, the transfer of authority to volunteer arena managers took time, as most of them could not arrive until a couple of weeks before the Games. Many of the managers criticized this late transition to arena management, and felt that the arena managers should have been involved earlier and given greater responsibility, including responsibility for their own budgets. However, Henrik Andenæs, Vice President in charge of the planning organization, was very clear when we interviewed him after the Games:

> *We couldn't have made the transition much earlier; maybe a month or two, but not any more. I am afraid we would have been unable to keep the tight budget control throughout if we had changed to more autonomous units at an earlier stage. Maybe that could have worked for a permanent organization, as then it would have been easier to trust and delegate authority. In this type of project organization, it is more a question of an extreme 'economy of negotiation' ('forhandlingsøkonomi'), where each unit tries to grab as much as possible. A fight for funds across the arenas would probably have led to sub-optimal solutions. And I am sure it would have been more expensive! (Løwendahl and Nordhaug, 1994: 66-67)*

Hiring and mobilizing human resources

One of the key factors of success in LOOC was the hiring of appropriate people for every single task. Even though from the outside a budget of NOK 7 billion seemed to allow almost unlimited hiring of experts and back-up people, the fact of the matter was entirely different. LOOC was bound by government regulations, including salaries, and could not attract people by offering extraordinary remuneration. However, this never seemed to be a problem, as every position open attracted a large number of highly qualified applicants. By the fall of 1993, LOOC had a total of 700 employees, including external experts hired on full-time contracts. Most of the employees were people with substantial experience, who wanted to be part of a large project. They immediately saw the opportunities to deliver high quality and visible work, and expected to improve their CVs both through the functional tasks and through the large project experience. Many people were hired into 'positions' which they largely had to define themselves, and worked hard to develop a consensus on their own responsibilities relative to those of their colleagues. 'Figuring out the gray areas', was an expression frequently used, and 'living in (or being) the gray area' was another.

In addition to the employees, the Lillehammer Olympics could not have taken place without the participation of the large number of volunteers whose commitment was incredible. Only a total of 15 people, out of several thousand, left during the Games, primarily because they were ill. People were recruited through a number of channels, including newspaper advertisements as well as sports clubs all over the country. A large number of volunteers worked for a sport for which they already had substantial experience having managed competitions for years.

In addition to the volunteers, a large number of other organizations also had their own sub-organizations with numerous paid and unpaid workers with full-time commitment to the event. Obvious examples include the catering company (Partena), the Police, the Army, countless bus-companies, and the Norwegian Broadcasting Corporation (NRK) with its own sub-organization 'ORTO' which incorporated a number of other broadcasting companies. One of the most visible differences between the LOOC workers and workers committed to other sub-organizations was the uniform. LOOC workers regardless of level and arena were all dressed in the same gray uniform, an effort made to avoid sub-cultures. The effect was to create a feeling of togetherness and joint responsibility for the final outcome. Other stake-holders, such as Partena (the caterers) and ORTO (the radio and TV-people), had their own uniforms, whereas the police, the army etc. kept their official uniforms.

In addition, numerous public and private suppliers also had their own olympic sub-projects. One example was the food deliveries, where e.g. all the main suppliers such as GILDE (meat) and TINE (dairy products) had their own sub-projects.

Training

The functional training of employees in LOOC was virtually zero; major efforts were made to recruit people who could start working 'from scratch', as time was limited. The self-employment nature of many of the jobs provided was clearly indicated by the answer we got to the question: *how long does it take for a newly employed person to get 'up to speed' in the job?* A typical answer was: *if you've been here a fortnight, you are a veteran!* Yet training was provided, particularly related to the implementation phase. In addition, LOOC had been particularly lucky in terms of winning the 1994 Olympic Winter Games, as a large part of the planning organization was already in place before the previous Winter Games took place in Albertville in 1992. The organizing committee of the Albertville Olympic Winter Games, COJO, was happy to receive the support of their colleagues from Lillehammer, and as many employees as possible actively took part in the final weeks of preparations. This experience gave them some very important insights: they were not only on track, but ahead of where COJO had been at the same stage of planning, LOOC was about the same size as COJO, and, perhaps even more importantly, that even if the complexity increases tremendously with the organization of so many events simultaneously, the actual details of each event are pretty much the same as any other major international competition. As one of the employees commented: *Standing in line to buy a hot-dog means standing in line to buy a hot-dog, regardless of whether it is a regular Sunday or a day of the Winter Olympics!* In interviews in the fall of 1992, those who had not been able to participate or who were recruited after the Albertville Games, expressed concern about their inability to grasp the complexity of it all; the experience gained from having seen it 'live' could not be transferred to those who had not been there.

When the Games in Albertville were over, and as soon as the arena organizations were established the focus shifted from getting all the plans right to preparing for every possible detail which might go wrong. The newly appointed arena managers were the key to this process, but in addition a lot of training activities were designed to test the ability of the organization to handle contingencies. For the sports events, a number of competitions and test events were arranged throughout 1993. The complexity of simultaneous competitions, however, was more difficult to try out before the event itself, and therefore a large number of simulations were organized for coordination and top management functions. In total, 28 simulations took place throughout 1993, particularly in the late fall, when most of the workers had been assigned to their positions in the arenas (see Malmo and Bryde, in Løwendahl and Nordhaug, 1994, ch. 21).

Additional training was a major challenge for the organization, given the fact that the majority of the workers were volunteers who were unable to come to Lillehammer until a few days before the event itself. Evening and week-end training seminars in numerous locations were the only alternative, and in total between 30 and 40 thousand workers went through the same basic training, which included the history of the Olympic Games, understanding of service-provision and national culture, knowledge about the region, and knowledge about the event itself. Even top management were required to pass the basic training. In addition, training was provided by each functional department as well as by each arena.

Stakeholder management

The number of stakeholders claiming a stake in the Lillehammer Olympic Winter Games was incredible. The stylized stakeholder map below gives a small indication of the interest groups officially recognized by LOOC, but in addition they felt the pressure from 'anything from cat breeders to traditional needle-work organizations' to promote their particular cause through the Olympics.

Maybe the most important stakeholder of all was the government. As mentioned above, the initial intention of the Lillehammer committee was to carry out the games with local and private financial support only, combined with government guarantees. However, over time the content of the application evolved from 'compact games' based largely on already existing facilities to a national effort to provide 'the best Games ever' in 'the cradle of winter sports' (as Prime Minister Brundtland said in a speech). As a result, both the ownership, the financing and the control of LOOC became a matter of national concern. The Ministry of Culture was put in charge of overseeing the planning as well as the expenditures of LOOC, and responded by creating a project organization with 8-9 people responsible for the supervision of LOOC. The Ministry imposed their own reporting standards on the organization, including monthly reports, risk evelation reports, etc. In addition, LOOC interacted with a number of other Ministries and public sector organizations, both on the national and the local levels. Other Ministries involved included Transportation, Finance, and Environmental Affairs, and other public organizations included the Norwegian Railways (NSB), the Norwegian Army, the Police, the Norwegian Broadcasting Corporation (NRK), Norwegian Telecom (Telenor),

Figure 5.1. Stylized stakeholder map

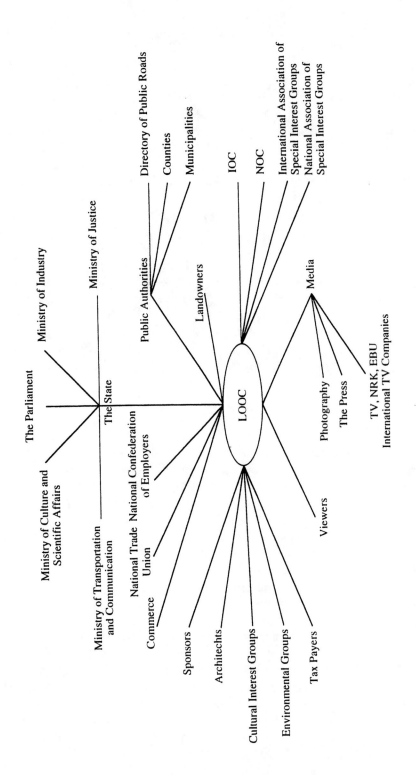

and many others. The governmental finances for LOOC were granted by the Parliament, and hence controlled by the Ministry of Finance. But in this respect, LOOC was pleased with the control-model adopted, in which they were held responsible vis à vis the Minister of Culture alone, and the Ministry of Culture, with their Project Director Henning Gorholt, took care of further coordination with the other Ministries, including the Ministry of Finance. Despite this fact, the national control authorities ('Riksrevisjonen') decided to set up a separate project organization to control LOOC, in addition to the auditors employed by LOOC directly (Ernst & Young).

But if the government representatives were challenging to deal with, the worst were probably the media. There were a lot of critics and skeptics, locally as well as nationally. One local newspaper was particularly critical, and seemed to be conducting something close to a journalists' vendetta against LOOC. More fundamental were the negative comments towards expected economic returns, especially locally. As early as in September 1991, Aftenposten (14.9.1991), the largest Norwegian newspaper, reported that the Olympic Games were unsuccessful. The event had by no means given the effect one had hoped for or expected, especially in terms of economic growth in the region. The mayor of Lillehammer, Audun Tron, had to reply to the criticism and said that:

> *The times have changed. The assumptions are no longer what they were four-five years ago. We lack neither good ideas nor capable people. We lack money. The banks lie with broken backs. But Growth is materializing, it is just delayed.*

Sigmund Thue, director of marketing in LOOC supported the notion of growth just being delayed, yet responded differently:

> *We have the money, we have everything. We just do not have the people to exploit the possibilities. We have planned a lot, but done little. Now we must organize the work, draw up the boundaries and delegate responsibility. It is time for results.*

Another major challenge came, rather surprisingly, from the employees' association. The story surfaced after an interview with a journalist, this time from the national business newspaper 'Dagens Næringsliv'. As late as in October of 1993, the paper brought the news of the "ruthless exploitation" of the employees, due to an extreme use of overtime in LOOC. The Labor Inspection reported a use of overtime more than four times higher than that stipulated in the Working Environment Act, despite the fact that the large majority of employees in LOOC were employed at middle management levels and never recorded nor reported use of overtime. Stein Indsetviken of the Labor Inspection said to the paper (18.10.93) that:

> *It appears that the use of overtime in LOOC is out of control. We have the impression that the employees are driven hard. LOOC should long ago have sent us an application about the expanded overtime. LOOC is breaking the overtime regulations!*

One of the responses of management was to make Christmas Vacation mandatory – a move which was highly needed as the Opening Ceremony was only weeks away.

The actual event itself; almost like fireworks

The last days before the opening ceremony were tense, as several final details were not in order. One of the biggest problems arose with accommodation for the volunteers, as the schools were emptied and turned over too late. Temporary accommodation had to be provided, and in some cases as many as 40-50 people had to share a single shower and toilet. But this was only for a day or two, and slowly every detail of preparation was more or less in place. On Thursday night, February 10th, many of the workers were invited to the trial presentation of the opening ceremony, and after climbing the narrow paths in several feet of fresh snow, hundreds of workers filled the Ski Jumping Arena. Getting there took much longer than expected, and more nerves were added regarding Saturday's Opening. It was incredibly cold; minus 25 or more, and the waiting time made everyone even more nervous. But the ceremony turned out to be wonderful. Freezing cold, but happy and hopeful, they all returned to work and/or to what would be their temporary housing for the rest of the Games.

The other major problem during the first few days had to do with transportation, the night-mare of every major event organizer, especially for events at sites without big-city infrastructure in place. The priorities were clear: press, athletes, and VIP-visitors were transported first, and in general they were satisfied with the service level. However, among the workers the situation was different. Buses sometimes never arrived, other buses went to the wrong arena, and loyal workers were furious about coming to work too late. Since private cars were not allowed into the city nor close to the arenas, everyone was dependent on the buses. Bus-drivers from all over the country were in Lillehammer, and some knew little or nothing about the local geography. But slowly even this problem was sorted out, and the buses started to arrive and leave on schedule. Even the bus-drivers smiled, and handled the problems as best they could; *If you say I will pass by that place, I guess I can stop there. Just say when...*

The opening ceremony was a tremendous success, and so was every single one of the early sports events. Participants were delivering the best possible quality sports, workers were actually smiling and delivering the best possible service, and visitors were crowding the arenas and the streets of Lillehammer, thereby making the gigantic feast happen. Event after event passed with no major set-backs. One of the main worries, the weather, turned out to provide only minor problems. The first week was so cold that some of the outdoor events were in danger of being postponed, but in the end only minor delays were necessary, primarily in the alpine slopes. Everything was running smoothly, and the arenas were really solving the majority of their problems locally. One example can illustrate this situation: In the middle of the Games we interviewed Bjørn Brenna, the director of finance, and were asked to come to his desk in the main operations center (HOS), where he was on evening duty. To our surprise, the core operations center of the entire Games was a quiet and relatively tidy meeting-room, and almost empty. During the couple of hours we were there, only one minor issue occurred, and Brenna laughed: *He would have solved that himself, if I hadn't been here and available,* he said.

The arenas began to get used to the idea that this was actually going to be 'The best Games ever', even though the nerves never disappeared until the closing ceremony was over. Many workers expressed surprise at the smoothness by which every little problem was solved, and to what extent they were allowed to find an acceptable solution without referring to managers higher up somewhere. There was a lot of local creativity involved when unexpected challenges turned up. Generally the arenas lived their own separate life-cycles with new and different challenges occurring as the sequence of sports events evolved. Some sports completed their competitions very early, such as luge and bob-sleigh, whereas others, such as Ice Hockey continued until minutes before the closing ceremony. As some were packing and handing back their mobile phones and other equipment, others were facing new problems as late as the final day. In Haakon's Hall, for instance, they suddenly needed to plan the details for a victory ceremony in Ice Hockey, since there is no winner until the very end. The problem was solved smoothly, but it created some humour in arena manage-ment, as they realized that nobody had planned for the 'flower girls'. What was routine in Hamar (figure skating or speed skating) was an exception in Haakon's Hall!

The closing ceremony was the same success as the opening, and when IOC President Juan Antonio Samaranch said that it had really been 'The best Winter Games ever', all the workers of LOOC as well as their partners felt they had succeeded. Now what was left was closing down the arenas, moving everyone out of their temporary housing and back home, returning or selling the equipment, moving temporary houses to places where they were to be reused, and so on. The closing down had also been pre-planned in detail from the early stages of the Olympic Games, and just like the planning hierarchy and the arena organization overlapped in the transition from planning to implementation, the close-down organization overlapped with the arena organization as soon as the arena started packing. Each arena had specially assigned people responsible for security, return of equipment, etc., and in addi-tion, a senior manager was appointed to be in charge of the final closing-down. He had his own project team to support his efforts, with particular support from the Army and other security people.

Post-event evaluation

One of the challenges in terms of evaluating the effects of the XVII Olympic Winter Games in Lillehammer is the fact that the actual goals and criteria for evaluation were never agreed upon, neither before nor after the games. Expectations varied substantially from one stakeholder group to another, and whereas some were extremely happy, others were disappointed. For a mega-event such as the Olympic Winter Games, it is important to look at post-event effects not only in terms of economic effects for the local or national business community. Since our main concern here is with the learning effects, as opposed to the economic effects, we will focus only on those in the following.

The organizer

Whereas most conventions and other types of events are organized by firms or organizations specialized in the organization of such events, one-shot mega-events which take place as rarely as the Olympic Games have to rely on hiring and mobilizing people on an ad hoc basis. Hence, in this case the 'organizer' is 'dead' – only small subsections live on, such as in the companies established in Lillehammer and the other local municipalities to continue utilizing the arenas. One interesting example may be the luge and bobsleigh arena in Hunderfossen, where they even offer summer rides on a bobsleigh with wheels. Norway had no experience whatsoever with modern bobsleigh competitions prior to the Olympics. In addition, some minor learning effects manifest themselves in terms of improved capabilities in running World Cup sports events and other International Championships, but this effect seems to have been much smaller than that which the local communities had hoped for. In Norway we even have an unresolved debate as to whether Lillehammer, Granåsen in Trond-heim or Holmenkollen in Oslo should be given the status as the National Ski-jumping arena. There is no question that Lillehammer has improved their competence in terms of running such events, but since the competence already existed in other cities which continue to compete for World Cups and other International Events, Lillehammer has not received as many post-Olympic sports events as they had expected.

Another part of the organizer is the IOC, as well as future organizers of Olympic Winter Games. Just like LOOC employees went to Albertville, a large number of Nagano consultants and employees came to Lillehammer to learn from the way the Norwegians organized the Games. Like Japanese students of quality assurance in any area of business, these observers and participants studied every single detail of the organization with such impeccable accuracy that it was sometimes the subject of internal jokes and story-telling. They had a complete organization set up to tap into the planning as early as four years ahead of the Lillehammer Games. One major problem, of course, was the language. Even though most Norwegians speak (some) English, they do not interact in English when doing their jobs together with other Norwegians. They did try to help the Japanese (future) colleagues along, but still, when the going got rough, they returned to the language in which they were most comfortable themselves. It is therefore difficult for us to assess the learning effect as seen from Nagano's perspective.

In addition, the IOC keeps records of how the Games have been organized in the past, and serves as an intermediary between one organizer and later ones. However, these documents only give partial insights into the complexity of all the little details to be handled during the event itself. The 'white books' are important to future organizers of olympic events, but since every organizer wants to be remembered for the successes, such ex post reports are unlikely to contain information about many of the most difficult and challenging aspects.

We believe it is unlikely that the event-specific learning is going to affect the decision of a future site to apply for the Olympic Games, and hence it is more important to look at the learning effects in a broader sense, both in terms of direct effects on firms and other organizations involved, and in terms of indirect effects through the added competence of the workers. In our view, the latter effect is often particularly underestimated when mega-events are undertaken or assessed.

Learning by employees and volunteers

Our study was designed to look primarily into the effects on individual competence, and we have documented a large variety of learning effects (Løwendahl and Nordhaug, 1994). In fact, when interviewed before the Games, the majority of the employees said they applied for the job because of the unique opportunity to build competence, in particular about working in cross-functional projects. Only a small minority of the employees said they applied for the job because they were particularly interested in the Olympic Games as a sports event. Still, we experienced substantial suspicion on behalf of people outside of LOOC as to the relevance of the learning from the event. Rather than look at the Olympic Games as a large, cross-functional project, they looked at it as an unusually complex sports-event which might have some positive economic effects for the local municipalities.

When we interviewed employees about relevant competence and learning effects, we emphasized a definition of competence including both knowledge (a primarily cognitive, information based component), skills (which are transferred through training), and aptitudes or talent (which both limit how good a person can become at something and how fast (s)he can learn). The interviews gave us a large number of inputs, and after careful analysis we ended up grouping them into six main categories:

1) *Task related competence.* This category included elements such as 'knowing how to set up an employment contract', 'knowing how to handle an advertising agency as a sub-contractor', 'knowing how to plan for a new transportation system', 'knowing how to

prevent unwanted persons from entering sensitive areas in an arena', etc. Since LOOC was primarily based on the ability of employees to apply what they already knew to new situations, it was only in a few functional areas that the challenge involved substantial task related learning. One important learning point was suggested by numerous young employees with a relatively limited experience before LOOC, and that was the increased understanding of multiple aspects of a contract. However, what most of the employees emphasized was the cross-functional learning; the repeated need to adjust to the requirements of people in other functions. Two examples may illustrate this: The experts in charge of the audio equipment for the opening and closing cermonies had to adjust a number of their 'ideal' positions for audio equipment in order to accommodate the requirements of TV cameras etc. Even if the sound was perfect, the solution could not be accepted if it put a loud-speaker at the forefront of some of the key TV images. Similarly, the police had devised a completely safe transportation route for the winners of medals from Håkon's Hall to the podium, but this required ugly fences and major areas being closed off to the public. Instead, in a cross-functional brainstorm, the idea of sledges with security people hidden inside emerged and gave a much better impression. Such cross-functional learning was pervasive throughout LOOC, and it is likely to improve the performance of the employees in their future jobs as well.

2) *Job mastery.* The second major category of learning effects at the individual level was related to mastering a complex and underspecified job, and even designing (and redesigning) your own position. Most of the employees spoke about the ability to handle frequent changes, the ability to handle a high level of stress, the ability to set priorities and deal with what is most urgent first, etc. Many employees also said that they never thought they would be able to handle so much hard work for such a long time without collapsing. They felt that they had tested their own limits, and experienced that their tolerance level was much higher than they expected. However, some also discovered that they had reached the limit, and learned not to take on more than what they could handle. These skills are clearly transferrable to other jobs and employers.

3) *Intra-organizational knowledge and skills.* From previous studies (see e.g. Nordhaug, 1993), we knew that an important part of individual competence had to do with the ability to get things done, get decisions made, work around the informal power structure of the organization, etc. We expected the effect of this kind of intra-organizational competence to be minimal in an organization designed to be closed down, but found the contrary: in order to 'make a career' in LOOC, with its unusually frequent reorganizations, it was critical to know who made the next decisions and to make sure those people knew about your own strengths and desires for the next stage. One example may be the assistant in the personnel department who became the personnel manager in the Hunderfossen arena; she was able to convince the right people that she had competence way beyond that which was evident from her previous secretarial position, was given a chance, and proved during both test-events and the Games that she could do an excellent job. Intra-organizational skills are difficult to transfer to other organizations, and such knowledge by definition cannot be transferred, but to the extent that individuals also learned how to find the appropriate information faster, this competence may help them in their future jobs as well.

4) *Industry and environmental knowledge.* Another key learning point frequently emphasized by employees was the tremendous amount of contacts they had to make

with other stakeholders external to LOOC. Suppliers, sub-contractors, consultants, part-ners, the media, the local and national authorities were only some of those mentioned. For many young employees, the work in LOOC provided an excellent opportunity to learn more about their previous clients as well as suppliers, such as the example of the young designer who came from an advertising agency and now found herself ordering art work from other agencies; 'I will be a much better partner for the clients in the future', she said, 'now that I have experienced what it is like to be the client myself'. In addition, hardly any employee of LOOC went through the planning and implementation phases without having to deal with the media. Even the purchase of basic office supplies could suddenly become the topic of a newspaper debate, and it was critical for all involved to know both what to say and when not to answer any questions. In addition, the mere presence of the LOOC employees recruited from all parts of the country sometimes provoked aggressive comments from local people; 'who asked these yuppies to come here and turn our quiet town upside-down'? seemed to be the perspective of some of the most negative. As a result, even going out for a meal or to a disco required of the employees that they mind both what they say and what they do. This kind of learning is difficult to achieve without having experienced the reactions of real journalists, and hence has proven helpful for many employees in the years following the event.

5) *Relational competence.* Maybe one of the most important categories of competence mentioned by the employees is the dimension dealing with the relationship between one employee and the other relevant colleagues involved. The examples were numerous, and included skills such as 'explaining to someone with a different expertise why your point is so important', 'ability to develop mutual trust', 'the ability to handle and solve conflicts in a diplomatic way', 'the ability to fight for your own perspective long enough to find the ideal solution, but also to compromise when necessary in order to achieve the best overall solution', 'ability to work with others in a cross-functional team', 'ability to make people laugh', etc. These are clearly the type of skills most employers look for when they hire new employees, and they are difficult to assess in recruiting. To the extent that LOOC-employees collected personal references for their competence from colleagues as well as superiors, they could document interpersonal skills to a much larger extent after the event than they had previously been able to do.

6) *Meta-competence.* The sixth and final category of competence elements included numerous examples of competence which may enhance (or impede) individual learning, such as creativity, ability to be systematic, skills in analytical thinking, empathy, ability to make quick decisions, etc. Most of these are aptitudes and cannot be learned per se, but some of them can be enhanced through training, and some may definitely be discovered when a person is put to the test. Many LOOC-employees were tested more than they expected on their ability to adapt to new circumstances and to adjust rapidly, and they said the realization that they were able to handle a large amount of uncertainty and pressure would help them in future change processes.

The six categories of enhanced individual competence are hopefully used to the benefit of other employers after LOOC. One challenge which concerned top management in particular shortly after the event, was how employees with unusually rich and complex experience could find new challenges with other employers, when they had already 'gone through the roof' dompared with a normal career development. The COO, Henrik Andenæs, emphasized the importance of finding new challenges in terms of learning, and said that some employees should definitely move 'sideways' into new jobs at the same level but with additional challenges in terms of developing competence they did not have. An unknown industry, for instance, could provide new challenges. Very few of those (already in the minority) who were granted a leave of absence from their previous employers wanted to go back. This is both a positive indicator of a learning effect, and an unfortunate indicator of the lack of ability and/or interest with the previous employer in terms of gaining the positive inputs from employees with substantially enhanced individual competence.

Another important learning point emphasized by many, was the ability to work in a major project 'owned' by the public (government as well as the local municipalities), but with business-like responsibilities for budgets and results. Most of the managers experienced this duality as extremely difficult in the beginning, but after the event they were positive to the experience. E.g. managers from the private sector gained much more respect for public bidding procedures, public access to (most) information, and the importance of listening to the requirements of all relevant stakeholders. Since there were so few managers from the public sector, the learning from this side was limited to very few people, and we will not elaborate further on this topic here.

If we were to highlight a few of the most frequently mentioned examples of competence added to or enhanced, these are some of them:

- Project (management) experience
- Cross-functional team experience
- Experience in defining your work ('sub-project') and negotiating responsibilities and boundaries
- Experience in handling (and planning for) media attention
- Experience in handling large contracts
- Ability to change quickly and 'find your own space' in an organization which changes every day, and where new colleagues arrive on the scene every day
- Experience in dealing with public routines and requirements (with positive results)

In addition, learning about the organization of sports events clearly took place among teams of volunteers from local sports clubs, thus increasing their competence relative to future sports events. Even the uniform from the Olympics seems to carry authority in local winter sports competitions, now as late as five years after the Games! Beyond the effect on sports organizers, it is difficult to pinpoint the learning effects on volunteers, as most of them only participated for about three weeks.

Learning by other organizations

In addition to the learning described by individual employees and volunteers participating in the organization of the Lillehammer Winter Olympic Games, a number of other organizations used the Games to test out and develop project based solutions for their own operations. We did not study the learning effects on sub-contractors, local and national government and others, but through the interviews carried out after the Games as well as additional insights provided by participants in other contexts, we may safely conclude that learning was not limited to employees and volunteers involved in LOOC. All of the major sub-contractors talk about the 'Olympic experience' as something important, not only to their status (and in a few cases profitability), but also to their organization and even more to the culture of their organizations. Sub-contractors we have come across after the Games include, but are not limited to, Norwegian Telecom, ABB, TINE Norwegian Dairies, GILDE Norwegian Meatproducers, Partena Caterers, NSB Norwegian Railways, NRK Norwegian Broadcasting, and The Norwegian Police. Suppliers who were involved often fought for the contracts by bidding so low that the economic result was minimal, but in addition they used the Winter Olympic Games to develop their own organizations, as well as to improve their practices and their reputation. In addition, they certainly made the most of this opportunity to invite key customers and partners to visit their own suborganizations during the Games.

Other learning effects are likely to be found locally. As visitors to Lillehammer long before, shortly before, during, and after the Games, we were impressed by the internationalization and the improved service orientation of Lillehammer's hotels and restaurants, and we experienced a 'boom' in the year before the Games. Some of the new attitude still remains, and of course the investments in the infrastructure are still there. However, it is sad to see how few of the new more internationally oriented restaurants survived. No matter how much you learn, it is difficult to change the hard facts of the size of the local population and its willingness to spend time and money retaining the international aspects of the city. Unfortunately it seems that many of the individuals who learned most moved away from Lillehammer's tourist business when they realized that even after the Olympics tourism was largely cyclical and inadequate for the new investments made. We refer to the chapter by Spilling for a more detailed analysis of local economic effects.

The learning effects in surrounding organizations are certainly not limited to the private sector. In the ministries as well as in the local municipalities they also talk about important learning effects, and several future public projects, most notably the new Oslo Airport at Gardermoen, were planned according to the model of LOOC. Since we did not study these effects at all, we will not speculate further on the implications of such effects.

Indirect learning transferred to other organizations

One of our main interests, as stated in the introduction to this chapter, was to study the transition from planning to implementation, in order to inform other organizations in a period of transition of what we could learn from this mega-event. Unfortunately, we experienced a surprising lack of interest in the pre-event phase for this kind of learning, and our efforts to conduct a large research project on these effects were stranded due to a lack of interest both from the Norwegian Research Council and from the companies which might benefit in the long run. Among others, we talked to the managers in charge of a group of companies, called 'Birkebeinerlauget', companies which were suppliers to the Games but who also wanted to gain additional effects, both in terms of image effects and in terms of learning. They discussed two sub-projects: one regarding 'best practice' in sub-contractor relationships (including logistics etc.), and the other regarding competence. The group decided to prioritize the first, and possibly 'revert to the competence issue if we have the time later...' The same mentality existed in the research council, where we were told to 'come back with a new application next year'. But this project of course had to be undertaken parallel with the Olympic Games, not four years after, and as a result, was conducted with minimal financing by the institutions employing us: (BI and NHH) and LOOC.

We believe the lack of interest in the learning effects at the organizational level may stem from a lack of understanding of the kinds of learning which may result from such mega-events. Many people expressed skepticism, such as 'this is too unique', 'who needs to know how to interact with the IOC', 'who cares which kind of Oysters Mr Samaranch prefers, …' The actual learning effects as listed above, and at the organizational level particularly in terms of how to handle the transition from a planning hierarchy to a competence based implementation organization, could have been extremely helpful to other firms, yet the opportunity was largely missed. Today, five years after the Games, we see what we expected to see, namely organizations of all shapes and sizes trying to become flat, flexible and centered around knowledge or competence. Unfortunately, our project did not have the necessary funding, neither during nor after the Games, to cover the costs involved in an in-depth analysis of the implications. However, let us just highlight one insight here, namely the 'competence-based transition'.

We believe that the transformation of LOOC from a planning hierarchy to a flat, decentralized structure for the implementation of the event itself was quite unique. Most organizations, even today as we are rapidly moving into a post-industrial society (Løwendahl and Revang 1998), still take a top-down approach to reorganizations and respect hierarchical positions and seniority way beyond their potential impact in the new organization. When Petter Rønningen reorganized LOOC from planning to implementation, he made a couple of rather brave moves: he disregarded seniority, and he disregarded the positional hierarchy and all the status involved. Imagine the first reactions of a senior director, one of the first to be hired into the organization, when Rønningen tells him that he will not have any position of importance at all during the actual Olympic Games! And imagine the reactions of his colleagues and friends, who are used to stable hierarchies; 'what went wrong'?, they asked. And 'how could he be demoted in such a way'? We believe that the reorganization process was a key factor of the success, and that Rønningen's ability to choose people with the right team-building competence for the local arenas was critical. Maybe it was even critical to choose managers who did not have any stakes at all in their budgets from the planning hierarchy? The transition opened a number of new opportunities to those who were positioned well enough to be recruited by the new arena managers. It would be naive to think that the new organization was optimal in terms of matching competence and local requirements, as there was no way the organization could support the new managers in these complicated choices (including numerous volunteers who were not even on site when the decisions were made). But the principles were unusual, and did point in the direction of future competence-based organizational transitions, and that is what we believe may be the most important in-direct learning point from this event.

If an organization fundamentally changes its tasks (as LOOC did, when it went from planning to delivering), management needs to consider people with the appropriate competence for a radically different future organization when they 'man' the new organization, as opposed to the historically demonstrated success in the previous organization. Predicting future competence requirements is difficult, and predicting future success and learning capacity of individuals recruited for completely new and different tasks is even more difficult. Yet, we believe that the LOOC study illustrates the principles of such a transition quite well, and at least the attempt was made to create an organization where the most competent individual (whether employee, volunteer, or externally hired) was recruited for each position in the new hierarchy. In some cases, LOOC underestimated competence elements or personal characteristics which turned out to be important, such as when the ticket controllers in Lysgårdsbakkene needed not only to control tickets and show people to the right section, but also to physically force twice as many people into a section than that which people felt was appropriate. With backpacks and winter clothing people were much 'bigger' than what was expected when the number of tickets to be sold per section had been calculated. Sweet and gentle women were hired to control tickets, and had to be both retrained and supported by the police, in order for the audience to be squeezed into its limited space. But in many cases, competence and creativity presented itself in unexpected places, such as when the same ticket controllers realized they needed to be able to distinguish their colleagues from all the other employees wearing the same uniform, and spent the entire night making orange arm-bands to make themselves visible.

Two major learning points result from this: On the one hand, it is important to build the new organization based on the competence required, rather than on past successes. On the other hand, competence is more available than one often expects, and people who are trusted and given the responsibility and authority to find a good solution very often do so, even if the solution may be different from the expected. Even today, very few organizations are built on these principles, and few transition managers are brave enough to short-cut the hierarchical structure of status and position!

5.4 Conclusion

We see the Lillehammer Olympic Games as a realistic laboratory for organizational learning, and highly recommend that future mega-events include research into the learning effects at all levels in order to secure the transfer of such learning to all relevant stakeholders. Unfortunately our study did not find the necessary support for an in-depth analysis of such effects, but hopefully future mega-events will include a thorough analysis of the learning effects *as well as* the economic effects.

Learning effects are difficult to measure and document, and may easily become an excuse for organizing a mega-event which costs far more than it imparts to society at large. However, since this study was conducted, major improvements have been made in terms of concepts and methods for assessing 'invisible assets' (Itami 1987) such as knowledge and competence (Nonaka and Takeuchi 1995; Sveiby 1997). It is not impossible to assess qualitatively the effects on individual as well as organizational competence – in mulitple organizations. It just requires the willingness to invest sufficient time and resources into documenting these effects carefully, as we now (luckily) have a tradition established for assessing the direct and more accessible economic effects of events.

References

Eisenhardt, K. (1989). Building Theories from Case Study Research. *Academy of Management Review, 14*(4), 532-550.

Erichsen, B. (1994). *Kulturkollisjon.* Oslo: Grøndahl Dreyer.

Erichsen, B., Hugdahl, L., Lundsgaard, A., Seeberg, T.B, Sønsteby, G., & Verde, L. (1994). *Fruer på Veggen – LOOC fra Innsiden.* Oslo: Aschehoug.

Glaser, B.G. & Strauss, A.L. (1967). *The Discovery of Grounded Theory; Strategies for Qualitative Research.* New York: Aldine de Greuter.

Haanes, K. (1997). *Managing Resource Mobilization: Case Studies of Dynal, Fiat Auto Poland and Alcatel Telecom Norway.* Copenhagen Business School: Ph.D. Thesis 9-97.

Hervik, A., Asheim, G., & Björnland, D. (1990). *Samfunnsøkonomiske perspektiver på OL.* Senter for Anvendt Forskning (SAF), NHH, Bergen og Møreforskning, DH, Molde.

Itami, H. (1987). *Mobilizing Invisible Assets.* Boston, MA: Harvard University Press.

Løwendahl, B.R. (1992). *Global Strategies for Professional Business Service Firms.* Unpublished Ph.D. Dissertation, University of Pennsylvania. Available from UMI Dissertation Services.

Løwendahl, B.R. (1997). *Strategic Management of Professional Service Firms.* Copenhagen Business School Press.

Løwendahl, B.R. & Nordhaug, O. (1994). *OL 1994 – Inspirasjonskilde for Framtidas Næringsliv?* Oslo: TANO Aschehoug.

Løwendahl, B.R. & Revang, Ø. (1998). Challenges to Existing Strategy Theory in a Post-Industrial Society. *Strategic Management Journal. 19*(8), 755-773.

Nonaka, I. & Takeuchi, H. (1995). *The Knowledge Creating Company.* Oxford University Press.

Nordhaug, O. (1993). *Human Capital in Organizations.* Oslo: Scandinavian University Press.

Pettigrew, A. (1988). *Longitudinal Field Research on Change: Theory and Practice.* Paper presented at the National Science Foundation Conference on Longitudinal Research Methods in Organizations, Austin, Texas.

Spilling, O.R. (1996). Mega-Event as Strategy for Regional Development: The Case the 1994 Lillehammer Winter Olympics. *Entrepreneurship and Regional Development, 8,* 311-343.

Spilling, O.R. (1997). Long Term Impacts of Mega-Events – The Case of Lillehammer 1994. In *Proceedings from the Talk of the Top Conference,* July 7-8, Östersund, Sweden.

Sveiby, K.E. (1997). *Managing and Measuring Knowledge-based Assets.* San Francisco, CA: Berrett Koehler.

Chapter 6

Financial Effects of Events on the Public Sector

Tommy D. Andersson and Lars A. Samuelson

ETOUR , Sweden & Bodoe Graduate School of Business, Norway
Stockholm School of Economics, Sweden

6.1 Background

Economic impact analyses are made for various beneficiaries and at various levels. At the first level, the effects directly attributable to the event as such are evaluated. Secondly, as events have impacts on the region involved, as well as on the public sector and the society at large, the effects on these levels will also be taken account of. Welfare effects on the society of events may be studied by cost/benefit analyses. Such analyses may also be used by the event propagators when they try to convince decision makers of the advantages of an event.

Figure 6.1. Three levels of evaluation of events according to a 'bottom-up' perspective

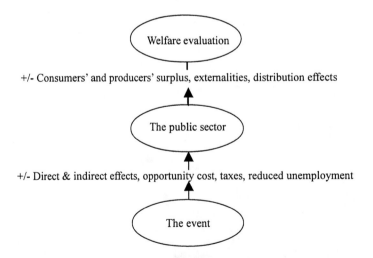

There is an interest from public units in evaluating – ex ante and/or ex post – the effects of events on the public sector. The literature so far has mainly studied events from other perspectives, either one limited to the direct effects of events, or one wider perspective treating the welfare effects for society as a whole. The evaluation of the effects of events on the public sector is not as straightforward as in evaluating the direct effects. Neither is it as complicated as determining the welfare effects. It therefore seems reasonable to clarify the principles and procedures in evaluating the effects on the public sector.

As shown in Figure 6.1 more effects are taken into account in a public sector evaluation than in an evaluation of the event as such and even more effects are included in a welfare evaluation.

The purpose of this chapter is to define a general model to be used in evaluating the financial effects of large events on the public sector. Variables that will enter into the evaluations will be defined below. The model will be exemplified with a case study of the proposal by the City of Stockholm to host the Olympic Summer Games in 2004.

6.2 Theoretical Framework

A general model of the most important variables to take into account when evaluating the effects on the public sector of large events is outlined (Figure 6.2).

Figure 6.2. A general model of the effects of events on the public sector. Boxes with bold text represent the effects that have an impact on the public sector

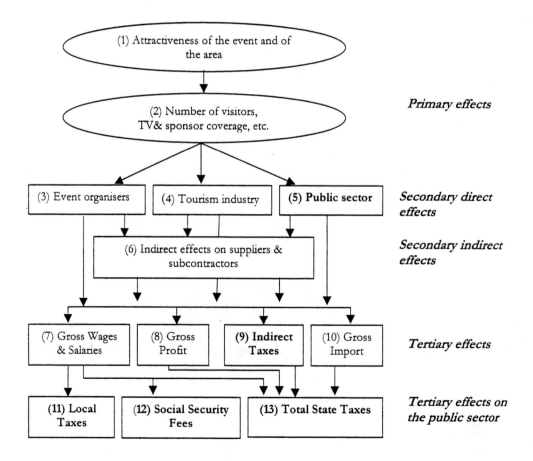

The general structure of, and the logic behind, the model are as follows: the attractiveness of the event from different perspectives (1) determine the *primary* effects that generate demand from visitors, TV and sponsors (2). This demand means revenues and costs to different *secondary* beneficiaries such as the event organization (3) and the tourism industry (4). There may also be some *effects directly on the public sector* (5), e.g. financial contributions to the event and effects on public services such as health care and police services. Secondary organizations will have to purchase resources of different kinds from different suppliers and this will result in various so-called indirect effects (6).

The distribution of value added among the four primary input factors: (7) Salaries & Wages, (8) Gross profit, (9) Indirect Taxes (e.g. VAT), and (10) Import are of greatest importance to the public sector. These four "basic economic elements" (Andersson, 1999) constitute the tax base and are treated differently in different countries. Thus the tax effect for the public sector will vary between countries according to tax legislation and other institutional arrangements prevailing in each country. In the final stage of this model, the tax effects for the public sector are determined, i.e. taxes and fees levied by the municipalities (11), the social security system (12), and the state (13). Added to the effects directly on the public sector (5) the overall effects on the public sector can be determined.

Primary effects: In the process of estimating the future or actual effects of events, the first variables to determine are related to the magnitude of the primary effects (1 and 2): How many visitors will be attracted by the event? How much money can be raised from TV and sponsors? These estimates are common to all events and often included in an event budget.

Secondary effects: These effects comprise *direct* and *indirect* effects. Getz (1997) gives an overview of the ways estimates of direct tourism effects are carried out. As an aid for calculating direct effects, some countries, e.g. Canada and Sweden, publish so-called Tourism Satellite Accounts showing normal amounts spent by visitors and tourists of different kinds and on different objects (see Nordström 1995).

There may also be some direct secondary effects on the public sector (5). Examples of such effects are financial contributions to the event and effects on public services such as health care and police services. These effects may to some extent be financed by the event. Another part may be financed by visitors (e.g. payments for health care received). The remaining part will be financed through public budgets. One should check for expenditure switching (Faulkner 1993). Government may merely switch public spending from one activity to another and that will have no net effect on the economy. If, however, public spending will have to be financed through a tax increase, the extra tax amount levied should be calculated at the marginal cost for public funds. The so-called dead weight losses should be accounted for which in Sweden is often done by adding 30% to the amount raised (see Varian 1993). If, however, all financial effects on the public accounts affect the amount of taxes levied, all these effects, positive as well as negative should be adjusted by this factor.

Opportunity cost is defined as "the revenue from the best alternative use of the resources utilized". If a small event is analyzed, it may be the case that all resources used would otherwise have been idle. For example: free capacity in hotels and restaurants is used, no public subsidies are granted, an otherwise empty sports stadium is used, etc. The opportunity cost will then be very low. Mega-events, on the other hand, where e.g. total hotel capacity is booked in advance, may have clear push-away effects and the revenue foregone from pushed-away normal tourists will then constitute a large share of the opportunity cost.

Significant 'displacement effects' on normal tourism by a mega-event have been shown by Hultkrantz (1998).

It has been argued that these 'pushed-away' tourists will still come, but at another time (Crompton 1995; Getz 1997). Visitors from outside the region may thus only change their visit in time or location. If this is the case, these effects should not be included in the opportunity cost. It is, however, also possible that they do come as usual and also take the opportunity to watch the games. In such cases these tourist expenses (except for the entrance fees) should not be included in the gross effect of the event even if they attend the event. 'Time-switching' and 'Casuals' act in different directions and may, to a certain extent, cancel one another out.

The opportunity cost of public funds used for a large event is usually a subject of the public debate preceding the decision to host a future event or not. People opposed to hosting an event often point to financial needs of hospitals and schools whereas advocates of hosting the event point to the presumed positive economic impact. To determine the value of the best alternative use of public funds used to support an event may simply be too hypothetical and too difficult. The best solution may therefore be to assume that the amount used for e.g. an event would otherwise have been distributed according to the average pattern of spending public funds. This is described by the input-output tables in the columns of the 'final demand sectors' as well as in other statistical sources. Assessing the opportunity cost is an area where further academic work is needed and some important steps in this area are taken by Hultkrantz in the following chapter of this book.

Indirect effects: In order to make a fair estimate of the indirect secondary effect (6), one should first determine the net financial contributions related to an event. By comparing the direct secondary effect to the opportunity cost, it is possible to clarify what amount represents an increase in the amount spent in the region and the state and what amount represents only a change in the use of these contributions from one activity to another. Only the net increase in the funds spent should be taken into account when calculating the indirect effects.

Obviously, money spent from outside the region is a net contribution and will induce indirect effects. It is important that the borders of the region are clearly defined when the classification is made. Of course there will be different amounts included if we look at a small region such as the city of Stockholm or the country of Sweden. In the case of Sweden, visitors from abroad will bring money to the country. What should be determined is the net increase in money spent by visitors due to the event considered as a basis for determining the indirect effects.

Money spent from sources within the region will in general represent a change in the object of spending and will not be a net increase in the level of spending. Examples of this kind of money are spending by visitors from the region and state grants (when studying the effects on the country level).

In calculating the indirect effects one should also take into account that the magnitude of the indirect effects varies between industries. So the direct effects on each industry affected by the event should be determined and a multiplier, that shows the effects on the revenues of the indirect industries for each direct industry, should be used. Such multipliers are available in several countries on different levels of aggregation. The applicability in a certain case has to be determined (Getz 1997, Ch. 14).

There are two different ways of calculating multipliers. Both are based on the mathematical properties of infinite series and they are both the result of work by outstanding economists.

- The Keynes' (1933) type of multiplier assumes a marginal propensity to consume and assumes this to be valid for the whole economy. The marginal approach seems appropriate for an analysis of an event but it may be less precise to assume the same marginal effects for the tourism industry as for any other part of the economy. Specific multipliers for the tourism industry have been developed for various countries (Archer 1976; Archer Fletcher 1990). 'Leakage' is a central concept and determines the size of the multiplier. The smaller the area studied the greater the leakage and the smaller the multiplier. The comprehensive multiplier for Sweden has been estimated at somewhere in excess of 50% whereas on a regional basis multipliers of 20-35% have been used.

- The Input-Output type of multiplier (Leontief 1936) is based on a detailed analysis of 50-100 industries. The number of industries depends on the scope of the national tables produced. In Sweden, input/output tables are produced every fifth year on a national level with details for a little less than 100 industries. The multipliers vary between industries from 10% to 170%. Input-Output tables are based on the average behavior of each industry regarding input requirements from other industries and from primary input factors such as labor and capital. Whereas the detailed analysis by sector is an advantage of the Leontief type of multiplier over the Keynes type, the average approach of the Leontief multiplier may be less appropriate than the marginal approach of the Keynes type, particularly so when the economic effects of an event are analyzed.

Each column in the input-output table in Table 6.1 shows from where each industry gets the input needed to produce output. The symbols a_{ij} represent the input that industry j gets from industry i where i = 1, 2, ..., m. The symbols v_{ij} represent the primary factor input (i = W, P, T, I) that industry j also has to pay in order to produce output.

Consequently, each row describes how output a_{ij} from industry i is consumed by each industry j = 1, 2, ..., m, as well as how output c_{ij} from industry i is consumed in the final demand sector by j = H, I, G, and E. Table 6.1 describes an input-output table in general terms. Later on, in the case study, a specific Swedish input-output table will be applied to the case.

Table 6.1. A basic input-output transaction table (cf. Fletcher, 1989)

Industry	Industry					Final Demand			
	(1)	(2)	(3) ....(m-1)	(m)		Households	Investments	Govmt	Exports
Industry (1)	a_{11}	a_{12}	a_{13}·················· $a_{1m\text{-}1}$	a_{1m}		c_{1H}	c_{1I}	c_{1G}	c_{1E}
Industry (2)	a_{21}	a_{22}	a_{23}·················· $a_{2m\text{-}1}$	a_{2m}		c_{2H}	c_{2I}	c_{2G}	c_{2E}
Industry (3)	a_{31}	a_{32}	a_{33}·················· $a_{3m\text{-}1}$	a_{3m}		c_{3H}	c_{3I}	c_{3G}	c_{3E}
....	...	...	... .		....	....	....	.....
.....	....	...	... .		....	....	....	.....
....	...	...	... .		....	....	....	.....
Industry (m-1)	...	...	... .		....	....	....	.....
Industry (m)	a_{m1}	a_{m2}	a_{m3} ·············· $a_{mm\text{-}1}$	a_{mm}		c_{mH}	c_{mI}	c_{mG}	c_{mE}
Wages & Salaries	v_{W1}	v_{W2}	v_{W3} ············· $v_{Wm\text{-}1}$	v_{Wm}		u_{WH}	u_{WI}	u_{WG}	u_{WE}
Gross Profit	v_{P1}	v_{P2}	v_{P3} ············· $v_{Pm\text{-}1}$	v_{Pm}		u_{PH}	u_{PI}	u_{PG}	u_{PE}
Taxes	v_{T1}	v_{T2}	v_{T3} ············· $v_{Tm\text{-}1}$	v_{Tm}		u_{TH}	u_{TI}	u_{TG}	u_{TE}
Imports	v_{I1}	v_{I2}	v_{I3} ············· $v_{Im\text{-}1}$	v_{Im}		u_{IH}	u_{II}	u_{IG}	u_{IE}

As indicated by the names of the coefficients in Table 6.1, the input-output table can be divided into four matrices: $\mathbf{A}$ (a_{ij}), $\mathbf{V}$ (v_{ij}), $\mathbf{C}$ (c_{ij}), and $\mathbf{U}$ (u_{ij}).

- $\mathbf{A}$ describes the inter-industry transactions and this matrix $\mathbf{A}$ is used to calculate the indirect effects and the Leontief type of multipliers. The technique used for this involves calculating the 'Leontief inverse' $(\mathbf{I}\text{-}\mathbf{A})^{-1}$ (cf. Miernyk, 1965 for a basic introduction).

- $\mathbf{V}$ describes the transformation from turnover to value added. Each element v_{ij} represents the primary factor input (i = W, P, T, I) that industry j will, on average, use to produce output. The element v_{ij} is expressed as a percentage of the amount of output.

- Another kind of indirect effect will appear when employees, in industries that are affected by the event, receive increased pay and spend incremental amounts on consumption. These effects are described by the matrices $\mathbf{C}$ and $\mathbf{U}$ and particularly by the column 'Households'. Increased pay may be related to higher salaries, more overtime work or formerly unemployed now receiving paid employment. Indirect effects of this kind, called *induced effects*, can also be estimated with multipliers.

The matrix $\mathbf{A}$ describing inter-industry transactions is used to calculate the direct + indirect effects. The 'Leontief inverse', $(\mathbf{I}\text{-}\mathbf{A})^{-1}$, describes how direct effects 'grow' when they are circulated an infinite number of times in the economic system. Thus when $(\mathbf{I}\text{-}\mathbf{A})^{-1}$ is multiplied by a matrix, $\mathbf{S}_{nx1}$, describing the net direct effects, calculated as the difference between the direct effects (3+4+5 in Figure 6.2) and the opportunity cost, the result, $\mathbf{N}_{nx1}$, will describe the net direct + indirect secondary effects for various sectors of the economy. In matrix notation this Model (1) is written as:

$$(\mathbf{I} - \mathbf{A})^{-1} \times \mathbf{S}_{nx1} = \mathbf{N}_{nx1} \dots\dots\dots\dots\dots (1)$$

$\mathbf{S}_{nx1}$ = a column describing the net direct secondary effect calculated as the gross direct secondary effect (3+4+5 in Figure 6.2) minus the opportunity cost.

$\mathbf{N}_{nx1}$= a column describing the net direct + indirect secondary effect. This column thus includes the multiplier effect and describes the net effects by n sectors.

Tertiary effects

Input-Output tables describe, not only inter-industry transactions, but also how the value added is shared among the 'basic economic elements': Salaries & Wages, Gross Profit, Taxes & Fees, and Import. This information can be used to describe the final effect (i.e. after an infinite circulation in the economy) in terms of the 'basic economic elements'. This calculation technique (Andersson 1999) will thus transform the original amount of money generated by the event into exactly the same amount of value added (+ import). By using the column describing the net direct + indirect secondary effects, $\mathbf{N}_{nx1}$, and multiplying this column by the matrix $\mathbf{V}_{4xn}$ that transforms turnover to value added and import, the net total economic impact will be expressed in terms of the four 'basic economic elements'. In matrix notation, Model (2) can be written as:

$$\mathbf{V}_{4xn} \times \mathbf{N}_{nx1} = \mathbf{E}_{4x1} \dots\dots\dots\dots\dots(2)$$

V_{4xn} =   a matrix of coefficients describing the tansformation into value added + import. $\mathbf{V}$ is a sub-matrix of the input output matrix of technical coefficients.

N_{nx1} =   a column describing the net direct + indirect secondary effect. This column includes the multiplier effect and describes the net effects by sector.

E_{4x1} =   a column of four amounts of money describing the final distribution in terms of 'basic economic elements' from e.g. tourism or a specific event.

Tertiary effects on the public sector in terms of tax revenue

Since taxes are based on various forms of value added, the last step in the analysis of tax effects will be to apply tax rates, customs duty, and social security fees to the 'basic economic elements'. In matrix terminology Model (3) can be described as:

$$P_{3x4} \times E_{4x1} = T_{3x1} \dots\dots\dots\dots\dots\dots\dots\dots\dots\dots\dots\dots\dots(3)$$

P_{3x4} =   a matrix of coefficients describing how the three types of taxes and fees are levied on the four basic economic elements i.e. the primary factor inputs.

E_{4x1} =   a column of four amounts of money describing the final distribution in terms of 'basic economic elements' calculated from the input-output table and the net direct + indirect economic effects from e.g. tourism or a specific event.

T_{3x1} =   a column describing the final amounts of local taxes, state taxes, and social security fees.

Total effects on the finances of the public sector

When the effects on the 'basic economic elements' or the primary input factors, which constitute the basis for taxes and fees, have been estimated, the effects on taxes and fees can be determined using Model (3) described above. Total effects on the finances of the public sector can now be summarized as follows:

- Direct secondary effects such as extra costs and/or revenue for public services and financial support (corresponding to 5 in Figure 6.2).
- Tertiary effects in terms of increased tax revenues and social security fees as described by T_{3x1} (corresponding to 11+12+13 in Figure 6.2).
- Savings due to reduced unemployment payments and other kinds of support.

6.3 Empirical Study

The example chosen is the proposal from the City of Stockholm to host the Olympic Summer Games in year 2004. This proposal was widely discussed in Sweden and several investigations have been carried out in order to estimate the economies of the event as such and the effects on the public sector. One study also tried to determine the welfare effects of the event (Abelin and Lundgren 1995).

The event organization (the Committee for the Project Stockholm 2004) has estimated the direct effects of the event as well as several other effects. These estimates have been revised by other actors participating in the evaluation of the event proposal, e.g. by the National Audit Bureau. A synthesis of the different estimates will be presented below as well as the major points of dispute. The budget from the Committee as of 1996-05-22 is used as a basis.

It perhaps goes without saying that in cases like Olympic Games not all efforts needed to carry out the games will result in payments. It is especially recognized that a lot of effort is made by volunteers.

The figures mentioned are stated in billions of Swedish Crowns (BSEK) and in the price level of April 1996. The exchange rate used is 1 USD = 7,50 SEK. Most payments are made in the years 2001-4. Analyzes involving payments over a period of several years will normally be based on discounted amounts and in the case of public investments a social discount rate will normally be used (see Battiato 1993). The input data used for this case study is however based on estimated amounts that have been added; present values have not been calculated.

Effects on the public sector in Sweden from this event will appear both on the regional and the national level. As the purpose of this case study is to define the effects on the Swedish public sector, the example will have the nation as its object of investigation.

Secondary effects

Secondary effects include most of the effects on the business sector. Three major beneficiaries will be analysed. Furthermore, there will be indirect effects on the business sectors that will eventually benefit all sectors. These effects will also be analyzed but only after due consideration has been taken to opportunity cost.

Effects on the event organization (3)

The budget for the event is based on estimated revenues of about 12 BSEK and costs of a similar amount. The income side is dominated by TV rights (5 BSEK), a lottery (3.5 BSEK), local sponsorships (1.1 BSEK), and ticket sales (0.70 BSEK). The income from the lottery was guaranteed by the State to make the financial commitment necessary to satisfy the requirements of the International Olympic Committee. Around 50% of revenues will come from abroad, mainly pertaining to the TV rights. Certainly more funds will flow into the Stockholm area from other parts of the country but, as stated above, the focus is on the effects on the national level. There are two dominating cost items 'Organization services' and 'Construction' that split the cost budget in two and one can calculate with 6 BSEK going to the Construction industry and 6 BSEK to the Services industry.

Effects on the tourism industry (4)

The tourism industry will benefit greatly from the event. According to estimates made, revenues will increase by 8.8 BSEK but when only the expected increase in the number of tourists from abroad has been taken into account. Most of this increase is expected to materialize during the years after the Olympic Games. During the Games, revenue from international tourists is expected to reach 1.4 BSEK which roughly corresponds to 1 million guest-nights. Since the number of tourist beds in Stockholm is limited, one should expect considerable 'displacement effects' and high opportunity cost (see below) during peak periods in the tourist industry.

Effects on the public sector (5)

There will also be some effects on the public sector not covered by the budget of the event. These refer for example to police work and customs services. The National Audit Bureau has estimated the additional costs at 1.2 BSEK. No analysis has been made of how these costs should be financed. Presumably there will be a change in activities for the departments involved for some time; others will probably realize some overtime work. Increase in the demand for health care services is also probable. To the extent that health care services are related to foreign visitors, the extra costs will be covered by extra revenues. For athletes, however, health care services should be provided free of charge.

Opportunity cost

About 50% of the revenue for the event organization is thus conceived of as equivalent to exports and represents a net increase in the financial means available to the region and to the nation. The other 50% is raised within the country and represents only a change in the object of spending. Thus the largest share of the opportunity cost is related to the alternative use of 6 BSEK that is raised in Sweden. To determine the economic impact of the alternative use is a challenging problem that is discussed in depth in the following Chapter 7 by professor Hultkrantz. In this case study, it is argued that the Swedish money could alternatively be used for either investment or consumption.

Since national financial support of the Olympic Games is often looked upon as an investment in tourism, a relevant alternative may be to use the 6 BSEK to boost the on-going marketing efforts for tourism to Sweden. It may be possible to calculate the advertising elasticity to get a fairly good estimate of the opportunity cost measured as the increased income from tourism that would have occurred if 6 BSEK was invested in traditional marketing of tourism to Sweden instead of supporting the Olympic Games.

An alternative approach is to look at the 6 BSEK as being withdrawn from the normal use of government and business funds as well as household consumption. This is often the argument used by opponents of hosting an event when they claim that resources would have been better used in hospitals, schools and other parts of the welfare sector. The average patterns of spending by government, private business as well as household sectors are described in the input-output tables (represented by c_{ij} in Table 6.1) which makes it possible to calculate the economic impact of the opportunity cost when consumption is assumed to be the relevant alternative use of the funds. In this case, no 'export' will be generated when the alternative is assumed to be consumption and the 'consumption alternative' is therefore likely to cause less impacts and a lower opportunity cost and hence a more impressive net impact.

In this study, the opportunity cost will be estimated according to the 'consumption alternative' discussed above, mainly because no clear-cut alternative was formulated by decision-makers. This probably means that the national net effect will seem more favorable than it would have done had the 'investment alternative' been used to calculate the opportunity cost.

Net direct secondary effects (Direct secondary effects – Opportunity cost)

The values used for the analysis are based on the following assumptions:

Effects on the event organization are 12 BSEK of which 6 BSEK goes to the Construction Industry and 6 BSEK to the "Other Services". *Opportunity cost* of the event organization is 6 BSEK of which 4.9 BSEK is household consumption and 1.1 BSEK business investments. These amounts represent the expenditure on the lottery, tickets, souvenirs, stamps and other merchandise that would be used to raise money from households. For the enterprises, money that otherwise would have been used for investments, would be used for e.g. sponsorship.

Effects on the tourism industry are calculated to be 8.8 BSEK, including 1.4 BSEK during the Olympic Games, and the economic effects have been distributed among different sectors of the economy according to statistics regarding tourists' average spending (Lodging: 20%; Shopping: 12%; Transport: 37%; Food: 10 %; Restaurants: 17%; Other activities: 4%). *Opportunity cost* due to 'time-switching' and 'displacement effects' (Hultkrantz, 1998) is estimated to be 2.5 BSEK distributed according to the same statistics as the direct effects. This is a rough estimate - as is the estimated increase in tourism after the Olympic Games.

   Thus the direct secondary effects will be 12 + 8.8 = 20.8 BSEK and the opportunity cost will be 6.0 + 2.5 = 8.5 BSEK. Table 6.2 describes these effects for various sectors of the economy.

   Table 6.2 illustrates that the net direct secondary effects may be positive as well as negative, which implies that there are 'winners' as well as 'losers' when the direct effects are analysed. Since the alternative use is estimated on the basis of the average household and business consumption, certain sectors of the economy, particularly the goods producing sectors, will notice a reduced demand when 6 BSEK are being 'redirected' and used for 'other services' to organise the Olympic Games.

Table 6.2.   A description of the secondary effects of the estimated economic impact of Olympic Games 2004 in Stockholm. The third column describes the vector S_{nx1} from Model (1). All values in BSEK

Industry	Direct Effects	-	Opportunity Cost	=	Net direct Secondary effects
Base Industries	.880		.774		.106
Wood & Chem.	0		.209		-.209
Metal Industries	0		.411		-.411
Construction Industry	6.000		.472		5.528
Retail Industry	1.060		1.090		-.030
Hotel & Rest. Industry	3.250		1.084		2.166
Transport Industry	3.250		1.091		2.159
Finance & Estate	0		1.003		-1.003
Other Services	6.360		2.367		3.993
SUM	**20.800**		**8.500**		**12.300**

Indirect effects (6)

By calculating the 'Leontief Inverse' $(A-I)^{-1}$ of the Swedish input output tables and multiplying this matrix by the 'Net Direct Secondary Effect' described in Table 6.2, the indirect effects for each sector of the economy can be obtained. Furthermore it is possible to state where the indirect effects will appear. Table 6.3 shows that whereas the direct effects mainly affect the service and the construction industries, the indirect effects will affect the base industries and the goods producing sectors to a much larger extent. Consequently, several of the industries that appear to be 'losers' in an analysis of net direct effects, as in Table 6.2, will come out much better when indirect effects are also included in the analysis. No induced effects have been estimated in any of the investigations in this study.

The estimate of the indirect effects has been widely discussed. In one of the first proposals from the event organization these effects amounted to 27 BSEK. A 50% multiplier was used. This estimate was criticized mainly with regard to the basis on which the multiplier was applied. This basis included an estimated increase in export of goods and services of 21 BSEK, which was supposed to be due to increased goodwill for Swedish products generated by the event. This item was later on withdrawn. The initial estimate of the effects on the tourism industry to 20 BSEK was later on also considered to have been too optimistic. Different multipliers have been used in order to take into account the different characteristics of the industries involved. On average a 60% multiplier was used. Based on the data (Table 6.3) the average multiplier for the event can be calculated by comparing the totals in the first and the second columns (7995/12300 = 65%). One reason for this comparatively high multiplier is the small import 'leakage' in the service sectors that are predominantly affected by the event.

Table 6.3.   The net direct secondary effects and the indirect effects calculated by using the column S_{nx1} and the 'Leontief inverse'. The third column corresponds to N_{nx1} in Model (1)

Industry	Net Direct Effects	Indirect Effects	Direct + Indirect Effects
Base Industries	.106	.934	1.040
Wood & Chem.	-.209	1.922	1.713
Metal Industries	-.411	1.125	.714
Construction Industry	5.528	.096	5.623
Retail Industry	-.030	.558	.528
Hotel & Rest. Industry	2.166	.175	2.341
Transport Industry	2.159	.884	3.043
Finance & Estate	-1.003	.393	-.610
Other Services	3.993	1.909	5.902
SUM	**12.300**	**7.995**	**20.295**

Tertiary effects

Tertiary effects in terms of the 'basic economic elements' will be calculated, using Model (2), mainly to provide a basis for estimates of tax effects, but also because these concepts yield information that may be interesting *per se*.

Tertiary effects including effects on taxable income and other bases of taxes and fees

The next task is to determine the net effects on Gross Salaries & Wages and other bases of Taxes & Fees. Model (2) generates an estimate of 'basic economic elements' based on the section V_{4xn} of the input-output tables that describes the transformation into primary input factors (Table 6.1) and on N_{nx1} the net direct + indirect secondary effects (Table 6.3). The result of the matrix multiplication of Model (2) is a column E_{4x1} describing the final effect in terms of the four basic economic elements that represent value added + import (Table 6.4). It is worth noting that the sum (12.3 BSEK) is exactly the same as the net direct secondary effect above (Table 6.2). This is a characteristic trait of the method and illustrates how, after an infinite circulation in the economic system, the net effect will dissolve into the four basic economic elements. 'Import' is comparable to 'Leakage' in traditional multiplier models with the difference that 'Import' describes the accumulated effect whereas 'Leakage' describes the effect at each 'economic period'.

Table 6.4. The distribution of tertiary effects among 'basic economic elements'. All values in BSEK

Basic Economic Elements	
Gross Salaries & Wages	6.720
Gross Profit	2.780
Indirect Taxes – Subsidies	.980
Import	1.820
SUM	**12.300**

'Indirect taxes' are comprised mainly of VAT and seems to be surprisingly low considering the Swedish VAT rate of 25%. One reason may be that the Hotel and Restaurant industry has a low VAT rate and that the food industry, that will have considerable indirect effects, is subsidized. The event organization proposed that the event should be exempt from VAT. This proposition was discussed but no political decision was ever taken which is the reason for using a normal VAT-rate in this case study. Gross Salaries & Wages is the dominating item which reflects one of the characteristics of the service sectors. Gross profit seems large but it should be noted that this is a gross amount to be used for depreciation / investments, interest rates, company taxes, and owners' profit.

Tertiary effects on the tax revenues of the public sector

Next, the four 'basic economic elements' will be used as a basis for calculating taxes. Income tax on salaries and wages in Sweden is levied by municipalities using a flat rate and by the state through a progressive rate. Social security fees are levied by a flat rate of approximately 33% on gross salary. In Sweden a tax equalization system is used for local taxes meaning that increases in tax revenues for one municipality will be reallocated to the benefit of all others. So even if the city of Stockholm hosts one big event and realizes tax increases these amounts will be reallocated to all other municipalities through the system.

The state will also receive more taxes if companies achieve higher profits as a result of the event and there is a flat rate of 30% of the profit. In Sweden, companies do not pay any local taxes. Indirect taxes go to the state and include customs duties. The data used are hypothetical (Table 6.5) and are based on assumptions of how high the average state tax rate would be on gross wages & salaries as well as gross profit.

Table 6.5. Hypothetical Swedish tax rates applied to the four 'basic economic elements'. This table corresponds to the matrix $\mathbf{P}_{3x4}$ in Model (3)

	Gross Wages	Gross Profit	Indirect Tax	Import
Local Tax	21%	0%	0%	0%
Social Security Fees	31%	0%	0%	0%
State Tax	7%	6%	100%	0%

When $\mathbf{P}_{3x4}$ (Table 6.5) is multiplied to $\mathbf{E}_{4x1}$, the result will be a column $\mathbf{T}_{3x1}$ (Table 6.6) with three rows displaying the tax revenues for municipalities and the state as well as social security fees

Table 6.6. A column showing the tax revenues and social security fees calculated according to Model (3). All values in BSEK. This table corresponds to the matrix $\mathbf{T}_{3x1}$ in Model (3)

Public Revenue	
Local Tax	+1.410
Social Security Fees	+2.080
State Tax	+1.620
SUM	**+5.110**

The total of 5.11 BSEK implies a comparatively low average tax rate (42%) for this project considering that the average tax rate in Sweden is well above 50%. One reason may be that the indirect tax is estimated net of subsidies.

Savings from reduced unemployment

In the final stage the effects on unemployment payments are calculated. The state, as well as the municipalities, will be affected by reduced unemployment payments. A forecast of the expected net increase in employment was based upon known relationships between revenues and employment in the industries involved. A simple calculation of this kind will probably overstate the effects on employment since overtime work and increased intensity of work by the current work force will account for a considerable part of the extra work needed.

According to the memo of 1996-12-20 from USK (a separate investigations and statistical bureau belonging to the city of Stockholm) there will be about 40,200 extra yearly employees. A more realistic figure will be 28,000 which represents the estimated effect on employment given that there is an excess of formerly unemployed people. It is, however, possible that the supply of highly skilled labor in the construction industry is scarce. In that case the increase in extra employment is overstated and the event will cause some other projects to be postponed or cancelled. The above mentioned memo estimates a deficit of 1,500 yearly employees. So the net increase in employment can be estimated at 26,500 yearly employees.

To estimate a total effect, the economic value of the reduction in unemployment needs to be assessed. To get a correct assessment requires an investigation into average cost, net of taxes and social security fees, for unemployed people. USK (1996) has estimated this amount to be SEK 99,000 per man-year of unemployment, which will bring the total value of the reduction in unemployment to 2.6 BSEK.

Total effects on the finances of the public sector

The model for estimating the effects on the public sector, advocated in this chapter, is based on three types of economic effects. Total effects are analyzed in terms of:

a) Direct secondary effects such as extra costs and/or revenue for public services;

b) Tertiary effects in terms of increased tax revenues and social security fees; and

c) Savings due to reduced unemployment payments and other kinds of support.

The discussion around the case study has been based mainly on data supplied by USK (1996). Other data are hypothetical and, in some cases, pure guesswork. The main objective with the case-study has however been to illustrate the model and the output the model yields rather than to provide a reliable estimate of the actual financial effects. To arrive at a reliable estimate of the Olympic Games Proposal would need a much closer scrutiny of the input data than it has been possible to pursue in this study. However, the three parts of the analysis are displayed and a total result has been calculated (Table 6.7).

Table 6.7. A calculation of estimated total effects on the public sector of Olympic Games 2004 in Stockholm. All values in BSEK

	Financial effects on the public sector		
a)	Direct secondary effects		- 1.2
b)	Tertiary effects:		
	Local Tax	+1.410	
	Social Security Fees	+2.080	
	State Tax	+1.620	+5.1
c)	Savings from reduced unemployment		+2.6
	Total effects on the public sector		**+6.5**

Discussion

This event seems to be a profitable project for the public sector judging from the total effect (table 6.7), but several of the items require closer scrutiny. This case study has been based on input data mainly from USK (1996) and if this input is unreliable, so is the output from the model.

- More than 3 BSEK comes from a budgeted surplus of a national lottery and this amount was guaranteed by the State that controls most national lotteries. If this guarantee implies that the State will reduce their surplus from normal lotteries to support the 'Olympic Lottery', the 3 BSEK will in fact represent a Government support and 'Direct secondary effects' should be less than – 4.2 BSEK instead of – 1.2 BSEK (cf. Table 6.7).

- As mentioned above, the organizing committee asked the Government for a VAT exemption. If such an exemption was to be granted by the State, this would probably mean at least 1 BSEK more of Government support.

- Tourism is estimated to increase by 8.8 BSEK before, during and after the Olympic Games. An increase in international tourism of about 1.4 BSEK during the Games implies about 1 million international guest-nights and taking into consideration that Stockholm has a limited amount of hotel rooms and that the majority of hotel guests will be Swedish, 1.4 BSEK may be an overstatement . The remaining 8,8-1,4=7.4 BSEK increase in international tourism represents a major item in the total effect of the Games and such an assumed effect has very little scientific support from studies of previous mega-events. Furthermore, these payments should be discounted to present value. Tourism may increase in Stockholm (and has in fact experienced considerable growth over recent years) but to credit the Olympic Games for such growth may be incorrect.

- The assumed opportunity cost based on consumption rather than investment also helps to support a high positive net effect. We could for example assume a 'Tourism Lottery' as an alternative to the 'Olympic Lottery'. Thus 3 BSEK would alternatively be used to market incoming tourism to Sweden, and the 8.8 BSEK in Olympic tourism would be matched by an alternative effect that would reduce the net direct Olympic effect considerably.

- Another major item is the reduction in unemployment by 26,500 man-years. This is based on the assumption that all salaries & wages will be used for new employment, which seems to be a rather unrealistic assumption.

Taken together, these points would easily erase all the profit calculated to be 6.5 BSEK (Table 6.7). The quality of the output from the model presented in this chapter does of course depend entirely on the quality of the input used for the model and, as mentioned, input data come from other sources (USK, 1996).

6.4   Conclusion

To evaluate the effects of an event, it is in most cases not enough to merely take account of effects attributed to the focal organizational unit. The effects in the society at large will also be important so that the public sector may support or prohibit the event.

The importance of taking into account the effects on the regional economy and on the public sector at large varies with the evaluation of the attractiveness of the event. Four cases can be identified (Table 6.8).

Table 6.8.   Effects for the event and the public sector

		Business profit of the event	
		Favorable	**Unfavorable**
Effects for the public sector	Favorable	A	B
	Unfavorable	C	D

Cases A and D are trivial whereas the other two are not. In case B, a private unit will not realize the event. As, however, this event will have positive influences on the public sector, this sector may compensate the loss of the private unit turning the event into a profitable one. In case C finally, a private unit finds the event to be profitable, but it may have large negative impacts on the public sector. This will motivate this sector to try and stop the event. The event may for example necessitate large public investment in infrastructure or it may require large efforts on behalf of the police or other services to secure law and order (or other kinds of so-called externalities).

It may be of interest to relate this discussion of the interdependence between the analyses on the private and public level to the major findings of North and Thomas (1973) in their historical account of the rise of the Western world. They argue that economic growth will not occur unless there are mechanisms to closely align social and private rate of returns. We can see that with regard to large events such alignment will not in many cases occur automatically. The institutional framework is not designed in such a way that this will take place by itself. Separate analyzes will have to be made and separate transactions may be designed and negotiated in order to reach alignment between the rate of returns.

When an event is organized by a unit belonging to the public sector, the overall evaluations are similar to the private case. One difference may be that no extra transactions will be needed to enforce alignment. It will be enough to verify the situation by the evaluations made. But in some cases different public units may be involved in creating a demand for extra transactions when needed. An example may be a city organizing an Olympic Games that are calculated to run at a loss. If this loss is well outweighed by positive effects on the state level, a transaction compensating the city may be negotiated.

With regard to The Olympic Games, the International Olympic Committee (IOC) requires the host state to formally guarantee the fulfillment of the games. The state will thus bear the financial risk of the event which, of course, is another reason why the effects on the public sector should be evaluated as a complement to the event calculation. The Olympic Summer Games in Los Angeles in 1984 represents an exception when Los Angeles got the games more or less as an emergency since no other nation was willing to organize them. No guarantee to fulfil the games was made before Los Angeles was appointed host. Later on, President Ronald Reagan, however, wrote a letter stating that "the U.S. government would stand by the Olympic Games and the Olympic Charter" (Ueberroth 1985, p. 118).

There may also be a general interest from the focal public unit (e.g. a city) to evaluate the effects of events on the general development of the region. From such a perspective it may be considered too narrow just to focus on one event; it may be seen as more appropriate to evaluate a certain strategy involving a program of different kinds of events. In such a program, for example the inclusion of certain events may have an impact on the attractiveness of the city and of other events from a tourist's as well as from an event organizer's point of view. In this paper the focus was, however, limited to the effects of events regarded as independent projects.

Comparing this model with other models, the most important feature is that the purpose of the model is to determine only the financial effects on the public sector (parts 5, 9 and 11-13 in Figure 6.2). Other models deal for example with the effects for the event organization (part 3) or have a wider purpose such as determining the effects on the society at large. Such cost-benefit analyses determine the benefits to the whole of the society with measures such as consumers' and producers' surplus and relate those to the costs involved. They also include all kinds of externalities, i.e. effects on the society that will have no effect on the accounts of the event or the society, at least not in the short run. An example of such an externality is pollution (cf. Burgan and Mules 1992; Collins 1991, Mules and Faulkner, 1996 and Williams and Giardina, 1993). A cost-benefit analysis will also take account of potential distributional differences between individuals in the society when resources are used in one way as compared to another. Analyses of this kind will not be treated here, although there are many methodological similarities between these cost-benefit analyses and the ones discussed here.

A cost-benefit analysis of an event normally includes considerable positive values for externalities such as the joy and pride that the local residents experience from the festivities surrounding the event. For many local sports enthusiasts, the consumer surplus of attending The Olympic Games at home is high compared to the ticket price. The value of new employment may also be much higher than the net financial effect since many unemployed suffer not only economically but also psychologically. Estimating the effects of events on the public sector has been shown to raise many methodological questions. With the help of a general model and an example it has been possible to identify the major tasks and problems involved. Clearly, in order to put forward the major features of the estimate, several aspects have not been covered in this paper. For example the time value of money has not been taken into account. What will the effect be on the political decision making if this is duly done?

Research in this area could progress in several ways. Firstly, it is of interest to refine the model and to apply it empirically in more cases. It should be possible to assess the financial effects for the public sector not only of events, but of any type of investment and economic intervention using this model. Secondly, a challenging task would be to find a comprehensive framework where the various kinds of calculations that may be made in connection with social events and similar activities can be integrated. In such a framework the budget of the event organization, the effects on the public sector and broader studies of the welfare effects should be building blocks that could be used according to the purpose of the investigation.

As now is known, Athens and not Stockholm was chosen to host the games in year 2004. According to a review, the costs of applying amount to a little less than 200 MSEK (OS projektet Stockholm 2004, 1998). It has also been argued that the costs for producing a similar amount of publicity through advertising and other PR activities as was achieved by being a candidate city, would have been much higher.

Perhaps it was more profitable for the City of Stockholm just to apply for the Olympic Games then it would have been to actually host the Games.

References

Abelin, C. & Lundgren, J. (1995). Samhällsekonomiska effekter av stora sportevenemang (Societal effects of big sport events). University of Uppsala. Master thesis.

Andersson, T.D. (1999). *An Alternative Model of Economic Impact Analysis – Using Dividends instead of Multipliers.* ETOUR W.P: 1999:7. Östersund.

Archer, B. H. (1976). The Anatomy of a Multiplier. *Regional Studies,* 10 pp. 71-77.

Archer, B.H. & Fletcher, J. (1990). Multiplier Analysis in Tourism. *Le Cahiers du Tourisme* Serie C, No.103, Centre des Hautes Etudes Touristiques, Aix-en-Provence.

Battiato, S.E. (1993). Cost-Benefit Analysis and the Theory of Resource Allocation. In A. Williams & E. Giardina (Eds.), *Efficiency in the Public Sector. The Theory and Practice of Cost-Benefit Analysis* Aldershot: Edward Elgar.

Burgan, B & Mules, T. (1992). Economic Impact of Sporting Events. *Annals of Tourism Research 19*(4), 700-710.

Collins, M.F. (1991). The Economics of Sport and Sports in the Community: Some International Comparisons. In C. Cooper (Ed.), *Progress in Tourism, Recreation, and Hospitality Management.* Belhaven Press.

Crompton, J. (1995). Economic Impact Analysis of Sport Facilities and Events: Eleven Sources of Misapplication. *Journal of Sport Management, 9,* 14-35.

Faulkner, H.W. (1993). *Evaluating the Tourism Impact of Hallmark Events.* Occasional Paper No 16, Bureau of Tourism Research, Canberra.

Fletcher, J. E. (1989). Input-Output Analysis and Tourism Impact Studies. *Annals of Tourism Research, 16,* 514-529.

Getz, D. (1997). *Event Management & Event Tourism.* New York: Cognizant Communication Corporation.

Hultkrantz, L. (1998). Mega-Event Displacement of Visitors: The World Championship in Athletics, Göteborg 1995. *Festival Management & Event Tourism, 5*(1/2), 1-8.

Keynes, J. M. (1933). The Multiplier. *The New Statesman and Nation, 1*(April): 405-407.

Leontief, W. (1936). Quantitative Input-Output Relations in the Economic System of United States. *The Review of Economics and Statistics, XVIII*(Aug.), 105-125.

Miernyk, W. H. (1965). *The Elements of Input-Output Analysis.* New York: Random House,

Mules, T. & Faulkner, B. (1996). An Economic Perspective on Special Events. *Tourism Economics, 2*(2), 107-117.

Nordström, J. (1995). *Tourism Satellite Accounts for Sweden 1992-1993.* Umeå: Umeå Economic Studies, No. 385.

North, D.C & Thomas, R P. (1973). *The Rise of the Western World. A New Economic History,* Cambridge: Cambridge University Press.

OS-projektet Stockholm 2004. (1998). (A final report from the project).

Riksrevisionsverket (National Audit Bureau), (1996). Comments on the Proposal for a State Guarantee and the Assumptions Regarding Hosting the Olympic Summer Games in Stockholm Year 2004 (RRV Dnr 22-95-3151).

Ueberroth, P. (with R. Levin & A. Quinn), (1985). *Made in America. His Own Story.* New York: William Morrow and Company, Inc.

USK (1996). Utrednings- och SatistikKontoret inom Stockholms stad; (Investigation and Statistics Bureau of the City of Stockholm), *Kommunalekonomiska konsekvenser av OS-projektet 'Stockholm 2004'* (Municipality Effects of the Olympic project 'Stockholm 2004') PM 1996-12-20.

Varian, H.R. (1993). *Intermediate Microeconomics,* New York: WW Norton & Co.

Williams, A. & Giardina, E. (Eds.) (1993). *Efficiency in the Public Sector. The Theory and Practice of Cost-Benefit Analysis* Aldershot: Edward Elgar.

Chapter 7
Event Economics: Top-Down Approaches

Lars Hultkrantz

Dalarna University & Uppsala University, Sweden

7.1 Background

Economics concerns the use of scarce resources, and therefore the choices that have to be made between different alternative uses of these resources. The fundamental question in the economic evaluation of an activity, such as an event, is whether the value of that activity exceeds the opportunity cost, i.e., the value of resources in the best alternative use. As a consequence, cost-benefit analysis of an event starts with analysis of the choice set – the available alternatives, and ends in comparison of at least two alternatives. Trivial as this may sound, it is often neglected in practice. An example is provided in Exhibit 7.1 showing the official so called socioeconomic impact assessment in connection to the bid for the Olympic Games in Stockholm in 2004. Irrespective of whether the estimated numbers are reliable or not it is clear that such an assessment is insufficient as there is no comparison made to a reference alternative without Olympic Games.

  The previous chapter has reviewed the traditional approach to event impact assessment, i.e., the multiplier approach, and outlined an alternative dividend approach which has several advantages. Both these approaches are constructive bottom-up techniques for computing an estimate of the overall economic impact. It uses data that is in some way specific for the event, e.g., expected attendance numbers, to construct this estimate. In *ex ante* analysis of an event, i.e., in assessments made before the event actually takes place, that is often the only feasible type of approach. To be informative, however, such assessment must be based on a careful identification of the actual economic choices to be made. The choice set of alternatives can, though, be quite complex, especially since it is changing over time. This issue will therefore be discussed in more detail in next section. Also in this chapter, we will give some consideration to the broader cost-benefit analysis context within which the economic assessment is made.

Exhibit 7.1. Summer Olympic Games in Stockholm 2004

In connection with the candidature of Stockholm City for hosting the 2004 Olympics, several so called socioeconomic impact assessments were presented. These focused on turnover effects. The first report presented by the organisers estimated the turnover impact of the games to SEK 100 billions. The table below shows a later more moderate appraisal made by an accounting consultancy firm.

Socioeconomic impact of Olympic Games in Stockholm. MSEK

The Olympic Games organization	5 800
Construction works	5 800
Tourism revenues, before and after the games	7 500
Ditto during the games	1 300
Other	400
Direct effects, subtotal	20 800
Indirect effects	12 400
Total effect	32 800

Source: Ernst & Young (1995).

Clearly, this does not show the net socioeconomic benefit of the project, although that was claimed. Resources used by the Olympic Games organisation would have an opportunity cost, for instance the efforts of various skilled experts necessary to arrange the mega project. Neither can the opportunity cost of the work input by construction workers in this capital city be expected to be zero. Tourists visiting Stockholm will give rise to both revenues and incremental costs, even if they are using idle hotel capacities etc. In a similar manner, indirect turnover effects do not show the indirect net benefit effect. Thus, the only thing that can be said (assuming that these values can be trusted) is that net benefits would have been less, probably much less, than the figures shown in the Table.

Frequently, the impact of an event will be recorded not only in measures that are event specific, but also in aggregate statistics that record the general economic activity in a region or in the tourist industry, such as industry turnover, regional GDP, tax revenues, regional employment, guest-night numbers, etc. Approaches that use such general data sources work top down, i.e., try to divide up the part of the change in such variables as can be attributed to an event. Analysis using such methods and data, is here called *intervention analysis*, since it studies how the development of a variable is affected by a specific intervention, here a special event. Such approaches will often be used in *ex post* analysis of the impact of an event, i.e., after the event has taken place. However, the reliability of *ex ante* bottom-up analyses will depend very much on the availability of good *ex post* analyses of previous events, so indirectly top-down methods are often a necessary input to *ex ante* impact assessment as well.

Unlike the bottom-up approaches, the neglecting of alternatives is not possible in top-down approaches, as the estimation of the counterfactual alternative is at the very core of these methods. In fact, different methods within this category are distinguished by the way in which the alternative development is constructed or estimated. An important observation for evaluation purposes is that an event is held at a specific site and is occasional. The event thus affects a unique place, while other regions or cities with similar conditions are not affected by the event and thus can be used as one or several control groups. Likewise, the effects of the event can be delimited in time, although there may be some effects before and after the occasion. This feature of events implies that they form *natural experiments*. The effects of an event can therefore be estimated from comparison of development of variables such as tourism revenues, guest-nights etc. at different sites/regions, and/or by comparison to a forecast of the counterfactual development based on *econometric analysis*. These two possibilities, and their combinations, are employed in intervention analysis, which will be discussed in the subsequence. First, however, we need to consider in more detail the role of alternatives in event analysis. Although top-down approaches must specify an alternative, it remains an issue what alternative reflects the relevant economic choice in the evaluation of an event. We therefore turn next to a discussion of aspects of specification of the choice set of an event.

7.2 Theoretical Framework

The planner's choice set of an event

Economic analysis is an instrument for decision-making, i.e. to guide decision-makers in making choices. It therefore presumes that there are choices to be made – that there are alternatives. As noted previously, although this seems to be a very obvious point, it is one of the most overlooked parts of economic event analysis.

Economic assessment when there is no explicit choice is *accounting*. Accounting, whether a business account or a satellite tourist industry account to the national account, can be very helpful in economic analysis as it provides economic data within a consistent framework. Economic accounts can sometimes be used directly for economic analysis to inform simply-structured choices, such as the decision of whether to continue an operation that is likely to perform in the future as it has in the past, or to discontinue and achieve zero net revenue. However, in most cases choice alternatives are much more complex. Not even annual events that are repeated on the same site/arena are likely to be the same from one year to another. External conditions (weather, prices, etc.) change and there will be deliberate changes because of learning from past experiences; to provide variety for the benefit of regular visitors; or just to reflect on new ideas as to how the event could be improved. The main alternative to an event may not be no event, but another event. Hence accounting data, if such are available, have to be transformed and supplemented in various ways before an economic analysis can be made. An economic impact analysis of an event can be a valuable input to an economic analysis but is not, for similar reasons, sufficient by itself.

There may often be a wide scope for variation of the organisation of an event. Different options may be available for timing, location, arena, program, accommodation and food, marketing, travel arrangements, etc. At different stages of the planning process it may therefore be necessary to specify choice alternatives at different levels of detail. In an initial phase, economic analysis will be needed for making strategic decisions, for instance on whether to organise an event or not, or choosing arena or season for the event, so the alternatives considered should reflect options at this level. At later phases, such strategic alternatives are no longer available, and a greater level of detail will be needed to reflect on the more fine-tuning aspects of the decision process.

The initial selection of alternatives is often of utmost importance to the final decision. Options that are discarded at this stage will seldom reappear in the analysis. On the other hand, the analysis may become very burdensome if many alternatives are left for subsequent evaluation. The selection of alternatives is therefore a delicate trade-off between the cost of the analytical effort and the cost of neglecting an important option.

The choice set as well as the effects of choices will be dependent on external conditions that are not known in advance. The initial planning needs therefore to delineate a limited number of scenarios. A scenario is a set of external conditions and their consequences that are mutually consistent. For instance, rainy weather may affect all outdoor activities in a similar way; the travel modal split chosen by the attendants has consequences both during arrival and departure; the distribution over various visitor categories, such as families, elderly, national groups, etc. will influence the size and characteristics of the demand for various activities, meals, lodging, and travel; etc.

The planning process may be such that some choices can be made contingent on what happens. For instance, pre-registration information may become available before the details of the program has to be decided upon. Other information will not be realised before its too late to adjust. The timing of vital information and of decisions that have *irreversible* economic consequences may be the single most important aspect of the planning of an event from the economic point of view. For instance, the difference between success and complete failure may be in the choice of the size of the arena. The economic risk of an event may therefore depend to a large extent on how long capacity decisions can be postponed and on how soon reliable information that indicates attendance numbers can be received. The reason for this is the *sunk* cost nature of many economic decisions. Costs that can easily be recaptured are not sunk, as for instance if the organisers have an excess supply of bottled beer that can be returned to the brewer. Goods that are idiosyncratic, e.g. T-shirts with prints specific to the event, or temporal, such as fresh food, often have only low or no reselling value, so the cost of such goods cannot be recaptured. Similarly, unused flight seats, hotel beds, arena space and such capacities are temporal services that have declining second-hand market values as the time for their use approaches, and have no value at all afterwards.

Thus, an economic decision that involves sunk costs may give rise to regret. The *expected regret cost* should therefore be considered. If it is possible to invest in an alternative that makes it possible to adapt to conditions that come up in a way that will reduce the expected regret cost, then this option has a value, *a real option value*, equal to the reduction of the expected regret cost.[1] Figure 7.1 illustrates this. Assume that an organiser can choose between two arenas for a summer music festival; Outdoor without a roof; *or* Indoor. Nature can then provide either Sun or Rain, with obvious ramifications for the entrance fee revenues, shown in the Figure. If the decision maker organising the event knows the coming weather, he would choose Outdoor in case of sun, and Indoor in case of rain. Further assume that there is an equal chance of these two states of nature. The Indoor arena is then the option that maximises the expected net revenues, as is shown in the Figure. A risk neutral or a risk averse organiser would therefore choose this arena (while a risk-loving organiser may possibly choose Outdoor, as this option is the one that brings the highest reward to a lucky decision).

In Figure 7.2, we now introduce a third alternative which is the Outdoor arena supplemented by a festival tent. In case of Sun, the existence of a tent will not attract additional visitors, so, because the tent is costly, Outdoor with tent provides a smaller net revenue than Outdoor

---

1) Dixit and Pindyck (1994) is an excellent textbook on real options.

Figure 7.1. Decision tree for a choice between two arenas (Outdoor and Indoor) when pay-offs (displayed in the diagram) are contingent on weather (Sun or Rain)

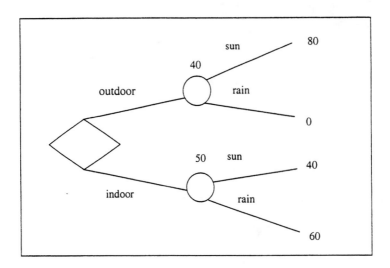

without tent. In case of Rain, Outdoor with tent attracts more visitors than Outdoor without tent, but less than Indoor. Therefore, this third alternative is inferior to both other alternatives if weather is known in advance. However, as depicted in the Figure, the third alternative provides larger expected net revenue than the alternatives and is thus the preferred option (except possibly to a risk lover). The tent reduces the regret cost of a unlucky decision (i.e., the choice of an outdoor arena when it turns out to be a rainy day or an indoor arena for a sunny day). This real option value exceeds the extra cost/revenue loss of this alternative.

Figure 7.2. Decision tree for a choice between three arena alternatives (Outdoor, Outdoor with tent, and Indoor) when pay-offs (displayed in the diagram) are contingent on weather (Sun or Rain)

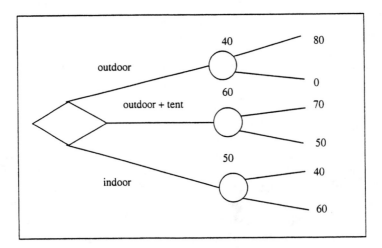

Another option of this type, elucidating the temporal sequencing of decisions and information is depicted in Figure 7.3. Here, it is assumed that the arena leasing contracts allows cancellation a short time in advance of the event. Hence, the organisers can make preliminary reservations to both arenas and then cancel one of them when a sufficiently reliable weather forecast is available. Of course this will probably be more expensive than if one arena is chosen from the beginning, but still this can be worthwhile given the real option value. Note that, decisions are not made just once but at several (here two) instances that differ with respect to the amount of information that is available. The decision maker thus has to evaluate not just a set of alternative arrangements (by comparison of their costs and benefits) but also the same arrangements that are chosen at different times.

Figure 7.3.   Decision tree for a choice between two arenas (Outdoor and Indoor) when pay-offs (displayed in the diagram) are contingent on weather (Sun or Rain) and arena reservation can be cancelled after the appearance of a reliable weather forecast

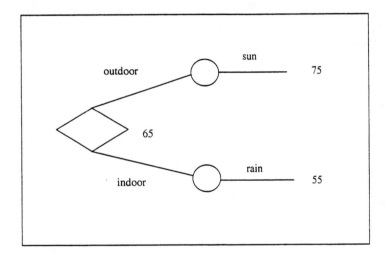

Decision trees, which in the examples shown here have very simplistic structures, can be used to summarise choice sets and scenarios. The complexity of the decision trees grows with; *i* the number of choices at each decision point; *ii* the number of scenarios (sets of external conditions); and *iii* the number of decision points. Whether complex or not, such a structuring of event planning is instrumental for several reasons:

1. Costs and benefits can be defined only in connection to the relevant decision alternatives. The fundamental cost concept for evaluation of a choice alternative is *opportunity cost,* i.e., the value of a resource in the best alternative use. For instance, the cost of an event arena is zero if it is already in place and would be empty during the time of the event; or equal to the net revenues that would be generated by another activity at the arena displaced by this event; or, finally, if not built, equal to the value of the resources needed to construct the arena.[2] Similarly, benefits of relevance for a choice decision are the additional benefits, compared to the best alternative option.

---

2) Of course, if it is not just a temporary arena used only during the event, revenues to the arena from subsequent use of the arena should be included.

2. The decision tree structure can be used as a basis for both sensitivity analysis (evaluation of alternatives under different scenarios) and for analysis of alternatives in terms of expected values (when different scenarios can be assigned objective or subjective probabilities).

By connecting decision points to a time scale, there is a basis for evaluation of the value of collecting information, the value of buying flexibility, and the value of postponing[3] decisions.

In this section, we have discussed the identification of the choice set, which is the first stage in economic assessment of an event. Before turning to the specific issues in intervention analysis, which is another stage of such assessment, we will briefly sketch the broader economic evaluation context in which these stages are a part.

Cost-benefit analysis

The general framework for making an economic assessment of a project such as an event is Cost-Benefit Analysis, CBA. CBA proceeds from identification of choice alternatives and scenarios; identification of consequences; quantitative, or qualitative, assessment of these consequences for different individuals or groups; economic valuation; calculation of comprehensive summary measures of the economic effects, such as net present value; to comparison and evaluation of these measures for different choice alternatives under different scenarios. If objective or subjective probabilities can be attributed to scenarios, then the final step analysis can be based on expected present value, otherwise uncertainty has to be handled by sensitivity analysis, which may or may not be part of the scenario construction.

Being a general framework, CBA encompasses a family of other economic assessment techniques as special cases:

- *All consequences can be valued. CBA values equal market prices.* CBA will use the same methods as the ones that are used in ordinary investment analysis made by business firms.

- *Resource sacrifice (i.e., cost of inputs) can be valued, outputs can not.* CBA for this case is called *Cost-Efficiency Analysis, CEA.* When there is one output only, CEA can be performed on unit cost measures. An example would be if a city considers several sites for a music festival that will be provided without entrance fees or other charges. In cases when there are multiple outputs, for instance if these different sites will allow various mixtures of local and non-local attendees, more complex CEA measures have to be used.[4]

- *The value of outputs can be assessed and CBA values equal market prices.* This is the scope of the so called economic impact analysis of tourism (see below). The emphasis here is on the various problems in estimating the sum of revenues that emerge from tourist expenditure on various items, for instance in connection with a visit to an event.

---

3) The mirror side (if the reference is a decision or action to be made in the future) is that advancing the decision/action can increase the value of later decisions. For instance an early announcement, preliminar registration, etc. may significantly reduce uncertainty when subsequent decisions are to be made.
4) Various programming techniques, such as Data Envelopment Analyzis, can be used in this context if there are sufficiently many choice alternatives (Charnes et al. 1994).

Of course, to be meaningful the results of the economic impact analysis have to be related to identified choice alternatives and their costs.

- *Some consequences can be quantified and valued, others not.* In point of fact, it is seldom the case that all consequences can be attributed an economic value. The CBA approach still requires that an attempt is made to identify and qualitatively assess all such consequences. Qualitative assessment can be in terms of the positivity/negativity of the effect (whether it is beneficial or detrimental to welfare), size (small, medium, large, etc.) or rank (better in alternative A than in alternative B, etc.). More advanced methods, so called multi-criteria analysis, proceed from such qualitative assessment to overall evaluation of the choice alternatives, for instance telling the decision-maker how much utility weight, in relative terms, she has to put on a specific attribute for it be decisive in selecting one alternative over another (Nijkamp and Voogd 1985). An outcome of the CBA process that does not present a one-dimensional bottomline to the decision maker by no means represents a failure. The role of the decision maker is to make the final trade-offs that normally remain. The task of the CBA is to reduce the number of dimensions for these trade-offs to a manageable number. The alternative is in reality often that the decision-maker makes her own simplifications by the use of heuristic decision rules, for instance lexicographic ordering discarding all aspects except a few.

Intervention analysis, which will be highlighted in the following, is needed in the CBA procedure for estimation of the impact of an event on volumes and values, i.e., visitor numbers or net revenues. However, it should be clear that these are just some aspects that are likely to emerge in economic assessment of events. In particular, the socio-economic net value of an event may not be identical to the net monetary revenues, because the social opportunity cost of resources may differ from market prices or because non-market valued resources, such as resources provided by the public sector, or environmental resources, are involved. This broader context will however not be considered in the following. The reader who wants a general introduction to the CBA approach is referred to textbooks such as Brent (1997).

Intervention analysis

As noted in the background, the analyst can choose between two basic approaches to the estimation of expenditure effects. *Constructive approaches,* discussed in the previous chapter, go bottom up and start by assessing the number of attendees, combining with estimates of duration of the stay, average expenditure per day etc. to finally construct a measure of expenditure, including direct, indirect, and induced effects. *Intervention analysis* goes the other way top down from aggregate data and tries to divide up the change that can be attributed to the event, i.e., the effect of the intervention.

A basic problem in assessing the effects of an event within a region or a nation during the period chosen for the analysis is the notorious lack of high quality data for such purposes. On the demand side, the prime variable that needs to be estimated is the net increase in cash flow expenditure generated by the event. This is a piece of cake to an experienced event organiser that sells a bundled full-service event package to the visitors, taking care of everything. However, typical event visitors make a large part of the bundling of the event composite good themselves; paying transport, meals, drinks, lodging, shopping, attractions, etc., to various enterprises at various places. Also, they are not buying these items at separated 'event markets' but from firms that simultaneously serve other customers; tourists as well as local residents.

So in many instances, total expenditure cannot be estimated from previous records in the accounts from a single firm or organization. When aggregate accounting data is available, the analyst still has the problem of determining what part of this is attributable to the event. That task is further complicated by the possibility that the total change in expenditure consists of both a direct effect caused by the event visitors' spending and an indirect effect of the event on other customers' spending. The indirect effect can be positive, for instance due to lower prices or greater supply diversity during the event; or negative, due to displacement, for instance because of increased congestion during the event that deters non-event tourists from the region.

The evaluation of an event must often be based on data sources that are not especially designed for this purpose. Often, several such sources can be found. Traffic flows are measured in various ways, e.g. as train, coach, ferry, and flight ticket sales, or as border crossings. Commercial guest-night numbers can be collected directly from individual hotels, camping sites, etc., or from regular statistical sources. Trips, guest-nights, and expenditure are sometimes recorded by regular tourist surveys to households. Tax authorities provide records of tax receipts. Household expenditure surveys and industry statistics are provided for the national accounting system. It may be possible to use business sales reports, firm accounts, etc. As such data is collected and reported on a regular basis, it will normally record the result of many activities, not just those that are related to an occasional event.

The event intervention is expected to affect such variables. The intervention analysis builds on either one or both of two features that are typical of special events we are considering in this book. First, the events, and the impacts of the events, are specific to a region or a specific site, i.e., there are other regions or sites that are not affected. Second, the event is occasional, which means that there is at least one complementary period before the event that is not affected by the event and, possibly, also another such period afterwards. Intervention analysis uses these features by computation of differences. In some cases these differences can be computed by subtraction alone. Such instances will be called *pure natural experiments*. In other cases the comparison is made with a counterfactual estimate constructed from an *econometric model* based on time-series and/or cross-sectional data.

The complexity required in the evaluation procedure is dependent on the multiplicity of the effects in time and space:

Some events are spread over a large geographical area, as for instance the World Soccer Games in Los Angeles 1994 that in fact took place all over the United States. An event arranged at a specific location may have impacts on many other locations. Travel to the event site may be a substitute for trips to other places, so that the number of visitors to these other places will be reduced because of the event, or complementary, i.e., included in round-trip travel generated by the event. Also, through the economic leakages discussed in the previous chapter, the economic impact of an event will propagate through the regional, national, and international economies, and therefore be spread in time and space.

Also the dynamic nature of the event impact can be different in kind. In many cases, one may anticipate that an occasional event has only an instant, transitory, effect. Such an effect is called a pulse. A polar case is a step, i.e., when the effect is permanent. In the former case, the dependent variable will not contain any memory of the intervention, in the latter case the memory will persist for ever. Using this taxonomy, it seems reasonable to expect to find cases when a memory remains for a while, but fades away as time passes. There are other possibilities as well. For instance, sometimes pre-event activities may give rise to some effects before the event. Figure 7.4a-c illustrates the three major cases and shows simple differential equations that can describe these dynamics. y_t denotes the dependent variable (e.g., the number of guest nights) while D is the instantaneous (in period s) pulse effect of the intervention, positive in period s and zero otherwise.

Figure 7.4. a-c Three different dynamic impact responses of an event on a dependent variable

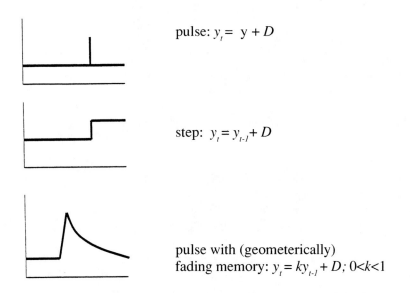

pulse: $y_t = y + D$

step: $y_t = y_{t-1} + D$

pulse with (geometerically)
fading memory: $y_t = ky_{t-1} + D; 0<k<1$

The ideal intervention analysis is based on data from a *randomised experiment*. Such analysis is often pursued in medical and psychological research, for instance in the evaluation of a new drug. The standard procedure splits a sample of patients randomly into two groups; the experiment group, that gets the real pill, and the control group that gets placebo. The target variables that the drug are supposed to affect, for instance blood pressure, are measured in both groups before, during, and after the treatment, as well as different individual background variables such as age, previous sickness history, etc. If the division in the two groups is truly randomised and the sample is large enough, then the impact of the drug (the intervention effect) can be derived as the difference of the target variables during the treatment, for a drug that has an instantaneous pulse effect only; or during and after the treatment for persistent effects. A check on this can be made by comparing the target variables before the intervention that then should be approximately equal. Likewise for the drug with only instantaneous effects, the target variables should converge afterwards.

Unfortunately, this scheme is seldom or perhaps never feasible for analysis of the impacts from an event intervention. However, enough control of other variables than the intervention variable may be provided for other reasons. When there is a transparent exogenous source of variation in explanatory variables there is a *quasi experiment* or *natural experiment* (in the psychological literature it is called correlational design, or static-group comparison), see Meyer (1995).

Since background variables are no longer controlled by randomisation, this has to be achieved in other ways. One possibility is to study *matching pairs* of two (or more) individuals that are similar with respect to background variables. In medicine, this is the reason for the huge interest in medical data for one-egg twins. If such comparison is not feasible at the individual level, still it may be possible to compare groups of individuals that are either homogenous with respect to some background variables, or are at least similar with respect to the distribution over background variables. Of course, this is the case that is most relevant to event analysis where the matching groups would normally consist of two (or more) cities or regions that are similar but only one being affected by the event. If the match is perfect, then the impact assessment could rely on a simple difference between the two groups. Normally, this is not the case but the conjecture can be maintained that changes over time will be similar (in absolute or relative terms). Thus the key figure is the *difference in differences,* i.e., the differences between the two groups with respect to change in the target variable between non- (pre- and/or post-) event period and the event period. Obviously such comparisons are pretty simple when the effect is of the pulse type, for which both the pre- and post-event periods can be used, or of the step type, while evaluation of more complex dynamic responses need qualified analysis of different subperiods before, during and after the event.

The difference in differences approach (or 'The before and after design with an untreated comparison group') can be extended in various ways, (see Meyer 1995). In particular, there may be major explanatory variables that can be identified and controlled by regression analysis, if the data includes multiple periods and/or multiple sites or individuals to provide enough time-series or cross-sectional variation. In developing such extensions, the preferred procedure is often to directly include the intervention by a dummy variable (or several, for instance if both effects on intercept and slopes in the regression equation is to be evaluated). The regression coefficient of the intervention variable then can be interpreted as the effect of the intervention. As in the case of matching pairs, the preferred data source is micro data for each individual, but in the absence of that, variables that describe mean and, perhaps, distribution of background variables in the experiment and control groups can be used. When there is both cross-sectional and time-series data, for instance if there is time-series data for several regions, the panel data models can be used. Such models often include a deterministic (fixed effect) or stochastic (random effect) intercept dummy variable to account for unexplained differences between individual sites.

If there is no unaffected control group (region) then the remaining possibility is to compare the experiment group (region) with itself, i.e., by using the occasional nature of the event intervention. The most simple case which still allows a pure natural experiment design is when the target variable can be expected to be constant in the absence of an event. Such cases are, however, rare. Instead, some form of statistical time-series analysis has to be used to make a prediction of the counterfactual development of the target variable. By using historical data, for the event region and/or other event regions, a prediction is made of the development of the target variables' absent intervention. This is then compared to the actual outcome.

Econometric studies of tourism demand[5] are often conceptually separated into two categories: economic models and forecasting models. Economic models, or structural equation models, focus on the relation between demand for tourism, measured for instance by expenditure, guest nights, arrivals, etc, and explanatory variables such as own price (destination price level travel cost from origin to destination), price of substitutes, disposable

---

5) An introduction to such models is provided by Sinclair and Stabler (1997), Ch. 3 (pp. 35-57).

income, etc. Some of these models are one-equation models, estimating the demand curve, and its shift variable relations, while others are multiple-equation models, describing allocation of for instance a travel budget for trips to various destinations. Economic models draws on micro economic theory and emphasize analytical insight. Forecasting models, in contrast, can be a-theoretical, i.e., be based on statistical relationships without any underpinning from economic theory. These models range from so called naive techniques, of which the before-mentioned assumption of forecasting no change[6] is one, various extra-polation methods, such as linear smoothing (Holt 1957), Box-Jenkins (ARIMA) models (Box et al. 1994), and structural time-series models (Harvey 1989). There are also multivariate techniques, such as vector autoregression (VAR), (Sims 1980).

The economic model – forecasting model dichotomy is, however, misleading, as it suggests that the two purposes, analytical insight and prediction, could not be, or should not be, unified. This is false for two reasons. First, to express a truism, only the predictable can be predicted. Every forecasting model is vulnerable to structural breaks, when some exogenously determined shift occurs that is not captured by variables in the model. A forecasting model that does not include the major strategic exogenous variables and their structural relation to the variable to be predicted is likely to be more exposed to structural breaks. Second, the validity of the analytical insight suggested by an economic model has to be tested. An essential validity test is the (out-of-sample) forecasting ability of the model.

Bearing on the latter argument, Witt and Martin (1987) and Witt and Witt (1995) made the important, and seemingly devastating, observation that the economic models of that time for explaining international tourism travel demand failed in forecasting performance, when compared with naive forecasting techniques. However, the models evaluated by them lack dynamic components. Economic theory provides guidance as to which explanatory variables to include in demand models, but has little to say about the dynamic processes in and between these variables. The analyst, therefore, has to go beyond the static economic model and statistically estimate a dynamic relationship as well. Several techniques are available for that purpose. One extends the static one-equation demand model by inclusion of lagged endogenous and explanatory variables. This method is called the autoregression distributed lags (ARDL) approach and is the one-equation correspondence to VAR. An example of an application to event evaluation based on this is Hultkrantz (1998) which will be presented below. Other possibilities are the previously mentioned transfer-function techniques. Holmes and Shamsuddin (1997) followed this road, using an ARIMA representation of the stochastic model component in evaluating the impact of the World Exposition 1986. A third possibility, which is the most elegant, and perhaps the most promising in terms of forecasting ability, see Kulendran and King (1997) is the Error Correction Model (ECM). ECM distinguishes between the long-term, equilibrium-oriented, relation between the economic variables, and the short-term out-of equilibrium adjustment.

Evidently, intervention analysis can be performed in several ways, depending on purpose, available data, time and resource constraints. We will present two examples using the case of the World Championship in Athletics in Göteborg 1995 (WCA95) to demonstrate that important insights on the impact of an event can be extracted in a fairly simple manner,

---

6) In fact, some economic series are so called Martingales, or more specifically follow a random walk (or Brownian motion), which implies that the best forecast that can be made one period ahead is the present value. Prices on informationally efficient markets (at least in an exchange economy with no production) have this property, so in the case of for instance a stock market price, the naive forecasting model really has a theoretical foundation.

especially so when the experiment group control group design is provided by the natural features of an event.

7.3 Empirical Study

A natural experiment (treated and untreated group design) example

WCA95 was held in Göteborg at the beginning of August, which is a peak time for touristic visits to this town by both foreigners and domestic residents. A mega-event such as this could therefore be expected to act both as attractor and as repellent on tourists. 'Regular' tourists can be deterred for several reasons; because of capacity limitations giving higher prices for travel, accommodation, and meals and/or shortage of available rooms and seats, increased traffic congestion, deterrence of tourists looking for peace and quiet, etc. It is therefore very difficult to come at net effects on tourist flows from this event with a constructive analysis. In our two examples, we will therefore use intervention analysis for this purpose. In both examples we will use the official Swedish statistics for the number of guest nights by residents from various countries in different regions in Sweden. In the first example here we will employ the two group natural experiment designs to study the impact on the total number of commercial guest nights. In the next section we will provide another example in which a forecasting model is estimated to evaluate the impact of visitors from abroad to Göteborg.

In this example, we use the county of Stockholm as the match to Göteborg. As Göteborg is the second largest city in Sweden, being both much smaller than the capital city and larger than the third largest city, another possibility would be to compare Göteborg to a group of smaller cities. Stockholm resembles Göteborg in several ways, being another metropolitan tourist destination in the same country, but there are of course many differences. For instance, Göteborg is closer to Denmark, Norway and the Continent, while Stockholm is closer to Finland and, being the capital city, is considerably more 'metropolitan' than Göteborg. Whilst Göteborg is not far behind Stockholm as a domestic tourist destination, Stockholm attracts far more visitors from abroad.

As discussed previously, a general problem in choosing a matching region is to find another region that is not likely to be affected by the event. In general, such dependency can be expected to be larger the bigger the event and the closer the pairs are in distance. WCA95 clearly was a mega-event so some repercussion on visits to Stockholm is to be expected. The cities are situated some 400 kilometres apart, so at least it is not self evident that most visitors to the event in Göteborg would have included a stay in Stockholm in the same trip. However, while complimentary trips may be a small problem, a worse difficulty may be substitution of trips between these two destinations. We will return to this problem later.

Figures 7.5a-b show results from application of the matching pairs approach on the number of commercial guest-nights, which is an obvious input to the computation of the increase of tourist expenditure brought about by the event. As it contains guest-nights by all visitors, not just visitors to the event, it captures both direct and indirect effects, as defined above. The quasi-experimental comparison is based on the maintained assumption that the relative change in tourist numbers would be similar in both cities, except for the effects of the WCA95 event. A validity test of this assumption is made in Figure 7.5a, in which the pairwise comparison is made for a non-intervention month, viz., July. As can be seen, this turns out in a favourable way; i.e., the change in number of guest-nights is the same. With some confidence

Figure 7.5 a. Guest-nights in July (1994 = 100)

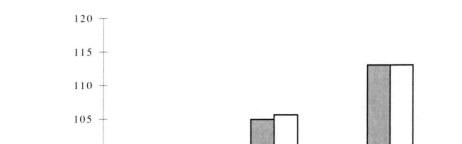

in the method, we can analyse the numbers during the intervention month, shown in Figure 7.5b.

From this, we see that guest-nights numbers increased by 13.7 percent in the Göteborg region compared to the same month previous year, while the increase in Stockholm was just 1.5 percent. Hence, this indicates that the effect of the event was a 12 percent increase in this variable. However, as often in non-randomised experiments, we can find ambiguity:

- Göteborg stays on a higher level than Stockholm in 1996, as well. This may indicate that either something else has enduringly raised Göteborg's attraction power in August or that the WCA95 had an enduring positive effect. A more detailed examination of the guest-night numbers shows that the number of foreign visitors to Göteborg in 1996

Figure 7.5 b. Guest-nights in August (1994 = 100)

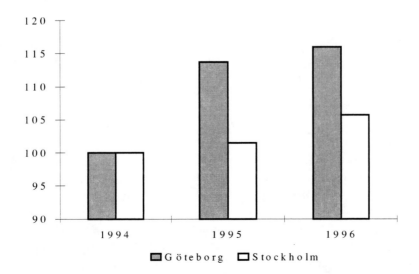

actually fell below the level implied by the development in Stockholm. Instead there was a sharp increase in domestic residents' guest-nights. This suggests that the 1995 numbers were the direct cause of the event, while the 1996 numbers were the result of an indirect effect, due to temporal displacement of visits to Göteborg by domestic tourists.

- The Stockholm increase in August is 1.5 percent (Figure 5b), which is less than the July increase at 5.6 percent (Figure 5a). This indicates that the commercial lodging in Stockholm was negatively affected by the WCA95 event in Göteborg; i.e., by substitution of trip destinations. Hence, the comparison made above is likely to exaggerate the net effect of the impact of the event in Göteborg. A conservative, and probably better, estimate of this effect can therefore be made on basis of the July figures; i.e., around 8 percent (13.7 - 5.6).

- A more profound problem is that these simple comparisons do not allow estimation of confidence intervals. We therefore have no basis for making statistical inference; i.e., to determine whether a noticed difference is likely to be the result of stochastic factors or of the event. To make that, it is necessary to analyse longer data series, as made in next example.

In conclusion, this example suggest that the natural experiment feature of events may allow an easy-to-use way for evaluation of the net impact of an event by the difference in differences method. However, as also has been illustrated the method has some limitations, and careful analysis is needed in the selection of the unaffected control region(s). Some of the short comings can be overcome by econometric methods, which is what we turn to in next example.

An example of the use of an econometric model based on time-series data for evaluation of net impact from an event

The illustration of an econometric approach is borrowed from Hultkrantz (1998) study of the effect of WCA95 on the number of foreign visitors' guest nights in the Göteborg region. The focus of this study is on short-term ramifications, or more exactly effects from July 1995 to January 1996. The data used is the monthly number of guest nights by visitors, from the USA, Germany, Norway, Denmark, Finland, respectively, and all other countries in total, spent in hotels, motels, resort hotels, and youth hostels in the county of Göteborg and Bohuslän.

The actual development is, in this study, compared to a short-term forecast. This is derived with an autoregressive distributed lags (ARDL) single-equation model. The endogenous variable to be explained is the logarithm of guest-night numbers while the explanatory variables are the logarithm of a destination price variable and three pulse dummy variables, one for the WCA95 event and the two others for two shocks that affected international tourist travel to Sweden in the years before this event, viz, the Chernobyl accident in 1986 and the Gulf War 1991.

Since the emphasis is on short-term development, it is not necessary to include long-term relationships, i.e., from explanatory variables that affect long-term equilibrium but are less important to short-term adjustment, such as national income levels, development of accommodation, tourist attractions and activities, images, etc. of Göteborg and/or Sweden. Any monthly measures of these variables would anyway be very crude, for instance, national disposable income is provided in quarterly frequencies only. Since such variables are omitted, one cannot expect to find a relationship between the variables that are included that is consistent in the long term (a so called co-integrated relation). Instead of estimating a model at the variable level, one has to confine the study to relations between differences. Formally, the analysis is made with variables that are stationary, so variables are differenced until they are stationary. The tests for stationarity are called unit-root tests and are easy to perform (Said and Dickey 1984). A typical result is that a monthly or quarterly tourist travel demand variable needs to be differenced first one period and then possibly also by the annual (4 or 12) difference, while price and income variables need to be differenced one period only. The practice of differencing demand variable twice, even if supported by the unit-root test, has sometimes been critized as over-differencing.

The ARDL modelling framework is described in most econometric textbooks, (e.g., Greene 1993, p. 538). It is convenient for the not so advanced econometric analyst as it can be done with the ordinary least-squares (OLS) method. To replicate the study of this example, therefore, only knowledge corresponding to an introductury textbook in econometrics (such as Carter Hill et al. 1997) is needed. However, an important problem is that the dynamic representation with a multitude of lagged endogenous and explanatory variables provide a rich variety of possible models. To restrict data-mining abuse of this potential it is essential to use a somewhat rigorous model in selecting the final model by successive testing of the estimated models. Such a procedure is the general-to-specific procedure (Hendry and Doornik 1996), which has been used here.

Hence, the estimation procedure started by testing for unit roots in the logarithms of the guest-nights and price variables, using the Augmented Dickey-Fuller and/or Dickey-Fuller unit-root tests. It was found that all guest-nights variables had to be differenced first by the year and then by the month to obtain a stationary serial, while the price variables were stationary in the one-month differences.

Then we estimated a general dynamic model including numerous lags of the endogenous and explanatory variables. The last 12 months were saved to check the out-of-sample structural stability of the final model. After initial estimation with the full lag structure, insignificant variables were omitted one by one, after successive re-estimations, until no variable having a t-value lower than 1.65 was left. The reduced model was submitted to a diagnostic checking procedure, including testing of out-of-sample predictions. Finally, we made a so called Lagrange Multiplier (F) test for complete omission of the WCA95 variable in the models where that result is obtained. The final result is illustrated by one example, the estimated equation for visitors from Norway. This is shown in Table 7.1. The B:s denote the so called back shift operator, i.e., the number of months for the lagged variables (eg., B12 in the first row denotes the value of guest-nights variable one year before). The estimated equation shows that the short-term dynamic change in the number of guest nights depends (significantly) on the change in destination price, the WCA95 event, and the two negative shocks. The dynamic adjustment is complex involving a large number of lagged variables. In fact, the decaying coefficient structure of the lags of the endogenous variables suggests that a considerably more parsimonious model would have been possible with a Box-Jenkins ARIMA framework, but that is not so important in the present context. Table 7.1 also shows a list of diagnostic tests that were used in the general-to-specific selection process. The values that are reported, except for R^2 in the table are the p-values, i.e., the probabilities that can be assigned to the null conjecture that the residuals of the estimated equations are 'well behaved' with respect to absence of serial correlation, normality (Jarque and Bera), absence of heteroscedasticity, and, finally, out-of-sample forecasting performance (Chow test).

Table 7.1.   Estimated ARDL-equation for the number of guest nights by visitors from Norway in the Göte-borg region. The guest-night variable is differenced twice (one month and one year), and the price variable is differenced once (one month), t-values in parentheses

$$(1 + 0.54B1 + 0.43B2 + 0.24B3 + 0.29B4 + 0.11B5 + 0.14B8 + 0.13B10 + 0.29B12)$$
$$(8.05)\quad(5.3)\quad(3.10)\quad(3.90)\quad(1.73)\quad(2.60)\quad(2.25)\quad(4.93)$$

$$(1-B12)(1-B1)GUEST\ NIGHTS$$

$$= -0.002 - (1.47 + 0.87B2)PRICE - (032.B1 - 0.26B5 - 0.33B6)WCA95$$
$$(-0.16)\ (-2.90)(-1.67)\qquad(-2.20)\quad(1.75)\quad(2.19)$$

$$+ (0.28B2 + 0.32B4)GULF\ WAR - 0.36CHERNOBYL$$
$$(1.98)\qquad(2.28)\qquad\qquad(-2.57)$$

R^2 relative to difference and seasonals:	0.83
LM F-test for serial correlation from lags 1-7, p-value:	0.31
Jarque and Bera normality test c^2:	0.70
Test of heteroscedastic errors using squares. p-value:	0.69
Chow, p-value:	0.69

The coefficient that is of main interest is the one for the first lag (B1) of the WCA95 event. The dummy pulse variable was defined to occur in July, to account for any possible effects in the month before the event. The regression of the first lag of this variable therefore shows the immediate impact during the month of the event. As can be seen, this coefficient is negative, indicating that the net effect on visitors from Norway was a negative one. A similar negative effect was also found for visitors from Germany (not shown here, see Hultkrantz 1998). The Norwegian visitor numbers seem to have recovered during the subsequent winter (the B5 and B6 lag of the WCA95 variable in Table 7.1 represent November and December), while the reduction in German visitor numbers was reinforced in September. The Norwegian and German visitor categories represented 43% of the number of guest nights in August 1996 so these negative effects during August 1995 were important. It can therefore be concluded that the positive net impact found in the previous example can be attributed to an increase in the number of domestic visitors.

This example of econometric analysis suggests that this methodology becomes more complicated than the quasi-experimental approach. This is probably inevitable in most cases. However, modern software is now available for forecasting purposes[7] that do not require many econometric skills of the user, so these techniques are now becoming accessible for a much broader category of users than previously.

7.4 Conclusion

From one point of view, economic evaluation of the economic impact of events is a very complex issue. Events are specific and occasional, so economic accounting and other information gathering systems will be specific and temporary too, and not much can be learnt

7) E.g., Forecast Pro and Autobox.

from past records. However, these features of events also have a bright side for evaluation purposes as an event can often be seen as part of a natural experiment. While there may still be need for technically demanding statistical and economic modelling analysis this also means that fruitful analysis can be made with very simple means. Instead of paying attention only to specific data that can be gathered during the event, anyone planning an evaluation of an event should also look into the possibilities of using existing data sources. All aggregate time-series data representing variables that are likely to be affected by an event can be used to track the impacts of an event, if only they can be broken down in adequate regional categories.

References

Box, G.E.P., Jenkins, G.M. & Reinsel, G.C. (1994). *Time Series Analysis: Forecasting and Control* (3rd ed.). New Jersey: Prentice-Hall.

Brent, R.J. (1997). *Applied Cost-Benefit Analysis*. Cheltenham: Edward Elgar.

Carter Hill, R., Griffiths, W.E. & Judge, G.G. (1997). *Undergraduate Econometrics*. New York: Wiley.

Charnes, A., Cooper, W. & Rhodes, E. (1994). *Data Envelopment Analysis: Theory, Methodlogy, and Applications*. Boston: Kluwer Academic Publishers.

Dixit, A. K. & Pindyck, R.S. (1994). *Investment under Uncertainty.* Princeton, New Jersey: Princeton University Press.

Hansen, C. & Jensen, S. (1996). The Impact of Tourism on Employment in Denmark: Different Definitions, Different Results. *Tourism Economics, 2*(4), 283-302.

Harvey, A. C. (1989). *Forecasting, Structural Time Series Models and the Kalman Filter,* Cambridge University Press.

Holmes, R. A. & Shamsuddin, A.F.M. (1997). Short- and Long-Term Effects of World Exposition 1986 on the US Demand for British Columbia Tourism. *Tourism Economics, 3*(2), 137-160.

Holt, C. C. (1957). *Forecasting Seasonal and Trends by Exponentially Weighted Moving Average.* Office of Naval Research Memorandum.

Hultkrantz, L. (1998). Mega-Event Displacement. The World Championship in Athletics, Göteborg 1995. *Festival Management & Event Tourism, 5*(1/2), 1-8.

Kulendran, N. & King, M.L. (1997). Forecasting International Tourist Flows Using Error-Correction and Time-Series Models. *International Journal of Forecasting, 13,* 319-327.

Meyer, B. D. (1995). Natural and Quasi-Experiments in Economics. *Journal of Business and Economic Statistics, 13*(2), 151-161.

Nijkamp, P. & van Voogd, H. (1985). An Informal Introduction to Multicriteria Evaluation, In G. Fandel & J. Spronk (Eds.), *Multiple Criteria Decision Methods and Applications*. New York: Springer-Verlag.

Nordström, J. (1996). Tourism Satellite Account for Sweden, 1992-93. *Tourism Economics, 2*(1), 13-42.

Sims, C. (1980). Macroeconomics and Reality. *Econometrica, 48,* 1-48.

Sinclair, M. T. & Stabler, M. (1997). *The Economics of Tourism,* (London and New York): Routledge.

Smith, S.S. & Wilton, D. (1997). TSAs and the WTTC/WEFA Methodlogy: Different Satellites or Different Planets. Also, see Rejoinder (1), from the World Travel and Tourism Council, same issue pp. 281-288; and Rejoinder (2). *Tourism Economics, 4*(1), 71-78.

Witt, S. F. & Martin, C.A. (1987). Econometric Models of Forecasting International Tourism Demand. *Journal of Travel Research, 3,* 23-30.

Witt, S.F. & Witt, C.A. (1995). Forecasting Tourism Demand: A Review of Empirical Research. *International Journal of Forecasting, 11,* 447-475.

Chapter 8

Beyond Intermezzo? On the Long-Term Industrial Impacts of Mega-Events – The Case of Lillehammer 1994

Olav R. Spilling

Norwegian School of Management BI, Norway

8.1 Background

The purpose of this chapter is to analyze the long-term economic impact of mega-events.[1] The chapter is based on the case of the Winter Olympics organized in Lillehammer, Norway, in 1994, and the intention is to contribute to the understanding of what may be the importance of mega-events to local development in the host region. The background for this interest is that when the city of Lillehammer started its campaign for hosting the Olympic Winter Games, it was based on the assumption that the Games would be very important to the economic development in the region and that it would contribute significantly to industrial growth. Similar attitudes seem to be prevalent among other actors aiming at hosting mega-events. Therefore, it should be of great importance to develop adequate knowledge of the economic and industrial impacts of mega-events, and of the short- and long-term impacts compared to the huge costs of hosting such events.

Although there may be other arguments for hosting mega-events than the economic interests, like for instance political prestige or the mobilisation effects that mega-events may have, the economic and industrial aspect of hosting an event, will still be important.

In previous articles by the author on the impacts of the Lillehammer Olympics, attention has been paid to how the Games stimulated entrepreneurial behavior and (for some time) triggered the development of a more entrepreneurial climate (Spilling 1996a), and a broader overview with main focus on the short-term impacts (Spilling 1996b). In this chapter, focus is on the long-term impacts. The objective is to identify and discuss processes that was stimulated by the Olympics and that have lasted for some years, and to put these impacts into a wider perspective.

---

1) This chapter is based on previous research carried out at Eastern Norway Research Institute, Lillehammer, during 1990-95, and a smaller follow-up study during the spring term 1997. The article has previously been published, in an almost identical form, in Festival Management & Event Tourism, Vol. 5, No. 3 (1998).

8.2 Theoretical Framework

Impacts of mega-events

As have been outlined in chapter 1, there seems to be a general agreement on the definitions of hallmark events and mega-events, and the current analysis will take as its point of departure the definition provided by Getz (1997:6):

> "Mega-events, by way of their size or significance, are those that yield extraordinarily high levels of tourism, media coverage, prestige, or economic impact for the host community or destination."

When analyzing impacts of mega-events, many aspects of how the host community or region is affected, may be considered. In their conceptualizing paper, Ritchie and Yangzhou have developed a framework for analysing mega-events. Their approach suggested to distinguish between the following types of impacts: economic, tourism/commercial, physical, socio-cultural, psychological and political (1988:24-26), and a rather sophisticated framework for analyzing mega-events is suggested. In their discussion of strategies for 'longer term benefits', which is less developed than their general framework, they included the following aspects as the most important (1988:48-49):

- enhanced international awareness and knowledge of the region
- increased economic activity
- enhanced physical facilities and infrastructure
- increased social and cultural opportunities.

Getz has also discussed the economic impacts of events. He has distinguished between five different economic roles: place marketing, tourist attractions, events as animators, events as image-makers and events as catalysts (1997:51-61). Like most other analyzes of mega-events, an important perspective underlying Getz' analysis is the perspective of tourism. Events are analyzed in terms of how they can contribute to develop the actual place or community as a tourist resort with improved infrastructure and facilities, and how the event may contribute to market the destination, create a positive image and attract tourists and increase visitor spending. Another and supplementing perspective is how events affect the host community as a residential area, and how it through various mechanisms can improve the quality of life and attract residents and investors, and more generally serve as a catalyst for stimulating business and trade.

In this chapter the main emphasis is on the long-term *industrial* impacts, i.e. on what kind of contribution a mega-event provides to the long-term industrial development of the host region as a whole. The present analysis is open to examining all kinds of impacts that have contributed to the long-term industrial development. On the one hand, this includes impacts working directly with various, but specific industrial sectors among which tourism is important. On the other hand, it also includes other and in some cases more subtle impacts working indirectly with the long-term industrial impacts, like affecting the attractiveness of the region as a residential area, which may affect population growth, and through this indirectly create growing markets and stimulated growth in local service industries. However, to what extent this ambition may be fulfilled is constrained by certain methodological as well as practical aspects relevant to this study. This will be commented on later in the chapter.

While conceptual frameworks for analyzing mega-events are rather comprehensive, the current knowledge on actual long-term impacts are rather poor. Although there is a considerable number of studies analyzing various aspects of events and their impacts on the host regions (cf. for instance Brunet 1994), there is little substantial knowledge on the economic and industrial impacts of events (Travis and Croizé 1987; Spilling 1996). This is partly because many reports are pre-event analyzes that have estimated rather than evaluated the economic impacts of the events. These include many consultancy reports that for various reasons have not had a sufficiently serious approach to the issues.

Second, there seems to be a fundamental lack of continuity in the studies of mega-events, at least as far as Olympic Games are concerned. Many research groups have for some time been involved in analyzing mega-events. This interest often has been triggered by local issues, like plans for bidding for an event and the need for assessing potential impacts. However, no research group so far has pursued their interest for mega-event research for a sufficiently long time to generate a deeper understanding of the post-event long-term impacts. Typically, research related to the Calgary Olympic Winter Games in 1988 terminated shortly after the event, and analyses of the economic impacts of the Barcelona Summer Games in 1992 are updated to 1992 only (Brunet 1995).

Some studies have focused on the impacts of mega-events on tourism. A study of Innsbruck, Austria, where the Winter Olympics were hosted in 1964 and 1976, show that these particular games caused no long-term effect in the tourism traffic (Kirchner 1980 and Schulmeister 1976, referred to in Spilling 1996b). In both cases, the short-term impact was negative for the region of Innsbruck, only in the city itself was the impact positive. The negative impact was explained by loss of German tourists, who stayed away because of the Olympics. On the other hand, the year after the Olympics, there was an increase in tourism. The authors thus concluded, "taking the short- and long-term effect together, they cancelled each other so that the games had no net effect" (Socher and Tschurschenthaler 1987:112). These findings are also supported by an analysis of the impacts of bigger winter sports events (Brönnimann 1982).

Other studies support findings that hosting an Olympic event may lead to a displacement effect during the event, i.e. that 'normal' tourism is affected negatively, and that there is a tendency to overestimate the number of visitors that will be attracted by an event (Burns and Mules 1986). Pyo et al. (1988) reported that in the case of the Tokyo Olympic Summer Games in 1964, Japan experienced an overall decrease in the number of tourists compared to the previous year. In Los Angeles 1984, the number of visitors were significantly below what was expected, many hotel rooms remained unoccupied during the Games, and in the restaurant sector business was below average for that time of the year.

For the three Winter Games organized during the period 1988-1994, i.e. Calgary 1988, Albertville 1992 and Lillehammer 1994, Teigland (1996) has compared the impacts on tourism. His conclusion regarding Calgary and Albertville is that in both cases tourism grew to a new plateau after the games. In the case of Calgary this is explained as most probably an effect of the general economic development, and four years after the event tourism were back to the pre-game level (Teigland 1996:37). In the case of Albertville, tourism was up 10-15 percent two seasons following the event compared to the pre-event level. This may be explained by economic cycles and snow conditions, but also by improved competitiveness in the region, as the region of Savoie (Albertville) developed much better than competing areas in the Austrian and Italian Alps. However, Teigland asked if this might be related to other factors than impacts of the Olympics (p.43).

Regarding the development in Lillehammer, Teigland concluded that the host community might have stabilized on 25-30 percent above national level, but with very significant differences between the various destinations involved. His conclusion may also be regarded as very temporary, as his data covers only one year after the event (1995). This development will be discussed in more detail later in this chapter.

Long-term impacts

When analyzing the long-term impacts, the focus is on various kinds of economic activities that have been stimulated or affected by the Olympics that were organized in Lillehammer in 1994. However, when analyzing impacts of mega-events, a fundamental question may be asked if it makes sense at all to talk about long-term impacts related to an event. The very nature of events is that of temporariness, particularly so for Olympic events which are one-time events that cannot be expected to come back to the host region within any reasonable time horizon. The role of a mega-event is that of creating activity for some time and temporarily attract people and create awareness, before the whole thing closes down and economic activity and awareness can be directed towards the next event which is to be hosted somewhere else.

This situation has in a previous article been discussed as an *intermezzo* (Spilling 1996b); i.e. all activities related to the event take place over a relatively short period of time. The intensity when it is going on is very high, but when it is over, it's over. Travis and Croizé (1987) has characterized many of the actors playing a role in organizing a mega-event as 'nomads'; media people, sportsmen, professional organizers, interpreters, hosts and hostesses, spend little time on-site, they arrive a short time before the event and leave shortly after. And it can be added to this list that many of the core staff of the organizing committee follow the same pattern, and the same applies to many companies involved in the preparation and organization for the event. For instance, construction companies will move to a new construction site when they have completed their work. Or, as was the case in Lillehammer, consultancy firms and sponsors may temporarily set up an office to serve the event on-site, but will close down and move away when it is over.

The critical issue, then, is to what extent a mega-event creates or stimulates economic activity with a time horizon beyond that of the event. Based on previous research related to the Lillehammer Olympics (Spilling 1994), and to some extent in accordance with impacts suggested by other authors (Ritchie 1984; Ritchie and Yangzhou 1987; Getz 1997), the following mechanisms may be suggested: A mega-event may serve as a catalyst for:

- improving material infrastructures like roads, railways and telecommunications; this may give a competitive advantage for local industries after the event, at least for some time,
- providing significant sports and cultural facilities which will create opportunities for organizing new events after the game, i.e. provide the material basis for developing the 'event industry',
- developing a 'soft infrastructure' for hosting events, i.e. all kind of competencies for marketing and organizing events, this infrastructure may partly materialize in new service firms (see below),
- creating awareness of the region as an attractive host of sports and cultural events and related tourism activities,

- creating a more entrepreneurial climate and through this stimulating the development of existing firms and the starting up of new firms (Spilling 1996a), and
- creating awareness of the region as a dynamic area and attract people and companies to settle in the area.

In total, these factors open for a dynamic long-term development as a *potential* or *hypothetical* impact of a mega-event, but to what extent such factors actually work, need to be examined.

In an analysis of hallmark events, Sparrow (1989) has suggested two different scenarios for the impact and outcome of events related to the development in the tourism industry. His first scenario implies that the event only has temporary effects, and that development after some time returns back to a normal growth pattern, i.e. there are no long-term impacts. This type of impact is parallel to what presently is called *intermezzo*. The second alternative provided by Sparrow is that the event affects the long-term tourism development – the event "has created a new plateau for tourism growth and a higher level of growth as a result of hosting the event" (1989:257).

The two different models may serve as illustrators of two different *typologies* for impacts induced by a mega-event. To complete the picture, a third and supplementary model is suggested here. This model focuses on the possibility that a mega-event triggers a new and more dynamic development and stimulates a change in the long-term growth pattern of an industry.

Thus we have three different models for interpreting the industrial impacts of a mega-event. These models (Figure 8.1) will be applied in the following analysis:

1. Intermezzo: impacts are temporary and related to a) the planning and preparation for the event, b) the organisation of the event, and c) post event activities for bringing the area back to its normal situation.
2. New level of activity: the level of industrial activity is moved up to a new plateau significantly above that of the pre-event situation.
3. Permanent change of long-term growth rate.

The type 1 model – the intermezzo - will always occur when a region hosts a mega-event and will per see be of little interest when analyzing the long-term impacts. Here, the focus will be more beyond the intermezzo to see to what extent impacts of type 2 and type 3 may be identified.

The type 2 model – expansion to a new level of activity – is the type of impact one can expect when firms develop and expand their activities related to the event, and after the event can take advantage of being in a stronger market position than before the event. The typical example for this is the tourism industry where new facilities, like theme parks, museums and accommodation facilities, have been developed as a part of a strategy for serving a short-term demand during the event. After the event, the businesses may be able to maintain a long-term market due to a stronger position of the destination in the tourism market. This type of effect may also occur in other industries, like for instance manufacturing or consultancy services, which may have expanded their activities or developed new products or services due to the event, and then have been able to find new markets after the event.

In the case of Lillehammer an example of this is a regionally based company producing laminated tree constructions for large buildings. As a result of demand for new sports facilities, the company developed a much bigger construction than had so far been made in tree, and successfully delivered the new construction for two of the skating halls which were set up

Figure 8.1. Stylized models for regional impacts of mega-events

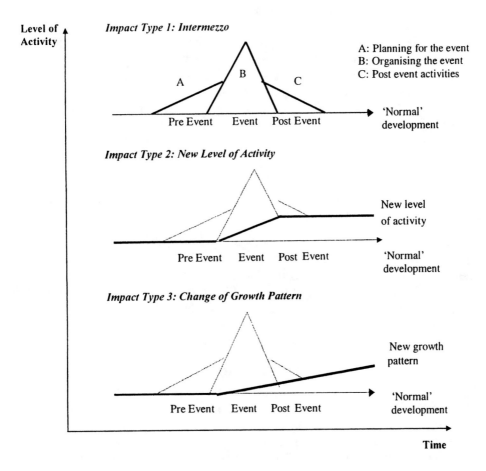

for the Olympics. This was the start for developing a new market, and after the Games similar constructions have been delivered for other large buildings.

Another example is a new consultancy firm started up after the event by two people working in the marketing division of the Olympic organising committee. The core business of the company is to provide counseling services specifically related to marketing strategies for future organizers of mega-events. The company has also specialized in counseling services related to acquiring sponsor services.

The type 3 model – change of growth pattern – is focusing on a potential effect that new dynamism is created in some industries in the region hosting a mega-event. The idea of the model is based on the observation that a mega-event may contribute to the development of a more entrepreneurial climate of the region. It may stimulate an economic and socio-cultural environment that is more conducive for starting up new businesses, as well as foster a learning process (Spilling 1996a). Partly this may be stimulated by improved infrastructures, partly by developing a more dynamic industrial structure, partly by becoming more attractive to outside people or businessmen to start their business in the area. For instance, this may be possible in the tourism sector. When the mega-event triggers the expansion of the industry to a new level of activity after the event, this may in turn trigger more development as new companies see more opportunities and develop new or additional markets adding to those already developed as a direct result of the mega-event.

Other sectors may also, hypothetically, be relevant, as for instance IT-related businesses as this sector is of great importance for organizing a mega-event. In the case of Lillehammer it has been claimed by local people that the upgraded IT-infrastructure developed for the Olympics together with the expansion of some local firms have stimulated the starting up of new firms after the event, and a long-term growth impact of the event is suggested. (This effect will be discussed later in the chapter.)

8.3 Empirical Study

Method

The results presented in this chapter are based on a follow-up study based on a previous research project reported in articles (Spilling 1996a; 1996b). In the original project, the development related to the planning and organizing of the Winter Olympics in Lillehammer was followed up for some years, but the project had to be finalized by the end of 1994, shortly after the event. Since then, and for the purpose of the analyses presented here, some supplementary data have been collected for the post-event development.

When analyzing the long-term industrial impacts of a mega-event, operationalisations are critical. In this case, a point of departure for operationalisations has been the examination of the long-term goals that were formulated by regional actors themselves. The main reason for hosting the Winter Olympics in Lillehammer in 1994 was expectations regarding the impacts the event would have on the regional economy. The Olympics were expected to become *the single initiative that more than other known policy measure will contribute to the growth and development of this region towards the end of the century.*[2] However, this has to a limited extent been operationalised in concrete objectives for what should be developed in different sectors. Expectations have been fairly general, different actors have had different expectations, and to a less degree overall goals for regional development have been formulated in an authorized way. The author's own interpretation of these goals can be summarized in the following points:

- Develop the region of Lillehammer as a significant destination for events, particularly as a national and international centre for winter sports events.
- Develop the region as a significant tourist destination.
- Stimulate industrial growth and development, create new jobs and reduce unemployment; in particular expectations related to the tourism industry, the media industry and knowledge-based institutions and businesses, but also other sectors like manufacturing have been relevant.

The data applied here are partly obtained from secondary sources, mainly Statistics Norway, where data on capacity and guest nights in the tourism industry are obtained as well as data

---

2)   The Norwegian Government's White Paper on regional development, 1988.

on the total population and unemployment. Partly, data have been obtained directly from companies and actors affected by the event. This group includes the owners of sports and cultural facilities who have provided data on the number of visitors, the organizers of local events who have provided data on visitors, and companies in tourism and other industries who have provided estimates of the employment effect of the Olympics. During the pre-event period various surveys were undertaken to identify which firms were affected by the Olympics. After the Olympics, this has been followed up through individual contacts to verify and adjust the estimated long-term impact of the event.

When estimating the long-term impacts of an event, one will be faced with a fundamental problem of interpreting to what extent a particular development may be identified as an impact of the event or not. The research approach has been based on in-depth knowledge of development processes in the region, and on continuing efforts in interpreting causal effects, partly just through observation, partly by discussing the development with the actors involved. In some cases the development in the Lillehammer region has been compared with other regions or cities to see if the development in Lillehammer has been significantly different compared to the development in other areas.

The fundamental problem here is the problem of attribution, i.e. which parts of an observed change may actually be attributed to the event under examination. For clarification of this problem, a model developed by Storey (1990) may be feasible, see Figure 8.2. Economic development is a continuous and complex process, and obviously not all changes observed may be attributed to a particular event, or employment initiative which is the focus of Storey's analyses. Thus, a distinction is made between 'dead weight' elements, i.e. developments that would have occurred independent of the actual initiative, and elements that may be attributed to the initiative. In addition to this, other policy measures may also work and should be considered as having a potential effect on the development being analyzed.

When analyzing impacts within a national context, it may be important to analyze to what extent jobs or other effects attributed to an initiative are transferred from somewhere else in the economy, or are established outside the region. Among those jobs actually new to the local economy, it may also be important to consider any potential replacement effects in other parts of the local economy, i.e. the entering of new firms or jobs may mean increased competition to other firms in the local economy.

In the case of Lillehammer, it has been fairly easy, in the short-term perspective, to identify which firms or expansions in firms that may be attributed to the Olympics. However, in the long-term it is far from easy to interpret in an adequate way the long-term effects that may be attributed to the event.

The attribution problem may be illustrated by drawing upon knowledge from the stage theory or life cycle theory of firm development and knowledge developed by the firm formation literature on dynamic processes. The stage theory of firm development is rather commonly applied in explaining processes of development related to firms or products (cf. Storey 1994), or it may be related to processes of entrepreneurship (cf. Johannisson and Nilsson 1989). The basic idea of this model is that there is a limited time span for economic activity. Whatever economic activity there is, it will not last forever. For an industry to survive in the long run, products and markets have to be renewed, firms have to restructure and reorganize, and much of the process of renewal is maintained by a significant exchange of economic activity – firms are entering and leaving the business arenas.

Although the basic principles are commonly accepted and recognized, the extent to which these processes take place are less recognized. Entry and exit rates of firms are around ten percent on an annual basis (SME Observatory 1993; Spilling 1997). On average, only fifty

Figure 8.2. Storey's model for evaluation of local employment initiative (Storey 1990)

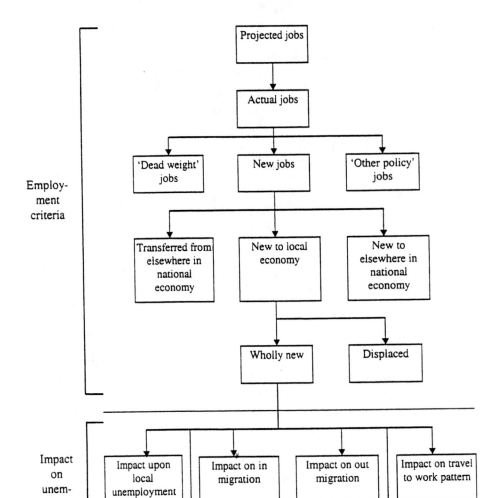

per cent of new firms survive the first five years, and as much as thirty per cent of new firms are out of business after 2-3 years. But the exit of firms does not necessarily mean the disappearance of the resources of the firms, they may be reorganized and appear in different firms. Or put another way, industrial development is a continuing process of organising and reorganizing resources. To develop firms and industries is not a one-time process, but a continuing process. Thus, it is in principle very difficult to talk about 'long-term effects', as it is probably impossible to attribute the long-term development of any business to any short-term event. An event may trigger a development of firms for a limited period of time, and it may facilitate the restructuring of firms and industries. But it cannot per se provide the basis for any long-term development, only the start of the long-term development.

What may be possible, however, is that an event may serve as a catalyst for developing infrastructures that may have some long-term impacts, or it may foster learning processes and develop competencies which are important as a basis for the long-term development. But, again, this basis has to be renewed and restructured in order for it to cope with the threats and challenges of long-term development.

Thus, it is not possible to quantify the 'long-term effects' of a mega-event in an objective way. This will to a certain extent be based on personal intuition and interpretations, preferably based on in-depth knowledge of the regional industrial structure and processes that have been stimulated by the event.

The Lillehammer Olympics[3]

To understand how a region is impacted by a mega-event, both the characteristics of the region and the event have to be known, as the same type of event may turn out very differently in regions of different size and industrial structure.

The region of Lillehammer is located in Eastern Norway around 180 km north of Oslo. The city of Lillehammer has some 24,000 inhabitants. When the neighboring municipalities are included, which together may be regarded as the core region that hosted the Olympics, the total population adds up to some 124,000. Thus, the Lillehammer Olympics took place in a region much smaller than most other regions hosting the Winter Olympics in previous years.[4]

Figure 8.3.   The Olympic region

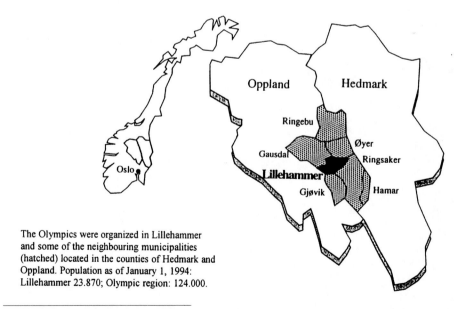

The Olympics were organized in Lillehammer and some of the neighbouring municipalities (hatched) located in the counties of Hedmark and Oppland. Population as of January 1, 1994: Lillehammer 23.870; Olympic region: 124.000.

---

3) This section is almost identical to a similar section in a previous article "Mega-event as strategy for regional development – the case of Lillehammer 1994", (Spilling, 1996).

4) Previous Winter Games have all taken place in regions with a bigger population base. 1992 – Albertville in France; 1988 – Calgary in Canada; 1984 – Sarajevo in previous Yugoslavia. Only in 1980 were the Winter Olympics hosted by a region with a smaller population than Lillehammer, namely Lake Placid, USA.

Being a small region with few sports facilities and an infrastructure of limited capacity, it was a major challenge to organize the Games. For instance, during the Games, the Olympic organization itself counted for a total of about 12,000 people, there were 30,000 official guests, up to 200,000 persons visited the region per day, and a total of 2.8 million persons were transported by the transportation system organized for the events (Table 8.1). And most of this activity took place in the city of Lillehammer, while the rest of the region to a significantly less degree was affected.

Table 8.1.   Key figures on the Lillehammer Winter Olympics 1994

Economy	(billion NOK)
The Olympic budget	7.4
Other public expenditure	2.8
Private investments	1-2
Revenues	2.7
Organization	(persons; total 12,000)
LOOC	881
Volunteers	9,054
Military forces	2,100
Official guests	(persons; total 30,000)
Participants/coaches	3,600
Media	8,000
Sponsors/suppliers	14,000
Police	2,800
IOC/VIP	1,600
Spectators	up to 200,000 per day
Sold tickets	1.2 million
Total number of spectators	2.2 million
Transported persons	2.8 million
Events	
Olympic disciplines	61
Cultural events with admission fees	285
Total number of cultural events	1,485
Media coverage	
Lands/regions with tv-coverage	134
Average no. of watchers, estimate	669 millions
Highest tv-ratings in some countries	(%)
Norway – closing ceremony	53.1
USA – figure skating	48.5
England – figure skating	45.3
France – figure skating	32.2
Japan – 5000 meter speed skating women	30.0
Germany – figure skating	20.4

Source: 1) Final Report from LOOC to the Ministry of Cultural Affairs. 2) Proposition for Stortinget (the Parliament) No. 1, 1994-1995, Ministry of Cultural Affairs, The Olympic Winter Games 1994.

There are many aspects of the development related to hosting the Olympics. It seems adequate to describe the development as consisting of stages, as outlined in Table 8.2. It started with an initial Klondike-like situation in the months following the IOC decision in September 1988. This was followed by significant periods of construction, hotel and tourism growth, and significant sales of a variety of goods and services related to the organizing of the Olympics, many of which were organized through temporary organizations set up for just a short period of time. After the very hectic days of the event, things calmed down. By the end of 1994 most activities related to the Olympics had come to an end, and the long-term activities after the Olympics which were triggered by the events have been fairly modest.

Table 8.2.   Stages of industrial activity related to the Olympics

Period	Stage	Industries/Actors	Activity
1988-1989	Initial Klondike		Broad specter of strategic maneuvering, new alliances and start-ups in the Olympic region.
1989-1990	Swedes	Swedish investors	Investments/purchases of property in Lillehammer and neighbouring places.
1990-1993	Construction	Construction and related industries	Planning and Construction of Olympic facilities, infrastructure, hotels etc.
1991-1994	Hotel expansions	Tourism industry	New hotels, refurbishing of existing hotels.
1993-1994	Temporary accommodation and restaurants	Private investors, tourism indystry	Significant temporary facilities for accommodation and restaurants were set up, partly working in the same markets as the permanent industries.
1993-1994	Tourism growth	Tourism	Significant growth in number of visitors to the region.
1993-1994	Olympic products, pins- and street-sellers	Manufacturing, retailing, individuals	Sales of Olympic related products, design products, souvenirs etc. Street sales of pins and other souvenirs.
1994-	Post-Olympic development	Tourism industry, organizers of Olympic facilities	Organizing and marketing the tourism industry and Olympic facilities.

The Olympics stimulated major investments and a significant consumption of goods and services. The official budget for the Olympics was about NOK 7.4 billion (approximately US$ 1 billion), additional expenditure on other public budgets accounted for another 2.8 billion, and considerable private investments and expenditures were made. In total it can be estimated that the Olympics stimulated economic activity of about NOK 11-12 billion (compares to around US$ 1.7-2.0 billion), of which about 5 billion was allocated for investments in physical facilities (infrastructure, Olympic arenas, accommodation). The costs of the Olympics were related to all kinds of goods and services, thus there were opportunities for all kinds of industries, and a variety of businesses have been affected by the Olympics.

Development as a center for events

The region of Lillehammer has in some respects succeeded in developing as a center for events, and is now hosting, on an annual basis, more international sports events than most other winter sports destinations. No other previous host of the Winter Olympics has ever hosted so many international sports events after the Games as Lillehammer has been doing. There are three main reasons for this development: 1) The region is endowed with a variety of high quality sports facilities, which makes it attractive to organize events in the region; 2) an organisational infrastructure has developed which has the competence and capacity for organizing these events, and 3) an economic system is developed that at least to some extent is able to tackle the economics related to organizing the events. However, the economics of many events are a significant problem, which will be commented on later in this section.

In the years before the Olympics, international sports events of any kind hardly occurred in the region. The most prestigious events hosted in the region would mainly be national events, occasionally national championships. As the new facilities were developed, this changed radically. During the winter season the year before the Olympics, several important sports events were organized in order to test the arenas and prepare for the Olympics. In the years after the Olympics, this situation has to some extent continued with 4-5 different world championships or world cup events every winter. In addition to this are a number of smaller sports events, and a number of large and smaller non-sporting events like concerts, exhibitions, trade fairs and smaller festivals. In fact, many of these events have turned out to be more interesting to the economic operation of the sports facilities than the international sports events that often are very costly to attract and organise (see later).

One part of the strategy of the region has been to develop mass sports events, as the economics of these kind of events generally are much better than the prestigious international world cup events. In this area, the region has good traditions, particularly related to the organization of 'Birkebeinerrennet', a cross country event which has been organized for more than sixty years, and for the last years has had more than 8,000 participants. Stimulated by the Olympics, other mass events have been developed, but with various degree of success (Figure 8.4).

There have been two very significant successes, the Inga Låmi cross country event, which is organized for female participants only, and which in 1997 attracted about 6,000 participants, and the Birkebeinerrittet, a 86 km off road bicycle race, which in 1996 attracted more than 4,000 participant. A third event, the Olympic Day Run, a 5 or 10 km street jogging event, turned out for some years to be a very great success, attracting at its best more than 11,000 participants. However, this mobilization has been very much related to the organization of the Olympics, and the interest for the event now seems to be fading. A fourth event, The Troll Ski Marathon, has never taken off. This is a 100-120 km cross-country ski race that has never attracted more than a few hundred people.

Generally, it may be concluded that the region has been fairly successful in developing a high level of activity related to organizing events. To some extent the development in this area has been like a type 1 impact, an intermezzo, as the number of events was highest during 1993-94. But there has also been a significant type 2 impact, i.e. the region has moved up to a higher level of activity and developed as an important destination for sports events in Europe.

However, this situation cannot be analysed without going into the economic basis for hosting sports events. Sports facilities are costly to operate, and many of the sports events are very expensive to attract. Neither is it free of charge to organize such events, although

Figure 8.4. Participants in mass sports events in Lillehammer 1987-1997

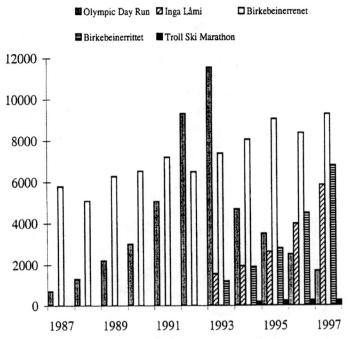

Mass sports events:

Olympic Day Run: 5 and 10 km jogging event, organized for the first time in 1987 (before Lillehammer had been approved as host for the 1994 Games) as a part of local mobilization for the Olympics.

Inga Låmi: Female cross-country event, 15 km, organized for the first time in 1993. The event was initiated as a spin off of organizing the Olympics.

Birkebeinerrennet: A classical cross country race, 55 km, organized since the 1930s, one of the most popular cross country races in Norway. Not influenced by the Olympics.

Birkebeinerrittet: Off road bicycle race, 85 km, organized for the first time in 1993. The race was initiated as a part of a strategy for organising more mass sports events, and is probably indirectly stimulated by the Olympics, but there is no direct link.

Troll Ski Marathon: A ski race never taken off due to the limited number of interested individuals.

volunteers do much of the work. *Event economy* has turned out to become a difficult issue for the various actors involved.

An important basis for operating the Olympic facilities has been the establishing of endowment funds, which were provided by the State Government in order to meet future economic problems in operating the Olympic facilities and to support regional development initiatives. In total, the funds have accounted for NOK 365 million, of which about 250 million has been allocated for the operation of the Olympic facilities (Spilling 1994). The main rule has been that interests earned on the funds could be used for subsidizing the operational costs of the Olympic facilities, and parts of the funds could be used for investments in the facilities.

These funds have been of great importance for operating the facilities so far, but they are far from sufficient. Only in one case, the Viking Ship (speed skating hall) in Hamar, which has been operated very successfully, is the economic situation fairly good. For all the other facilities there seems to be long-term problems. In one case (the Mountain Hall, Gjøvik), the local authorities have provided substantial annual subsidies, in another case (Kvitfjell Down Hill Facility), most of the endowment fund has been used for subsidies and investments, and the fund will probably be empty in one to two years. For the other facilities (in Lillehammer), the situation is not dramatic, but also in these cases the endowment funds are significantly reduced, and there will probably be economic problems in the future.[5]

The main reason for this is that operational costs exceed revenues generated by the Olympic facilities. The number of visitors has declined significantly after the Olympics (see next section), and there are significant economic problems related to at least some of the major international sports events organized in the facilities. World cup events in alpine and ski jumping have suffered significant economic losses, which is due to a combination of very high expenses in hosting these kinds of events, lack of good sponsors and low attendance. Subsidies provided by local authorities or endowment funds have even been required for organizing some of the events. And local sports clubs are very reluctant to take the responsibility for organising new events.

An example that may illustrate the problem of the region is related to local efforts for attracting the World Championship in alpine disciplines. This event, which is seen as very attractive and prestigious, is regarded as important to 1) generate activity in the alpine facilities, 2) serve as a means for marketing of the facilities, and 3) demonstrate to the outside world the position of the Lillehammer region as an outstanding organizer of sports events. The first attempt at attracting the World Championship in 2001, which cost NOK 3 million, was in vain, and currently a new campaign with a budget of NOK 5 million is being organized for hosting the 2003 events.

Development of tourist destinations

The tourism industry has by far been the regional industry most affected by the Olympics. As has been analysed in some previous reports and an article (Spilling and Vonlanthen 1992; Spilling 1994; 1996) a very significant short-term as well as long-term growth in hotel capacity has occurred. Parts of the region have experienced a significant growth in the number of visiting tourists, and to some extent there has been a development of tourist attractions. However, the development has been very diversified, and as tourism development to a large extent is about destinations, the most adequate picture of the development induced by the Olympics is given when related to the various destinations of the Lillehammer region.

Compared to other regions that have hosted the Winter Olympics, the Lillehammer region has a very small tourist industry. By the end of the 1980s, and before the Olympics had any impact, the total bed capacity of the region added up to 8,400 beds.[6] This changed radically as a result of the Olympics. For the Olympic region as a whole there was an expansion of different kinds of permanent accommodation facilities by 75% up to a total of 14,600 beds. Most of this capacity, but not all, was developed directly as a result of the Olympics, and most of it has been in operation after the Olympics.

In addition to the permanent capacity, a significant number of temporary accommodation facilities were set up for the Olympics and removed or converted for other purposes afterwards. This capacity added up to 15,000 beds, i.e. the same level as the permanent capacity.

---

5) It has been the intention of the author to provide and exact update of the status of the endowment funds. However, in spite of several inquiries, it has not been possible to obtain adequate data from all the companies operating the facilities.

6) In contrast, the two previous organisers of the Olympic Winter Games, Albertville (1992) and Calgary (1988) had around 300,000 and 37,500 beds respectively.

In addition to this, there were also a number of private initiatives offering temporary accommodation in private houses and holiday houses.

According to our classification of types of impact, the accommodation industry has experienced impacts of type 1, intermezzo, and type 2, growth to a new level of activity. The various destinations of the region have been affected in very different ways. Virtually all temporary accommodation facilities were developed in the destinations of Lillehammer, Øyer and Gausdal, and very little outside this area (see map in Figure 8.3). Much the same is the status for the permanent capacity, which has mainly been developed in the same three destinations. Some minor development has taken place in the Kvitfjell area (down hill facility in Ringebu north of Lillehammer), while the city of Gjøvik virtually has had no development of hotels related to the Olympics. In Hamar, a new hotel was set up before the Olympics, but this was probably independent of the Olympics.

The development of the tourism demand, here measured as number of recorded guest nights in hotels and other commercial accommodation facilities,[7] is quite clearly affected by the Olympics (Figure 8.5). The Olympic region as a whole has, from the end of the 1980s to 1996, experienced a growth of 68 per cent in demand. Much of this growth has occurred in the three core destinations Lillehammer, Gausdal and Øyer. Lillehammer and Gausdal have experienced a growth of around 70-80 per cent, and Øyer, which definitely has turned out as the winner, has more than trebled its total number of guest nights. Starting from a

Figure 8.5. Development of guest nights in the three destinations most affected by the Olympics

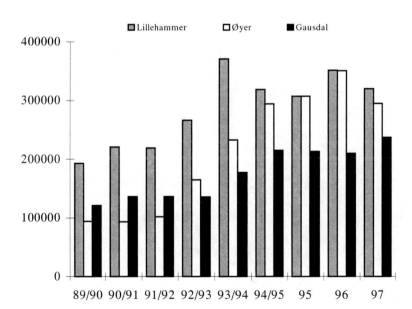

Annual number of guest nights. For the first years (1989-95), the periods go from May through April, for the last years the calendar year is followed. This means that there are four months overlap between 1994/95 and 1995. Data are obtained from Statistics Norway, Tourism statistics. Data for hotels and other commercial accommodation facilities with more than 20 beds.

---

7) The data includes guest nights in hotels, motels, apartments and camping sites with cottages with more than 20 beds. Ordinary camping is not included.

rather modest level, Øyer now is challenging Lillehammer as being the foremost destination of the region.

The performance of the Olympic region is significantly better than the national development of the tourism sector. For the nation as a whole, the number of guest nights grew by about 30 per cent in the same period (up to 1996). However, during 1997 the development in the region stagnated, while the national development still was growing, particularly in the cities. Thus, there may be indications that the impacts of the Games are fading out.

All three types of impacts have been demonstrated for the tourism sector. First, there was a considerable intermezzo in demand for guest nights directly related to the Olympics. This demand is only partly reflected in the statistical data as much of this accommodation took place in temporary facilities that did not report data to the statistical authorities. Second, we have the impact type 2, growth to a new level of activity, which seems to be the case of Lillehammer and Gausdal, and third, a significant acceleration of growth rate has occurred in Øyer, although this effect culminated during 1997. Without the Olympics probably very little of this development would occur, only smaller parts of the investments would have been realized.

The main long-term impact induced by the Olympics is due to a combination of heavy investments in new facilities – accommodation and activity facilities, like the alpine facilities – and the very significant awareness effect and interest for the region which was created by the Olympics. In particular, this has been the case for Øyer, where virtually a whole new destination has been developed. Before the Olympics, it had some smaller accommodation facilities and one major tourist attraction (Hunderfossen Family Park). By now the destination comprises a variety of facilities. A core facility, and an important catalyst for the local development, is the alpine facility which was developed for the Olympics, and after the 1996/97 season ranked as number three among the biggest alpine facilities in Norway. Next to this facility several new accommodation facilities have been developed, like a large hotel (one of the biggest hotels outside urban areas in Norway), a smaller hotel and several simpler accommodation facilities. Attractive for recreational activities, the area also has developed as a very popular location for holiday houses. Around 500 holiday houses have so far been built, and the area has turned out to be probably the most popular recreation area for higher income people from the Oslo region (two and a half hours' driving distance). Furthermore, new attractions have developed, like the bob and luge track and a road museum.

When analyzing the development of tourist attractions in the Olympic region, a distinction can be made between general attractions not directly related to the Olympics, and sports and other facilities that were set up for the Olympics and that turned out to have a potential as tourist attractions.

Regarding the first type of attraction, the general pattern in the region seems to be that the number of visitors in most cases was only marginally affected by the Olympics (see Table 8.3). This is also the situation in the case of the region's most significant tourist attraction, a family park, which did not reach an attendance level much 'above normal' during the 1993-94 period when the number of visitors attracted to the region by the Olympics was at its highest. Many smaller attractions in the region (not included in Table 8.3) seem to show the same pattern of development, i.e. no impact induced by the Olympics.

Two attractions, however, turned out to develop differently from this pattern, the Maihaugen Open Air Museum and the Lillehammer Museum of Art. Both institutions took advantage of significant support from the organizing committee (LOOC) to expand their facilities, as they hosted parts of the official cultural program during the Olympics. In the case of Maihaugen, the number of attendants on an annual basis grew from about 120,000-150,000

Table 8.3. Visitors at tourist attractions located in the Lillehammer area 1990-1997

Attraction	1990	1991	1992	1993	1994	1995	1996	1997
Hunderfossen Family Park	223 000	223 000	258 320	256 800	268 071	256 005	266 987	255 000
The Norwegian Road Museum			38 000	43 100	27 500	31 336	45 714	37 157
Lilleputthammer		60 000	65 000	35 000	42 000	51 200	50 000	
Motor Vehicle Museum				15 900	12 057	9 120	7 788	5 821
Lillehammer Museum of Arts				49 300	19 876	25 956	9 618	8 217
Maihaugen Open Air Museum	118 872	125 891	146 891	170 643	205 164	169 095	166 658	147 470

Comments:

Hunderfossen Family Park: The most significant attraction of the region, located near the Hafjell Alpine Facility; theme park, established in the 1980s, no major investments induced by the Olympics.

The Norwegian Road Museum: Established in the early 1990s in Øyer, next to Hunderfossen Family Park, location probably inspired by the Olympics, but investments independent of the Olympics.

Lilleputthammer: Miniature model of the city of Lillehammer, located in Øyer next to the Hafjell Alpine Facility; opened in the 1980s, no investment induced by the Olympics.

The Norwegian Motor Vehicle Museum: Established in Lillehammer in the 1980s, no investment induced by the Olympics.

Lillehammer Museum of Arts: Old institution located in Lillehammer, significant investments obtained through the Olympic Organization, new exhibitions opened in 1993.

Maihaugen Open Air Museum: Norway's largest museum located in Lillehammer, established in the first half of this century, significant investments obtained through the Olympic Organization, new concert hall and new exhibitions opened in 1993.

during the early 1990s, to its peak of more than 200,000 in 1994, dropping down again to a lower level in the years after. Similarly, the art museum had a temporary growth in attendance in 1993/94. In both these cases we can basically talk about a type 1 effect caused by the Olympics - intermezzo.

The other type of attractions, which have been directly created by the Olympics, have followed a different type of pattern (Table 8.4). First, it should be mentioned, that it actually was a surprise to local actors that the sports facilities had a potential as tourist attractions. As the facilities were not planned as attractions from the beginning, they had to be adjusted to be capable of receiving a large number of visitors. During the best years, 1993-94, when the Olympic facilities in total attracted several hundred thousand visitors, they ranked high on the national ranking of tourist attractions.[8]

The significant short-term interest for the sports facilities created a lot of optimism in the region regarding their long-term potential. Although some decline was expected after the Olympics, the decline turned out to be far more dramatic than expected. In most cases the number of attendants in 1996 was just a smaller fraction compared to the performance in 1994. One attraction, which was opened after the Olympics to memorize the event, even turned out to be an economic fiasco, eventually closing down and going bankrupt in 1996.

As far as they appear as tourist attractions, the Olympic facilities have followed a combination of type 1 and type 2 impacts. Partly it was an intermezzo, but still they constitute a

---

8) During the 1994 Summer Season (May-August) the Viking Ship was no. 25 on the national ranking, Håkon's Hall no. 31, the ski jumping tower no. 39, the ski jumping lift no. 52 and the Mountain Hall no. 71. *Source:* Norwegian Tourist Board.

Table 8.4.   Visitors at Olympic facilities 1992-96

Location/Facilities	1992 May-Aug	1993 May-Aug	1993 Whole year	1994 May-Aug	1994 Whole year	1995 May-Aug	1995 Whole year	1996 May-Aug	1996 Whole year
Lillehammer:									
Håkon's Hall		141 400	194 500	90 738		46 184	60 623	32 300	40 387
Ski jumping – tower	58 000	122 200	260 900	77 000			51 721		36 859
Ski jumping – lift		58 500	64 400	58 000		30 767		46 845	
Simulator			53 200				42 205		29 001
Information Center	146 320	220 680	403 700		220 000				
Experience Center					19 200		44 500		31 000
Øyer:									
Bob and luge track			23 000				17 589		17 624
Wheel bob			3 500				11 145		11 806
Hamar:									
The Viking Ship		171 000	300 000	127 200		57 200		42 996	
Gjøvik:									
Olympic Mountain Hall		67 672	165 000	41 136		38 311		28 402	

Data for the tourist season (May 1st to August 31st) obtained from the Norwegian Tourist Board ranking of most
visited tourist attractions. Other data obtained from the companies operating the facilities.
Olympic Facilities:
Håkon's Hall: Ice Hockey hall, opened in 1993.
Ski jumping facilities: Tower opened in 1992, and lift opened in 1993.
Simulator: Small facility offering a short multi-media program simulating down hill and bob racing.
Information centre: Centre providing information about the Olympics, opened in 1991, free admission, converted
into an experience centre in 1994.
Experience Centre: Centre with multimedia program and exhibitions related to the Olympic events. Significant
investment, opened in 1994, closed down and bankrupt in 1996.
Bob and luge track: Opened in 1993, a specially designed wheel bob offer tourist rides in the summer season.
The Viking Ship: Speed skating hall, opened in 1993.
The Olympic Mountain Hall: Ice Hockey hall build inside a mountain, opened in 1993.

group of attractions that have contributed to the tourist product of the region, and that represent
a new level of activity.

To summarize the development of the tourism industry: The Olympics have served as an
important catalyst for developing the tourism industry, particularly in the core parts of the
Olympic region. It has been a significant intermezzo, and there has been a number of
investments both intended and unintended which have contributed to this intermezzo. But
there has also been a permanent expansion and improvement of the industry, which now
seems to be operating at a level significantly higher than it was by the end of the 1980s,
where it would not have been today if the Olympics had not been organised. However, the
development during 1997 may indicate that the impacts of the Olympics are fading out, as
the region experienced a decline in recorded guest nights, which was in contrast to the
national development which still was showing growth.

Industrial development and job creation

The main argument for hosting the Olympics in Lillehammer was the long-term impact that was expected on industrial development. Originally, the expectation was to create a long-term employment effect estimated to around 1000 jobs immediately after the Olympics, and growing to 1200 jobs eight years after the event (Selstad 1984). This estimate was based on a simple analysis of how development would occur and how the different industries would be affected by the Olympics, which at that time were estimated to be much smaller than they actually turned out to be.

The analysis triggered a very intense debate among local interests. Actors opposing the idea of bidding for the Games criticized the estimate of the long-term effect, and presented an alternative analysis which suggested a much smaller long-term effect. On the other hand, people supporting the idea of the Olympics trusted the estimation of the long-term impacts, or at least did not put forward alternative data.

In retrospect, and based upon today's knowledge about what actually happened, it is easy to see that the analysis undertaken at that time was not based on proper insights into what kind of dynamic processes the Olympics would imply. The analysis lacked models for estimating the long-term development in various sectors.

In late 1994, half a year after the Olympics, using data from a survey and direct observation of a number of firms directly affected by the Olympics, a direct job creation effect of the Olympics at around 380 full time equivalents[9] was estimated (Spilling 1994). This estimate, however, did not include a potential effect of expansion in higher education,[10] and also local employment effects of growing population and multiplier effects were not included. On the other hand, the analysis neither took account of any possible displacement effect nor that public money, which was very important for the development, would have been spent in an alternative way to stimulate regional development if the Olympics had not been organised.

Reconsidering the analysis one year later, a total employment effect of between 300 and 400 full time equivalents in Lillehammer, and between 500 and 600 (low and high estimates) in the Olympic region as a whole was estimated (Spilling 1995, unpublished paper). According to this analysis, the most significant contribution to employment growth came from the tourism industry (100-200 full time equivalents), from organizations operating the Olympic facilities (80 full time equivalents), and the remaining full time equivalents were spread in different sectors, including the multiplier effects.

What seems to be quite certain about the employment effect related to the Olympics is that most employment generated by the event was highly temporary, and the long-term effect is rather marginal in view of the total employment of the region. Before the Olympics, employment related to the Olympics reached its peak in 1992 when it was almost 2,000, of which activity in the construction industry accounted for two thirds.[11] To put this figure in

---

9) This is equivalent to 570 jobs, i.e. 2/3 full time equivalents per job.

10) The mechanism here is that a huge media center set up for the Olympics were converted into high quality facilities for the local University College after the Games. These facilities may have served as a catalyst for expanding higher education after the Games and may have contributed to a relatively higher growth in the Lillehammer area compared to competing regions.

11) The estimations are provided by the local labor market authorities, who organized a survey four times a year where employment data were collected from all companies, organizations, institutions and local administrations that worked directly with activities related to the Olympics.

perspective, the total unemployment in the Olympic region was about 5,000 in 1992, and the Olympic related employment of 2,000 people did not account for more than about 2-3 per cent of the total labor force of the region. So, although the employment generated by the Olympics was important, it was still rather marginal in the regional context.

During the Games, when volunteers and military forces are included, the total number of people employed was about 12,000. This figure dropped to a few hundred immediately after the Games, and faded out with the closing down of the Olympic organization and the finishing of the reconstruction work 1-2 years after the Games.

As far as 'permanent' and 'long-term' employment is concerned, it is, as discussed earlier in the paper, difficult to present an exact and reliable estimate due to lack of knowledge of which activities can be attributed to the Olympics. Thus, the present analysis suggests an estimate with considerable uncertainty involved.

When reconsidering the data on the long-term development three years after the Games (1997),[12] the long-term impacts may be summarized in the following points.

The tourism industry is the most significant growth sector affected by the Olympics. Contact with the involved companies revealed that the employment status basically was the same in 1997 as reported in 1994, with some minor changes up and down. This gives reason to maintain the estimate of a long-term employment effect of between 100 and 200 full time equivalents.

The Olympic related organizations, i.e. organizations set up for operating the Olympic facilities and manage the endowment funds, originally reported an employment of 90 in 1994, which was reduced to 80 in 1995. In 1997 this has been even further reduced to 40 full time equivalents.

In the manufacturing and construction sectors and the producer services, some 20 companies reported a long-term employment growth as a result of the Olympics in our previous analysis. When approaching these companies again in 1997, the majority reported that they were no longer experiencing a long-term impact of the Olympics. Thus, the 'long-term' impact reported in 1994 has turned out to be temporary, and the long-term impact reported from these firms therefore has to be reduced considerably.

Producer services, also including firms related to IT and data processing, have been claimed, by local authorities in Lillehammer, to be a significant growth sector stimulated by the Olympics. However, when controlling the development in this sector, by examining public databases and combining it with knowledge developed in previous research, it turns out that the development in this sector is rather marginal as far as caused by the Olympics. There is a tendency to attribute much more to an Olympic effect, than there seems to be accurate knowledge based on considerations of what kind of mechanisms have been at work.

In total, the long-term employment effect created directly by the Olympics can be roughly estimated to be about 250-350 full time equivalents three years after the Games. This does not include employment generated by the growing population in Lillehammer, neither does it include multiplier effects. When these aspects are considered, we end up with a total revised estimate of the long-term impacts of between 400 and 500 full time equivalents.

---

12) The data have been checked by 1) direct contact with all companies that according to investigations in 1994 reported a long-term employment effect caused by the Olympics, and 2) contact with the local business agency of Lillehammer to obtain their assessment of the long-term impacts. The latter has been controlled by checking the current situation of new firms as it is recorded in a national database on firms (Dun & Bradstreet database).

Unemployment and population development

As the long-term employment effect has been a main interest of the Olympics, it is also interesting to see what has happened to unemployment in the region. When the decision of organizing the Olympics in Lillehammer was taken in 1988, the level of unemployment was rather low in Norway, about 2-3 percent, which also was the percentage in the Lillehammer region. But it was growing significantly, and in a few years total unemployment grew to a very high level more than three times higher than in the mid 1980s. In 1993 the development culminated, and during the period 1994-96 there was a significant decline of unemployment.

The various parts of the Olympic region have followed the same pattern, with one very important exception, namely the core area of Lillehammer, which, during 1992-94, and particularly in 1993, experienced a significantly lower level of unemployment than the rest of the region (see Figure 8.6). This, of course, may be explained as an effect of the Olympics. But it was a temporary effect, and supports the idea of the Olympics as mainly being an intermezzo. After the Olympics, the Lillehammer area for some time had a growing unemployment rate while it was declining in other areas, and for some time Lillehammer even had a higher level of unemployment than the rest of the region, but later this evened out.

Figure 8.6. Development of unemployment 1988-1996 (Data from Statistics Norway, Unemployment statistics.)

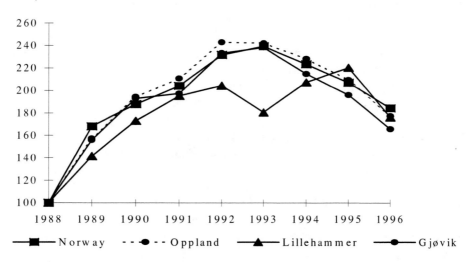

Another aspect of the impacts of the Olympics is how it has affected the population development in the Lillehammer area (see Figure 8.7). Although these data are difficult to interpret, and require a lot of knowledge on the current pattern of population development in Norway, it seems reasonable to interpret parts of the development as an effect of the Olympics. Figure 8.7 illustrates that the population of Lillehammer accelerated significantly from about 1988 to 1996. The growth rate is about 10 percent and it is significantly higher than the national average. It was also higher than most smaller towns in Eastern Norway. However, during 1997 this development culminated, and a decline was experienced.

When estimating the impact induced by the Olympics, it is important to be aware of the general mechanisms of population restructuring in Norway in the same period. Generally, there has been a population growth in combination with a concentration of population to the

Figure 8.7.   Population development 1980-1997 (Data from Statistics Norway, population statistics, data as of January 1st each year.)

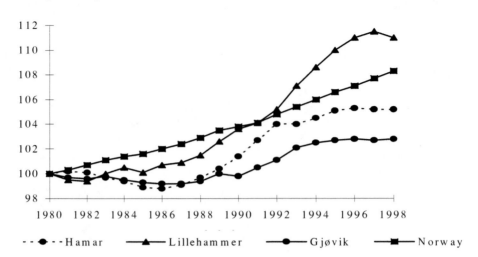

central areas of the country. The highest population growth occurred in the Oslo area. Smaller cities have had a smaller growth, while rural and more peripheral areas have experienced a decline. Some municipalities in the Oslo area have performed better than Lillehammer, but among cities with the same structure as Lillehammer, there are some with the same performance. Based on this, it may be estimated that the Olympics have created an additional population growth in Lillehammer of about 2-3 per cent more than what would be expected with a development without the Olympics.

Population growth means more demand for a variety of goods and services, and thus indirectly new jobs are created in private as well as public services. How significant this effect is, however, is difficult to explain. One possible result is that employment in the relevant services (basically retailing, personal and private services and local public services) has expanded a percentage equivalent to the population expansion. It might be, however, that the advantage of growing markets is taken out in higher productivity, and as far as public services are concerned, it might be that the service standards are reduced. We have no possibility to control this effect. However, the amin conclusion seems rather clear that there for some has been a type 3 impact on the population development – change of growth pattern. On the other hand, the most recent development may indicate that this effect is fading out as the population now has stopped growing.

8.4 Conclusion

The main conclusion derived from this analysis is that a mega-event is a temporary phenomenon, and that the main impacts of the Lillehammer Olympics may be characterized as an intermezzo. To the extent that there are long-term impacts, they are rather marginal in comparison with the total economic activity of the region. The long-term impacts are mainly related to the tourism industry and the organizing of events in the region. In both areas the region has developed its activities to a new plateau. There is a marginal growth in industrial employment that may be attributed to the Olympics. While there is no long-term effect on unemployment, there seems to have been a long-term impact on population, although this effect may be fading out (Table 8.5).

Table 8.5.   Summary of impacts related to the Lillehammer Winter Olympics

Sector	Type of impact		
	1. Intermezzo	2. New level of activity	3.Change of growth rate
Center for events	X	X	
Tourism – guest nights	X	X	(X)
Tourism – visitors to attractions	X	X	
General industrial employment	X	(X)	
Unemployment	X		
Population		(X)	(X)

When considering these results, it should be kept in mind that the Lillehammer region is fairly small, much smaller than most other regions that have hosted the Winter Olympics. The small size of the region may provide an important explanation to the observed long-term impacts. Due to the size of the region, a significant expansion of the tourism industry was stimulated by the Olympics, and this in combination with the setting up of new sports facilities has provided an important basis for the expansion of tourism and developing the region as a center for events. Although comparative studies have not been done, there is reason to believe that similar impacts would not occur to the same extent in larger regions with more developed tourism industry and sports facilities.

When the long-term impacts are evaluated, they should be considered against the background of the total expenses of hosting the Olympics. In total it is estimated that the national net deficit of hosting the Games was some NOK 5-6 billion (0.8-0.9 billion US$), and in this perspective a long-term employment effect of some 4-500 full time equivalents is rather marginal. This conclusion is even more significant due to the fact that major parts of the regional long-term impact are based on reallocation of resources within the country, like for instance population growth, parts of the growth in tourism industry and the operation of the Olympic facilities. What really is missing, and is in sharp contrast to the original expectations, is the development of new dynamism where businesses exploit new markets and contribute to national growth. Only smaller parts of the new activities have contributed in this way.

If the host region should be responsible for covering the deficit, serious economic problems would have developed. However, it was the Government that paid it all, and even provided the local authorities with extra funds for planning for the event, for operating the sports facilities after the event and even for stimulating local and regional industrial development. To the region, then, hosting the Winter Olympics has mainly been regarded as an advantage, but in the national perspective the conclusion in economic terms is the opposite.

Ritchie and Yangzhou have stated that (1987:48):

> "The efforts and resources required for a host region to stage a short duration mega-event such as an Olympic Games are out of all proportion to the returns which result directly during the period of the event itself. While these returns are not insignificant, they are clearly secondary to other and more substantial long term benefits which underlie the expenditures of resources involved."

And the authors indicated, although in very vague terms, that the long-term benefits following from a mega-event might be sufficient for making up for all the expenses related to hosting the event. In the case of Lillehammer, however, the opposite conclusion has to be drawn.

Looking beyond the intermezzo, which is the main mechanism of an event, it turns out quite clearly that the long-term industrial impacts are very marginal and in no way justify the huge costs of hosting the events.

If the main argument for hosting a mega-event like the Winter Olympics is the long-term economic impacts it will generate, the Lillehammer experience quite clearly points to the conclusion that it is a waist of money. Probably, this will also be the case for other smaller regions hosting similar events, and although we do not have reliable data on the long-term impacts from larger regions having hosted the Winter Olympics, the indicators we do have point in the same direction.

However, this does not mean that there are no other arguments for hosting a mega-event. The Lillehammer Olympics was a great experience, although not in economic terms.

References

Brunet, F. (1994). *Economy of the 1992 Barcelona Olympic Games*. Barcelona/Lausanne, Centre d'Estudis Olimpics Universitat Autónoma de Barcelona/IOC Olympic Study and Research Centre.

Brunet, F. (1995). Economics. In M. de Moragas & M. Botella (Eds.), *The Keys to Success. The Social, Sporting, Economic and Communications Impact of Barcelona'92*. Centre d'Estudis Olimpics Universitat Autónoma de Barcelona, Olympica Museum Lausanne and Fundació Barcelona Olímpica.

Brönnimann, M. (1982). *Die Touristische Bedeutung von Wintersport-Grossveranstaltunge*. Max Brönninmann (Eigenverlag), Bern.

Burns, J. P. A. & Mules, T. J. (1986). A Framework for the Analysis of Major Special Events. In J. P. A. Burns, J. H. Hatch & T. J. Mules (Eds.), *The Adelaide Grand Prix - The Impact of a Special Event*. Adelaide (Australia), The Centre for South Australian Economic Studies.

Getz, D. (1989). Special Events. Defining the Product. *Tourism Management,* June, 125-137.

Getz, D. (1997). *Event Management & Event Tourism*. New York: Cognizant Comunication Corporation.

Johannisson, B. & Nilsson, A. (1989). Community Entrepreneurs: Networking for Local Development. *Entrepreneurship & Regional Development, 1*(1), 3-19.

Kirchner, C. (1980). *Auswirkungen von Internationalen Grossveranstaltungen auf die Regionale Entwicklung. Dargestellt am Beispiel der IX. Und XII. Olympischen Winterspiele Innsbruck 1964 and 1976*. Bergheim: F.L. Doepgen.

Pyo, S., R. Cook, et al. (1988). Summer Olympic Tourist Market – Learning From the Past. *Tourism Management,* June, 137-144.

Ritchie, J. R. B. (1984). Assessing the Impact of Hallmark Events: Conceptual and Research Issues. *Journal of Travel Research,* summer, 2-11.

Ritchie, J. R. B. & Yangzhou, J. (1987). *The Role and Impact of Mega-Events and Attractions on National and Regional Tourism: A Conceptual and Methodological Overview*. Paper for 37th AIST Congress, Association Internationale d'Experts Scientifiques du Tourisme, Calgary.

Schulmeister, S. (1976). Olympische Spiele und Reiseverkehr. *Monatsberichte des Oesterreichischen Instituts für Wirtschaftsforschung, 8, 89-97*.

Selstad, T. (1984). *Lokale Konsekvenser av Olympiske Leker. (Local Impacts of Olympic Winter Games)*. Eastern Norway Research Institute, Lillehammer.

Socher, K. & Tschurtschenthaler, P. (1987). *The Role and Impact of Mega-Events: Economic Perspectives - The Case of the Winter Olympic Games 1964 and 1976 Innsbruck*. Paper presented at the 37th AIST Congress, Association Internationale d'Experts Scientifiques du Tourisme, Calgary.

Sparrow, M. (1989). A Tourism Planning Model for Hallmark Events. In G.J. Syme, J. Shaw, D.M. Fenton, & W.S. Mueller (Eds.), In *The Planning and Evaluation of Hallmark Events*. Aldershot (England), Avebury.

Spilling, O. R. (1994). *OLs næringsmessige betydning på kort og lang sikt. (Industrial Impacts of the Lillehammer Olympics)* Eastern Norway Research Institute, Lillehammer.

Spilling, O.R. (1996a). The Entrepreneurial System. On Entrepreneurship in the Context of a Mega-Event. *Journal of Business Research, 36, 91-103*.

Spilling, O. R. (1996b). Mega-Event as Strategy for Regional Development: The Case of the 1994 Lillehammer Winter Olympics. *Entrepreneurship and Regional Development, 8*(4), 321-343.

Spilling, O. R. (Ed.)(1997). *SMB 97 - fakta om små og mellomstore bedrifter i Norge.* (SME 97 – facts on small and medium-sized enterprises in Norway) Bergen: Fagbokforlaget.

Spilling, O. R. & Vonlanthen, P. (1992). *OL 94 og reiseliv. (The Olympics '94 and the Development in the Tourism Sector).* Eastern Norway Research Institute, Lillehammer.

Storey, D. (1990). Evaluation of Policies and Measures to Create Local Employment. *Urban Studies, 27*(5), 669-684.

Storey, D. J. (1994). *Understanding the Small Business Sector.* London and New York: Routledge.

Syme, G. J., Shaw, J., Fenton, D.M., & Mueller, W.S. (Eds.)(1989). *The Planning and Evaluation of Hallmark Events.* Aldershot (England), Avebury.

Teigland, J. (1996). *Impacts on Tourism from Mega-Events: The Case of Winter Olympic Games.* Western Norway Research Institute, Sogndal, Norway.

The European Observatory for SMEs. First annual report, 1993. European Network for SME Research, EIM Small Business Research and Consultancy, Zoetermeer, The Netherlands.

Travis, A.S. & Croizé, J.-C. (1987). *The Role and Impact of Mega-Events and Attractions on Tourism Development in Europe: A Micro Perspective.* Paper presented at the 37th AIST Congress, Association Internationale d'Experts Scientifiques du Tourisme, Auguste, Calgary.

Chapter 9
Event Strategies in Practice

In this, the last chapter of the book, we decided that someone representing a large city should present the event strategies of the city, which we, one by one, would comment on. Stockholm was chosen due to the numbers of events arranged there every year but also for practical reasons, as all the contributors have a good awareness of the city. The authority responsible for tourism issues in Stockholm is The Stockholm Information Service (SIS). Göran Långsved, the president of SIS was invited to describe the strategic considerations made by Stockholm when trying to attract various events or types of events to the city. We wanted an answer to the question of whether Stockholm City has an overall strategy and if that is the case, how it is formed. Also how this strategy is communicated to other actors.

Below follows an abstract from the speech of Göran Långsved.

Långsved started to discuss how the community's attitudes to and knowledge of the tourism industry has changed over the last ten years. At the end of the 80's the level of interest and knowledge was poor. Today, the community realizes that the industry has a great importance for economy, growth, and employment but also for social aspects. He means that the industry can e.g. generate employment for groups difficult to otherwise employ. Increased tourism leads to a living city with a decreased risk for deterioration. An advantage is that the tourism industry provides a good combination of public and private businesses.

Långsved describes SIS work with help of five circles. The first circle focuses on the leisure market, the other on the congress market, and the third on the event market. The circles below consist of product, which is the city including various part products where e.g. infrastructure and parks can be included. Finally, the last ring consists of services, such as tickets and maintenance.

Leisure tours are often sold as packages. Marketing is carried out mainly through catalogues delivered to many countries. Certain themes are selected for the congresses. These are medical, transports, and communication – themes congruent with important areas for the industry in Stockholm. The goal is to be one of the ten largest congress cities in the world by 2002 (today Stockholm is number 14).[1] To be able to attract congresses SIS invites resellers and journalists and has considerable contact with large international organizations.

---

1) The speech was held in February 1999. In November 1999, Stockholm is ranked as number nine, according to Göran Långsved.

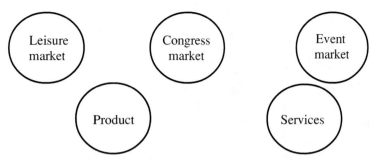

The areas selected for events are culture, water, and sport. Events are means to lift the product (Stockholm) by attracting a lot of attention. Events are one way spreading Stockholm's name . Långsved contends that it does not really matter if not so many visit e.g. the hockey game. Instead, one-minute of broadcasting time on Eurosport is worth more due to the high marketing value. Stockholm's candidature for the Olympic Games is an example of great mass media effects. Despite the fact that Stockholm did not get the opportunity to arrange the games, the candidature gained prestige and 'a ticket to the best room'. The candidature gave acceptance, which has made it easier to sell congresses today.

With help of congresses and events Stockholm is trying to reduce fluctuations in demand. One problem is the climate as it is e.g. not possible to arrange running competitions in Stockholm during March. They have to be arranged during the warm summer months. The best occupancy levels occur during the months of May, June, August, and September. Stockholm tries actively to organize events that increase the occupancy during the rest of the months. One example is 'Vikingarännet', a skating competition, which was arranged for the first time in February 1999.

The investment in infrastructure is important for tourism. The construction of The Stockholm Globe Arena has had great importance.

SIS tries to select events, which conform to the image they like Stockholm to be connected with -clean, quiet and close to water. They are wary of events related to soccer and motor sport as they are often connected with noise and trouble.

The methods of financing differ between various events. For the culture-capital year (for Stockholm 1998) funding was provided to a great extent from public sources (municipal and government) as private sources were not sufficient. The Water Festival, an annual event is financed with both municipal and private sources. Every event has to, as Långsved says, stand on its own feet as regards sponsoring. There is a network of sponsors and SIS works as a middleman between arrangers and the companies. Sometimes SIS aslo is a sponsor of its own.

A significant problem with events is to convince for example taxpayers, journalists, and politicians of the advantages of the investments due to the fact that the financing is often based on public money. It is questioned whether public money should be financing events or whether it is a better investment to build kindergartens or new roads. One reason for the debate is the difficulties in assessing the economic impacts. Also, there are difficulties in presenting the potential or real effects in an easy and pedagogical way in the media. Events are therefore vulnerable. It is easier to argue for investment in the leisure and congress markets.

How should one evaluate the success of investments? Långsved contends that it is difficult to evaluate success. Available measures are incomplete. SIS tries however, to show the importance of tourism, through presenting the number of guest nights, and effects on taxes- and employment.

In the following pages, some of the contributors to this book will comment on the event strategies adopted by Stockholm. We found four issues particularly interesting, which the rest of the chapter will focus on, respectively. These issues are:

1. Events as part of the destination marketing
2. Destination marketing as part of the communities competition
3. Attitudes of the locals toward events
4. The decision process of events related to public financing

9.1 Events as Part of the Destination Marketing

Lena L. Mossberg: Many others as well as Långsved have labeled events as image-makers. Creating a positive image is a vital step in attracting tourists. It is also rubbing off on other markets and interest groups. The profitable markets in Stockholm are, according to Långsved, leisure and congresses. The latter is the milk cow but the market depends on events to increase the attraction and awareness of the city.

A positive image can be created or enhanced through promotion and other forms of exposure, for example television. To use events in communication with various interest groups, including potential visitors, can be a successful means for destinations. For large destination events can contribute to the feeling of happenings that something is going on and that there is always something to do. Even for smaller destinations a 'destination of events' approach can be formulated. In the latter case events with specific attraction have to be arranged regularly. For such events each should be a special experience and it might be a 'once in a lifetime happening', such as if a mega star plays in the city arena. Small destinations with an event image are often connected with one specific recurring event, such as a rock festival, a ski run, or a soccer-cup. The event is a so-called hallmark event, i.e. the occurring event is " … tied to a specific place whereby the destination and the event become synonymous" (Jago and Shaw 1998:29).

Promotion and publicity is necessary to be able to attract visitors. Today many speak about the importance of relationship marketing. Relationship marketing is contrasted with transactional marketing. The traditional view of marketing, transactional marketing, is said to focus on attracting new customers, while relationship marketing aims at long-term lasting relationships. Relationship marketing is difficult to apply in event marketing to visitors, as it is not a continuous service. It is discrete services and consist of service episodes that are separate entities. The nature of an event is, especially if it is a one-time event, built upon attracting new visitors. A visit to an event is opposite to e.g. banking, insurance services, and telephone services and used only occasionally or just once. The latter are continuous services, often based on a contract. This has to be considered in marketing. The event visitor makes a decision each time about whether to go and which service providers to use. Due to this, there is often a need for intense, short-term promotion of the upcoming event. One-time events must manage communication carefully in order to achieve an early awareness. The communication, like advertising and other forms of promotion if well done can have positive effects on other markets as well. This ties in with Långsved's argument about events as a catalyst for the leisure and congress markets.

Another important means of communication is word-of-mouth, especially for recurrent events, like the Vasa ski race, Hultfredsfestivalen (a rock festival), and the Stockholm water festival. The activities during the event effect word-of-mouth among the visitors, which in turn affects image and repeated purchase. According to Balogly and McCleary (1999) is word-of-mouth recommendations from friends and relatives the most important source in forming touristic images. Similarly in a study by Webster (1991), about customers' expectations of various services, word-of-mouth had the strongest influence, followed by earlier experience and, in third place, advertising and sales promotion. The importance of 'being there' is important for many groups and it can be related to word of mouth. An example is teenagers talking to each other in school about this 'must see' music event. Also, a visit to an event, in many cases, must compete with alternative activities. Instead of watching the event on TV, you visit the event with some friends. One can also assume that active participation plays a role in word-of-mouth communication. The more involved someone is during the event, the more he/she talks about the experiences and the destination. Someone just watching the event on TV probably speaks more about the event itself and not so much of the destination, especially if the individual has never visited the place. Word-of-mouth can also be considered important in connection with visitors from far away due to the complex buying process, which includes high risks and many decisions. Also word-of-mouth is often considered to be a more objective source of information in comparison with promotion. One has to bear in mind that word-of-mouth is uncontrollable and this is often the case with publicity too. It is not certain that the word-of-mouth or the publicity is favorable. One example is the Lousiana World's Fair. Local media were critical of the fair and the publicity was disadvantageous (Dimanche 1996).

Besides communication among and with certain interest groups, the size, the theme, the time of the year, and whether it is a one-time event or recurrent are other factors, which can influence the image effect. As presented in chapter three about the World Championships in Athletics in 1995, it appeared that foreign tourists in Göteborg (who did not visit the event) had the same opinion about the destination after the event as they had before – the destination image did not change. In this case it was evaluated whether the respondents changed their perceptions about the destination due to e.g. the mass communication (e.g. TV, radio and newspapers) and the strategic promotion in connection with this very large event. The international media coverage was intense, but little was said about Göteborg itself, since most of the media representatives invited were sports writers. Most of the sponsors were also of foreign origin and very limited information was provided about the city. Despite the fact that the destination image did not change for the foreign visitors in focus, it changed for other groups. It has, according to Göteborg & Co (the local tourism authority), been easier to attract other events, trade fairs, and congresses to the city ever since. Göteborg got the spilling over effect Långsved was talking about.

Only communication about the event itself might not be enough to attract visitors. The event can be seen as a package. Like a tangible product's package, the event and other elements at the destination 'wrap' or package the services and convey an external image of what the sum of beliefs, ideas and impressions are to individuals. Product packages are designed to communicate a particular image. It is the same idea with the 'wrapping' or packaging of an event. The individual needs more than just the event at the destination. The 'wrapping' or package is designed to portray the event through an interaction of many complex stimuli. It can be seen as a visual metaphor of what is offered, which is of specific importance for creating expectations. Tangibles can be used, such as arenas, conference centers, hotels, and tourist attractions. Visitors have limited knowledge about the event and everything around it if they have not visited the destination before. Therefor, the package is important in the buying decision process when selecting an event. According to Shostack (1977), "Customers cannot see a service, but they can see various tangibles associated with the service. They see service facilities, equipment, employees, communication materials, other customers, and price lists, among other things. All of these tangibles are 'clues' about the invisible service".

The 'wrapping' for Göteborg when bidding for and attracting visitors to events is 'closeness' (the image they like to be connected with). The messages communicated to all interest groups are focused on the closeness of the physical buildings, including walking distance between the arena, the hotels, the entertainment and shopping centers. According to Långsved, Stockholm tries to communicate cleanliness, quietness and closeness to water and they avoid events that do not correspond to these elements. Another example is the bid for the 2000 Olympics in Sydney. The bid company developed a 'green games' image based on natural resources and Sydney's relatively clean environment (Gordon 1994).

The communication strategy (including a package concept and image creation/enhancing for the destination) is of prime importance in attracting sponsors. The sponsors view the event not only as a way of increasing their sales and marketing specific products but also as a way of raising the company profile, and showing that they participate in the affairs of the municipality and creating good relations with the local inhabitants. Furthermore it is possible that the costs for this type of marketing are lower than they would be for other activities. Sponsorship can be a condition for establishing and organizing new events, and besides, many repeat events would not manage without that source of financing. The primary gain, Hall says (1992), from sponsorship of an event is the stability which suitable sponsors can offer, which makes it easier for the organization to manage and market the event. SIS in Stockholm has a 'sponsor bank' they work actively with. This can be assumed to be an advantage for all the actors involved.

Another important aspect in destination marketing and events considers selection of the target groups. In a survey (presented in chapter two) of different types of events, it was clearly evident that the spectators/participants come principally from the surrounding areas. The organizers and tourist authorities, like SIS have to ask themselves about what type of visitors they prefer. Is it the local market they are trying to attract or is it national or international tourists? Do the attendees at some events represent relatively homogeneous market segments in terms of for example age, gender and life style. Another issue is whether the visitors will come to the event in a private capacity or if it is a question of business entertainment. This difference is supposed to determine, for instance, how long they are going to stay, their interest in other activities at the destination, and their choice of hotels, restaurants, et cetera. In many mega-events there is a lot of business entertainment. This affects, to a large extent, the use of the capacity of the arena. Businessmen have tickets that are valid for several days but they do not occupy their seats all the time, which means that sometimes large sections of the arena are vacant. We can often watch tennis tournaments on TV, where the stands are empty, which, to a large extent, is a result of the ticket distribution. The discussion becomes essential in image creation. Perhaps events may be viewed as more successful when they draw more attendees. Also, just as other customers can have an important impact on consumer's perceptions of service firms (Zeithaml and Bitner 1996), so too can other event participants have an impact on one's experience and subsequent assessment of event image (Gwinner 1997).

The buying behavior of visitors to events also differs based on e.g. participation. Participants (like skiers and runners), spectators, media and other visitors must be distinguished. In a sport event, the athletes and the media have, for instance, different spending behavior in comparison to the spectators. Also shopping behavior differs between the groups and only some are interested in visiting attractions at the destination (Ritchie 1996:125). Another study shows that the activities vary from one member of the family to another (see for instance Rutherford and Kreck 1994). The whole party engages in certain activities together, while other activities are for only a part of the group. Thus, different attendees at the same event have different lengths of stay, activity and spending patterns (see e.g. Carmichael and Murphy 1996).

9.2 Destination Marketing as Part of the Communities Competition

Magnus Bohlin: As pointed out in the chapter addressing event travel, the location[1] of an event will in many ways affect the entire basis for the event. Location is in some respects absolute and in others relative. Place is absolute and this is particularly true when we refer to any given point in time, but when the time dimension is added to the coordinates of places, it is obvious that vital aspects of a location may change. For example, the occurrence of intervening opportunities may drastically change the viability of an event. Changes in infrastructure, particularly transportation may similarly change the prospects of a particular location for better or for worse. For events located in places where the indigenous population is small the transportation network will strongly influence the long-term viability of the event in question, as large parts of the audience will probably be made up of tourists. Thus, population distribution and density are key issues to address when assessing the potential of any location suggested for an event as is the accessibility to the place in question.

Events are to a large extent users of the same type of infrastructure as are conference and congress tourism. Accomodation, food, shopping and transportation are infrastructure elements used by these forms of tourism, and although there may be differences in kind if we scrutinize consumption patterns between conference delegates and event visitors, we will still record major similarities. A location which can offer both event products and conference products will obviously, *ceteris paribus,* gain a greater potential for using resources such as hotels, restaurants and shopping facilities more efficiently. This will of course rest on the assumption that demand for these products can be properly managed in time, reducing seasonality and securing a high rate of used capacity. Although little research seems to have addressed these matters it would probably be safe to suggest that larger urban centers will have a greater advantage compared to small centers when it comes to realizing event tourism combined with e.g. meeting and convention tourism. This issue relates to what is normally referred to as advantages stemming from agglomeration of activities. A question of particular relevance in this context is if one can relate this question to the central place theory as first proposed by Walter Christaller.[2] If limited to the supply of tourism products, the degree of centrality of a particular location would increase with increasing

---

1) The question of location relevance to event tourism has recently been dealt with by Johansson, C & Olsson, C., 1999, Evenemangsturism - En studie av turismens geografiska lokalisering. C-uppsats i kulturgeografi vid Turismprogrammet, Högskolan Dalarna.

2) For those not familiar with the theory of central places, please refer to any basic textbook on human geography.

supply (time aspect) as well as the diversity of this supply. If such an inquiry is also tied to the population function of places, one might be able to relate the size of urban centers to their potential for establishing themselves as proprietors of event and conference tourism. It is in this context that the policy of the city of Stockholm can be viewed. Långsved has pointed out that the main aim of events is to market the capital of Sweden as a primary location for meetings, incentive travels, conventions, congresses and conferences (the MIC market). Events may or may not generate any economic surplus on their own, but if they function as marketing vehicles, events can be paid for by the more lucrative products found in the MIC market. However, if non-profitable events are paid for with taxpayers money and benefits in the MIC market are difficult to trace accurately, there will be a possibility for potential political conflict, and the justification for circulating money this way may not be appreciated by the electorate.

   Other interesting fields are the types of economic arguments and preliminary calculations that are made before or in connection with a bid for a rotating event. Many items in a budget are uncertain, for instance costs of changes in exchange rates and proceeds from sale of admission-tickets and visitors spending (it is difficult to estimate the number of visitors). The items are especially uncertain when the time for planning is long. Besides, it is not certain that the process leads to obtaining the event. The question is: How many, long and expensive, processes for candidature are handled on the level of the national economy? In this connection it is relevant to mention a study which was made concerning the Winter Olympics in Lillehammer on expected effects on the national economy (Hervik, Asheim and Bjørnland 1990) and also another study on the calculations in connection with the Stockholm bid for the Olympics (included in chapter six in this book). However, it should be noted that changes in the economy even over a relatively short time span may radically change the outcome of an event. Thus, at the time when the national housing fair, Bo 91, took place in the province of Dalarna, the Swedish economy went into a strong recession. The visible result of this was that almost the entire conference program, which would normally have attracted a large number of architects and planners more or less caved in.[3] Significant changes in Swedish legislation affected the housing market simultaneously which aggravated the general economic downturn at the beginning of the nineties which led to the restructuring of building companies and closure of architectural firms. It is difficult to foresee such rapid changes and even afterwards it is difficult to suggest any measures which the event organization could have adopted to counteract these effects.

9.3 Attitudes of the Locals Toward Events

Monica Hanefors: The importance of the locals in an event hosting community must never be neglected. This became apparent in the study of the Skinnskatteberg Choir Festival (chapter 4) and Stockholm has its own similar example in their bid for the Summer Olympic Games for 2004. At an early stage, the bid committee presented an unrealistic economic forecast. It was criticized and had to be revised. This new forecast was also greatly criticized by, for instance, academics. This criticism was frequently reported in newspapers, radio and TV. These reports did not make it any easier to convince the already skeptical locals to agree to the arranging of the Games. Public opinion surveys showed that not more than 45 – 55 % of

---

3) Bo 91, Svensk Bostadsmässa i Dalarna 1991, Stiftelsen Bo 91, Slutrapport, p. 15-23.

the locals were in favor of Stockholm hosting the Games. The negative attitudes hidden in these numbers were probably based mainly on what the media reported, and are believed to be one important reason for why Stockholm was not given the opportunity to organize the Games.

It is, of course, difficult to make a direct comparison between what happens nowadays in Stockholm with what has happened in Skinnskatteberg – the differences are far too great. There is, however, one thing in particular to be learned from the Skinnskatteberg experience: local attitudes towards an event, or to several, must be taken into consideration in order to achieve acceptance of and lasting success for events.

When Långsved talks about events as *one way to spread the name of Stockholm,* a simple image model[4] comes to mind (Bohlin and Hanefors 1994). It was developed in connection with a study of a Swedish regional museum, where image was seen as a two-sided (ever-changing) phenomenon, created by both the museum itself *and* the surrounding locals/visitors. The reason for this was, of course, that when the museum gave certain pictures to its surroundings these were simultaneously interpreted by outsiders with individual backgrounds, knowledge, expectations, et cetera. The pictures given by the museum were made up by its inner identity and outer profile in interaction. The former being the 'soft part' of the museum, i.e. management, personnel, internal information and such, and the latter 'hard part' being museum building, exhibitions, openings hours and the like. If we, instead, use a similar model to understand the dilemma of Stockholm, there is no way for Stockholm Information Service, as an event organizer, to create a positive picture – not without having the 'soft' locals on their side. Stockholm's "local taxpayers, journalists and politicians" will keep on complaining about crowding, litter, increased noise, crime, social dislocation, and finances, and the image of Stockholm will suffer because of that.

The pedagogic trick Långsved seems to look for may be articulated, as in the case of Skinnskattberg, as knowledge and participation. According to the Skinnskatteberg Choir Festival study it is necessary both to add to the locals' knowledge through relevant information and to involve them and make them feel part of the Festival. It is true that there is an understanding of the importance of tourism in general, and that local attitudes in Stockholm have changed in a positive direction, but this does not seem to include the Stockholm events. Therefore, there is a need for more information, perhaps partly based on positive results from event research. For example, in a study focusing on resident perceptions of the Taejon International Exposition in Korea, by Jeong and Faulkner (1997), it is concluded that the event was perceived as generally beneficial. However, the authors point to short-term and long-term effects, which is noteworthy. In the former perspective, the benefits are temporary job opportunities, exposure to foreign cultures, and an increased variety of shopping goods and leisure opportunities. In the longer perspective, tourism and urban development benefits are the results. After the Seoul Olympics, the long-term benefits of hosting are increased park and recreational facilities, better opportunities for shopping, acceleration of the urban growth rate, and the improved appearance of the Chamsil area (Jeong 1997; see also e.g. Ritchie and Lyons 1990).

If the local residents are informed about such positive impacts, about both short-term and long-term effects of the Stockholm events, this knowledge will most likely create a greater understanding of the events. If they find out, for example, the amount of money that tourists

---

4) "Festivals and special events (...) are organized to create a positive image or enhance an existing one of a place and bring in money to the local economy" (Uysal and Gitelson 1994:3; see also Getz 1993:947-949 and 953).

bring into an area because of an event (Archer 1982), or that events stimulate sales by non-residents (Turko 1991 cf. Uysal and Gitelson 1994). And even better, if they can be informed that the Stockholm events do not need public money.

Even though it can be assumed that it is relatively easier to find volunteers in a small community like Skinnskatteberg, i.e. if this is the objective, reports on voluntary work in connection with big events can be found in literature. For example, in a study made by Gorney and Busser (1996) the effect that participation in a major special event has on a "resident's importance and satisfaction with community life" is examined (p. 139). They find, among other things, that new participants increased their satisfaction within community life after participation in the special event. Also Walo et al. (1997) argue that participation and assistance of volunteers sometimes constitute a key factor for the success of an event. Many volunteers are found among the local residents studied, and with their support the event generated value to the local host society, such as enhancement of the way of life, economy and environment. Williams et al. (1995) report, that during the Whistler's Men World Cup in Skiing, the volunteers were of the opinion that the pros of the event outweighed the cons. They also felt that the perceived positive effects benefit the community and its residents. In a similar manner Arthur and Andrew (1996) show how community involvement, and local participation, may be incorporated into the management of a sporting mega-event. They identify two essential areas. The first means a structured approach based on volunteer recruitment and retention strategies advocated by leading agencies, and the second is corporate sponsorship, i.e. involvement of local business in the sponsorship of the event.

There is only limited research on the locals in direct relation to economic effects even though indirect economic impact is apparent in most studies. Continued study with a focus directly on the impact that special events have on locals' views are asked for by Gorney and Busser (1996:147), and it is easy to agree. Far too often event research focuses on figures only and does not take into account that without humans – informed locals and volunteers – there would be no events. Jeong and Faulkner (1997:5) likewise argue that "perception studies should be an integral part of event cost-benefit analyses to the extent that they enable costs and benefits to be examined in relation to specific reference groups". The reason for this is that the "outcome of the cost-benefit assessment at the macro-level can provide a misleading indication of an event's impacts on a community if it obscures variations in the distribution of these impacts and, equally importantly, fails to appreciate the nuances of these impacts at the individual level" (op. cit.).

9.4 The Decision Process of Events Related to Public Financing

Financial demands and public information

Lars A. Samuelson: There are two major topics dealt with by Långsved that relate to financial aspects. Furthermore, these topics are heavily intertwined:

1. the role of events and the financial demands that can accordingly be put on events,

2. the inherent problems in estimating the effects of events and, partly due to that, the problems in describing these effects to the general public.

According to Långsved events are mainly seen as means to increase the attractiveness of Stockholm to tourists and congresses. As discussed above, events are thus one way of marketing a destination. From a financial viewpoint, events may be allowed to show deficits as long as their marginal impacts on the effects on tourists and congresses more than balance these deficits.

The critical problem here is to estimate the effects of events in the first place. Furthermore to evaluate the long-term effects on tourists and congresses. And, finally, there is the problem presenting these findings to the public.

The problems in estimating the effects of events have been covered in several chapters in this book. What is evident from the case of Stockholm is that *there are* problems in estimating the effects of mega-events such as Olympic Games. The problems are less when it comes to smaller and recurring events such as the Stockholm Water Festival. Probably the impact of these smaller events on the long term image of a city is also smaller which is why it is quite natural that these events, as demanded by the city of Stockholm, should stand on their own. Besides it is of interest to note the ambitions of Stockholm in trying to find events such as the 'Vikingarännet', to increase the visits to Stockholm during low season. Such events, if successful, will obviously make important positive contributions to the economy of the area.

The key problem, however, pertains to the estimates of effects of mega-events. Of course, such events occur less often which is why the problem may be conceived to be of less importance. But when they do occur, it will be important to deal with them correctly. One lesson from Stockholm is that after the publication of initial and rather rough estimates of the effects of Olympic Summer Games made by the committee preparing the Swedish bid, these estimates were scrutinized and found to be overoptimistic as described above.

A conclusion from this example is that in the face of great uncertainty it will probably be wise not to use a favorable preliminary estimate, showing great positive effects, as a part of the argumentation of the proposal. If and when such an estimate is found too optimistic the whole project will meet with bad will and negative attitudes. A better strategy may be to discuss the effects in general terms until thorough investigations of the effects have been conducted.

It is also a general experience that budgets for large projects often prove to be too optimistic. Besides Stockholm, this was the case for Lillehammer as described in chapter eight and we all know of many other similar projects. We also know, however, that whenever cost estimates are based on realistic specifications, it is nowadays also possible to make realistic cost estimates. A critical decision to make therefore regards the timing of when cost estimates should be made public.

Another aspect on the same theme is that our general knowledge concerning the effects of mega-events is still meager and so long as this is the case, the estimates for new events can only to a minor extent be based on the experiences from earlier events. This also goes for the methods to be used in these estimates.

Besides the difficulties in making realistic estimates, those proposing large events also have the pedagogical challenge of describing the effects in a way that is understandable for the general public. If an estimate only involves revenues and expenses directly attributable to the event and the figures show a surplus, the task would be simple. But for large events these figures often make up a deficit. And the debate often concerns whether it is justified to cover the deficit with public funds or not. As is shown in chapter six, possible revenues for the public will show up in accounts belonging to different public agencies (the state, municipalities and so on) and only as a result when primary effects have been identified and a certain algorithm has been used. Furthermore the effects will often materialize over several years adding to the pedagogical challenge of describing the effects in simple ways. As this use of funds also competes against alternatives that are very attractive and simple to understand for the citizen such as better care for elderly, children or the sick, the width of the challenge will be clear.

The only solution to this problem would be to develop the skill in communicating complex matters such as event budgets to the public. This would involve the presentation of a valid algorithm showing the amount of public funds to be put in a project and the positive effects of this on the number of jobs, guest nights and so on which will lead to monetary flows of certain magnitudes back to the public.

Göran Långsved made a presentation showing Stockholm to have a strategy according to which events as well as other forms of promotion would support Stockholm as a growing destination for tourists and congresses. With regard to the difficulties in evaluating single events a good idea may be, as suggested by Långsved, to focus on the development of key figures for the whole industry. The development in number of guest nights, visits to various museums and tourist attractions, and employment in the key industries, may be a very important way of assessing the impacts of events and other forms of promotion on the attractiveness of Stockholm as a tourist destination.

The advantages of public investment

Tommy D. Andersson: When Göran Långsved, who is the manager in charge of tourism development in Stockholm, discusses the problem of convincing people about the advantages of an event, this raises a number of issues. Göran Långsved expressed the following concerns:

> *A significant problem with events is to convince for example taxpayers, journalists, and politicians of the advantages of the investments due to the fact that the financing is often based on public money. It is questioned whether public money should be financing events or whether it is a better investment to build kindergartens or new roads. One reason for the debate is the difficulties in assessing the economic impacts. Also, there are difficulties in presenting the potential or real effects in an easy and pedagogical way in the media. Events are therefore vulnerable. It is easier to argue for investments in the leisure and congress markets.*

On one hand, it may be argued that 'profitable investments' in the commercial sense should not be on the political agenda. Investments in public goods, such as roads, certainly are on the political agenda and they may also be profitable in a wider economic sense and show a surplus in cost-benefit analyses. But these road investments are rarely profitable in a commercial sense. One idea that tends to surface in debates, is that when public income, in terms of e.g. taxes, generated by an event exceeds public subsidies then it will make the event 'a profitable public investment'. This is a qualitatively different and narrow definition of 'public profitability' compared to a cost-benefit analysis. If profitable public investments in this more narrow sense are acceptable, a huge market for public investments will open up. Not only local firms in temporary difficulties, but also any taxed activity can claim that a public investment will be profitable since it will generate taxes. True enough, this type of reasoning is frequently used albeit more often in areas with a desperate need for industrial activity than in large cities. The underlying logic is actually to grant 'tax freedom' since the idea is that an amount up to, but not exceeding, the amount of taxes to be generated could be used for investment in a project. It is not surprising that, according to the same logic, one idea launched in the budget for the Olympic Games 2004 in Stockholm was to finance the cost partly by 'VAT refunds'.

On the other hand, it may be argued that a big event, and particularly a mega-event, is in fact a 'public good' generating excitement, pride and pleasure for everyone to enjoy for free and consequently the advantages of the public investment should be assessed in a wider economic sense. Most local residents appreciate the festivity (free of charge) that surrounds a mega-event and take pride in the fact that their city is one of the foci of world attention for a day or two. Some will enjoy this more than others and some may not enjoy it at all, but this may also be the case for other types of public goods such as when a new road is built. Thus, when externalities are taken into account in a cost-benefit analysis, a public investment in a popular event may prove to be as profitable as e.g. the construction of a new road. This may be the case provided that the event has few negative externalities and that economic utility in the form of joy, pride and happiness is considered equally important as other economic values. This is surprisingly difficult to put across in the media. It is not easy to convince people that an enjoyable life is at least as important as other economic values such as stock market value and the value of pension funds. The 'primary surplus' discussed in chapter six is thus a major argument in favour of public investments in events. An investment in a popular and successful event may thus be Pareto efficient: Public authorities get their money back and are better off after than they were before the event. So are the business community and the general public that enjoy the festivities around the event for free. Pareto efficiency implies that nobody should be worse off after the event. A vital issue is therefore to look for 'losers'.

An argument against public interference is that the market will be disturbed since some firms will benefit while others will not. Hotels and restaurants are notorious free riders and, as illustrated in Table 6.2, direct economic effects do to a large extent go to these industries. In the perfect market, the tourism industry (mainly consisting of transport firms, shops, hotels and restaurants) would immediately realise the potential of events and work together to attract events. It is a task for research to find out why this very seldom happens neither in Sweden nor in most other countries. A good guess is that the fragmentation of the tourism industry makes co-operation difficult. One reason often raised by business owners is that the profitability in the business is too low to allow any excessive sponsoring of events. To be able to survive, public money to support tourism is necessary, according to owners of tourism businesses, especially so since other industries also get various forms of public support.

An event normally concentrates the demand geographically and there will be 'losers' also in the tourism industry as e.g. restaurants in the periphery will have less customers since their normal customers go to restaurants located at the event centre. The same is true on a larger scale for events that attract a large number of national spectators and generate a flow of business from peripheral regions to the event region. Particular caution should therefore be taken if state money, and not only regional public money, is used to subsidise an event. There is of course also the danger that if politicians from different regions decide to support events and interfere in the market economy, the result may be a zero-sum game between the regions. This may result in declining economic efficiency and an illustration of the 'Prisoners' Dilemma' where regions realise too late that things were better before they started to support events but where it is impossible to withdraw since that would give away the market to other regions (cf. advertising for washing powder). The analysis in chapter 6 pointed out that some industries that may be 'losers' in terms of direct economic effect when the opportunity cost is taken into account (Table 6.2). There will of course also be some welfare sectors that will face short-term budget cuts if public investment is directed to the tourism industry. If the event is economically successful and has a net positive effect on the public finances (after due consideration is taken to opportunity cost), the long-term effects may however be positive for the welfare sector.

To conclude this discussion about the advantages of public investment in events the following points could be made:

- A simple calculation in terms of 'money in' vs. 'money out' of the public tax chamber is not a sufficient argument to justify a public investment. The model presented in chapter six is thus only meant to be one of several pieces of information to be used for a decision.

- It may be argued that an event that brings excitement, joy and pride to a community is a type of (immaterial) public good and should consequently be assessed by a cost-benefit analysis where economic utility also must include an evaluation of excitement, joy and pride.

- In a well functioning market, public intervention into the tourism market should not be necessary. The firms should realise the advantages of co-operation and act together to attract events. It may be argued that since the tourism industry is fragmented and poorly organised, public authorities need to take an initiative to create economic value. This argument is however dangerous in the long run and needs to be scrutinized.

- An investment in a successful popular event may be close to Pareto efficient. Most economic actors, including tax authorities, the business community, and the general public, are better off after the event than they were before the event.

- An event creates a geographical concentration of the activities which means that on the periphery there will be several 'losers' both tax authorities, businesses, and the general public. This is particularly the case for an event that also attracts a large national audience. This means that Pareto efficiency requires that the event be financed from sources close to the event (preferably by the tourism industry located close to the event). Thus Pareto efficiency will be considerably reduced and turn negative when financial resources from the periphery are used to subsidise the event.

References

Archer, B. (1982). The Value of Multipliers and Their Policy Implications. *Tourism Management, 3*(4), 236-241.

Arthur, D. & Andrew, J. (1996). Incorporating Community Involvement in the Management of Sporting Mega-Events: An Australian Case Study. *Festival Management & Event Tourism, 1/2*(4), 21-27.

Baloglu, S. & McCleary, K. (1997). A Model of Destination Image Formation. *Annals of Tourism Research, 26*(4), 868-897.

Bo 91, Svensk Bostadsmässa i Dalarna (1991). Stiftelsen Bo 91, *Slutrapport*, pp. 15-23.

Bohlin, M. & Hanefors, M. (1994). *En kulturekonomisk studie av Bohusläns Museum. Image, publik och samhällsekonomi.* ITR-rapport No 1. ITR, Högskolan i Falun/Borlänge, Sweden.

Carmichael, B. & Murphy, P. (1996). Tourism Economic Impact of a Rotating Sports Event: The Case of British Columbia Games: *Festival Management & Event Tourism, 4*(3/4), 127-138.

Dimanche, F. (1996). Special Events Legacy. The 1984 Lousiana World's Fair in New Orleans, *Festival Management & Event Tourism, 4*(1/2), 49-54.

Getz, D. (1993). Festivals and Special Events. In M.A. Khan, M.D. Olsen, & T. Var (Eds.), *VNR's Encyclopedia of Hospitality and Tourism* (pp. 945-955). New York: Van Nostrand Reinhold.

Gordon, H. (1994). *Australia and the Olympic Games. The Official Story.* University of Queensland Press, Australia.

Gorney, S. M. & Busser, J. A. (1996). The Effect of Participation in a Special Event on Importance and Satisfaction with Community Life. *Festival Management & Event Tourism, 3*(3), 139-148.

Gwinner, K. (1997). A Model of Image Creation and Image Transfer in Event Sponsorship. *International Marketing Review, 14*(3).

Hall, C. M. (1992). *Hallmark Tourist Events - Impacts, Management & Planning*, London: Belhaven Press.

Hervik, A., Asheim, G., & Bjørnland, D. (1990). Samfunnsøkonomiske perspektiver på OL, Senter for anvendt forskning, SAF, Bergen & Møreforskning, DH, Molde.

Jago, L. & Shaw, R. (1998). Special Events: A Conceptual and Differential Framework, *Festival Management & Event Tourism*, 5(1/2), 21-32.

Jeong, G.-H. (1997). Residents' Perceptions on the Long-Term Impacts of the Seoul Olympics to the Chamsil Area Development in a Tourism Perspective. In *The Impact of Mega-Events,* proceedings, 7-8 July, Mid Sweden University.

Jeong, G. H. & Faulkner, B. (1997). Resident Perceptions of Mega-Event Impacts: The Taejon International Exposition Case. *Festival Management & Event Tourism, 4,* 3-11.

Johansson, C. & Olsson, C. (1999). *Evenemangsturism - En studie av turismens geografiska lokalisering.* C-uppsats i kulturgeografi vid Turismprogrammet, Högskolan Dalarna.

Shostack, L. (1977). Breaking Free from Product Marketing, *Journal of Marketing, 41*(April), 73-80.

Ritchie, B. (1996), How Special Are Special Events? The Economic Impact and Strategic Development of the New Zealand Master Games, *Festival Management & Event Tourism*, 4(3/4), 117-126.

Ritchie, B. & Lyons, M. (1990). OLYMPULSE VI: A Post-event Assessment of Resident Reaction to the XV Olympic Winter Games, *Journal of Travel Research*, 28(3), 14-23.

Rutherford, D. & Kreck, L. (1994). Conventions and Tourism: Financial Add-On or Myth? Report of a Study in One State, *Journal of Travel & Tourism Marketing*, 3(1), 49-65.

Turko, D. M. (1991). *Assessing the Spatial Distribution of Expenditures Attributed to a Large-Scale Special Event.* (Unpubl. Ph.D. Dissertation). Albuquerque, New Mexico: University of New Mexico.

Uysal, M. & Gitelson, R. (1994). Assessment from Economic Impacts: Festivals and Special Events. *Festival Management & Event Tourism, 1*(2), 3-9.

Walo, M., A. Bull., & Breen, H. (1997). Achieving Economic Benefits at Local Events: A Case Study of a Local Sports Event. *Festival Management & Event Tourism*, 4(3/4), 95-106.

Webster, C. (1991). Influences Upon Consumer Expectations of Services, *The Journal of Services Marketing*, 5(1), 5-17.

Williams, P. W., Dossa, K.B. & Tompkins, L. (1995). Volunteerism and Special Event Management: A Case Study of Whistler's Men's World Cup of Skiing, *Festival Management & Event Tourism*, 3(2), 83-95.

Zeithaml, V. & Bitner, M. J. (1996). *Services Marketing.* The McGraw-Hill Companies, Inc.